The Everyday Crusade

What is causing the American public to move more openly into alt-right terrain? What explains the uptick in anti-immigrant hysteria, isolationism, and an increasing willingness to support alternatives to democratic governance? *The Everyday Crusade* provides an answer. The book points to American Religious Exceptionalism (ARE), a widely held religious nationalist ideology steeped in myth about the nation's original purpose. The book opens with a comprehensive synthesis of research on nationalism and religion in American public opinion. Making use of twelve years' worth of national and state surveys, it then develops a new theory of why Americans form extremist attitudes, based on religious exceptionalism myths. The book closes with an examination of what's next for an American public that confronts new global issues, alongside existing challenges to perceived cultural authority. Timely and enlightening, *The Everyday Crusade* offers a critical touchstone for better understanding American national identity and the exclusionary ideologies that have plagued the nation since its inception.

Eric L. McDaniel is an Associate Professor and co-director of the Politics of Race and Ethnicity Lab at the University of Texas at Austin. He is the author of *Politics in the Pews: The Political Mobilization of Black Churches* (2008).

Irfan Nooruddin is the Hamad bin Khalifa Al-Thani Professor of Indian Politics in the Edmund A. Walsh School of Foreign Service at Georgetown University. He is the author of *Coalition Politics and Economic Development* (2011) and *Elections in Hard Times* (2016, with T. E. Flores).

Allyson F. Shortle is an Associate Professor of Political Science at the University of Oklahoma. She serves as the chair of the faculty advisory board for OU's Community Engagement and Experiments Laboratory (CEEL) and directs the Oklahoma City Community Poll.

Bro. Dickerson

Thank you for being such a great inspiration

'06

Edward

The Everyday Crusade

Christian Nationalism in American Politics

ERIC L. MCDANIEL

The University of Texas at Austin

IRFAN NOORUDDIN

Georgetown University

ALLYSON F. SHORTLE

University of Oklahoma

CAMBRIDGE
UNIVERSITY PRESS

CAMBRIDGE
UNIVERSITY PRESS

University Printing House, Cambridge CB2 8BS, United Kingdom

One Liberty Plaza, 20th Floor, New York, NY 10006, USA

477 Williamstown Road, Port Melbourne, VIC 3207, Australia

314–321, 3rd Floor, Plot 3, Splendor Forum, Jasola District Centre,
New Delhi – 110025, India

103 Penang Road, #05–06/07, Visioncrest Commercial, Singapore 238467

Cambridge University Press is part of the University of Cambridge.

It furthers the University's mission by disseminating knowledge in the pursuit of
education, learning, and research at the highest international levels of excellence.

www.cambridge.org
Information on this title: www.cambridge.org/9781316516263
DOI: 10.1017/9781009029445

First published 2022

A catalogue record for this publication is available from the British Library.

Library of Congress Cataloging-in-Publication Data
NAMES: McDaniel, Eric L., 1976– author. | Nooruddin, Irfan, author. | Shortle, Allyson
F., author.
TITLE: The everyday crusade : Christian nationalism in American politics / Eric L.
McDaniel, Irfan Nooruddin, Allyson F. Shortle.
DESCRIPTION: Cambridge, United Kingdom ; New York, NY : Cambridge University
Press, 2022. | Includes bibliographical references and index.
IDENTIFIERS: LCCN 2021053514 (print) | LCCN 2021053515 (ebook) | ISBN
9781316516263 (hardback) | ISBN 9781009029445 (ebook)
SUBJECTS: LCSH: Christianity and politics – United States. | Conservatism – United
States – Religious aspects – Christianity. | Nationalism – United States – Religious aspects –
Christianity. | White nationalism – United States. | Republican Party (U.S. : 1854–)
CLASSIFICATION: LCC BR526 .M29 2022 (print) | LCC BR526 (ebook) | DDC 277.308/3 –
dc23/eng/20211227
LC record available at https://lccn.loc.gov/2021053514
LC ebook record available at https://lccn.loc.gov/2021053515

ISBN 978-1-316-51626-3 Hardback
ISBN 978-1-009-01458-8 Paperback

For my mentor, Bishop Cornal Garnett Henning, Sr. – *E. L. M.*
For Esme and Emil: "Imagine there's no countries." – *I. N.*
For my mother, Brenda. – *A. F. S.*

Contents

Figures

Tables

Preface

On January 6, 2021, American citizens stormed the US Capitol, attempting to overturn the result of the 2020 election. Their goal was to disrupt the formal process of counting electoral college votes and thereby to block certification of Joe Biden's election to the presidency. They were encouraged in their efforts by the loser of the 2020 election. At a rally that morning, where his effort to overturn the election results was amplified by speeches from his family and state and federal senior government officials, Donald Trump repeated his lies that the 2020 election had been "rigged" and urged his supporters to "fight like hell" to save their country. Attendees walked to the Capitol with his words ringing in their ears, and hundreds breached the Capitol's security with shocking ease. Five people lost their lives, including Capitol Police Officer Brian Sicknick, as a result of that day's violence. In the days that followed, there was bipartisan denunciation of the attackers. Opinion pieces decried the tenuous future of the Republican Party leaders who had egged on these rioters. Such predictions were naïve. Republican lawmakers who were photographed screaming in terror on the day of the attack were later vociferous in their contention that criticisms of the rioters were "overblown."

The Everyday Crusade offers a provocative explanation for the anti-democratic impulses of otherwise ordinary Americans that surfaced so viscerally on January 6, 2021. We advance two main arguments. First, the political coalition represented by the rioters is unified and animated by a toxic narrative of racial and religious grievances under the umbrella of nationalism. White Christian Nationalists are today the base of the Republican Party, and those who attacked the US Capitol are drawn from their ranks. Second, tempting as it is to believe that this attack is an aberration and that it is unrepresentative of America, we argue that its instigators draw on a long tradition of American religious exceptionalism that dates back to the earliest days of colonial settlement of today's United States. In that very real sense, and with apologies to the poet, they, too, sing America.

The irony is that such revanchism sits alongside an increase in progressive support for voting rights, marijuana legalization, gay marriage, universal healthcare, reinvestment in racial equality, and decriminalization reforms. It is almost as if, on the eve of a progressive policy explosion, something deep within American society was awoken, ready to fight for continued cultural dominance – rebranded as "survival." This is no surprise. When Trump warned of American carnage at his poorly attended inauguration, he was issuing an unmistakable dog whistle to his supporters who worry that their two centuries plus grip over defining America is being loosened and affirming his willingness to champion them. When he promised them America First, he invoked their belief in American religious exceptionalism, a coherent intellectual framework that combines America's origin myths and explains its role in the world, and has done so from the nation's founding.

Our effort builds on rich theoretical and empirical research that has joined the effort to process the whiplash experienced by many of how we went from Barack Obama to Donald Trump and what the implications are for our understanding of American politics. Many of these works focus usefully on group identity mechanisms, explicating, as Robert Jones and Janelle Wong do, the insecurity of White evangelical voters in the face of demographic change, and, per Rachel Blum, the growing influence of extremist factions within the Republican Party. Either way, Christopher Parker and Matt Barreto make clear, the motivating force is the threat of losing status as a dominant group in society. Another tack has been developed by Samuel Perry and Andrew Whitehead, who, focusing also on the growing power and disquiet of White evangelicals, warn of the power of White Christian nationalism. Their explanation, like ours, builds on foundational comparative models of how the variety of ways religion and nationalism combine shapes national myths and impacts state institutional design.

This book owes considerably to the insights produced by the scholars cited earlier and by many more who have built the theoretical models of public opinion we work with here. Yet we believe our book offers a distinct interpretation of the restrictive and illiberal attitudes characterizing American public opinion from the 2000s to the 2020s. Public willingness to support undemocratic policies and candidates is not the sole purview of the nation's White evangelicals. In fact, heightened illiberalism in American public opinion has been occurring in an unprecedented era when Americans have increasingly left organized religion. The public's willingness to support undemocratic policies and candidates is likewise left unexplained purely by looking to the nation's Republicans or the rise of the Tea Party; as we will show, there are plenty of political independents and Democrats who subscribe to restrictive policies and authoritarian candidates. The answer is in the power of historically entrenched myths that comprise an ideology of American religious exceptionalism, which originated at the nation's founding. Under its banner, Americans – religiously observant and not; Christian or not; White or not – are susceptible to drawing on their internalized sense of a religious purpose embedded in their American identities to arrive at a shared sense that all is not well in their society and that, in fact, America's God-given purpose in the world is being undermined by those who would betray that sacred trust. The consequence is a battening of the hatches, a hardening of the walls that separate us from outsiders, and a willingness to countenance anti-democratic actions under the justification that it ensures the continuance of leadership determined to put America first.

We offer a new theory that specifies the ideological components that give a particular brand of religious nationalism sway over a large swath of the American public – one that moves beyond explaining White evangelical sentiment and into the ordinary lives of everyday Americans who sometimes even lack any conscious commitment to religious influences. Our approach offers an explanation based on foundational myths of America as religiously exceptional, characterized by a specific focus on the nation's divine purpose, place, and origin vis-à-vis the rest of the world. Through a historical analysis, we chart how several national origin myths of American religious exceptionalism were adopted into the national fabric at its founding, and then analyze how these relics have been time and again reproduced into the modern-day powerhouse influencing Americans' everyday political lives. The bulk of the book is dedicated to testing the observable implications of this argument in a variety of domains and through a vast array of national and state-level public opinion surveys that we have designed and conducted over the past decade. These rich original individual-level data are supplemented wherever possible with other surveys commissioned independently by reputed research organizations that generously made their data public for lucky scholars like ourselves.

Our hope is that the combination of theory and data serves to convince readers that American religious exceptionalism is an ideology of considerable import in contemporary American politics and that it deserves sustained attention from future scholars of America, as well as comparativists who can identify the opportunities to export this framework to diverse settings and thereby also to delineate its uniqueness. At the end of the day, American religious exceptionalism is first and foremost American, but America is not the first – nor will it be the last – society to believe that they too were chosen peoples. From India and Pakistan to Israel and Iran, the challenge of religious nationalism for democracy is apparent. We hope this book offers some insight useful to scholars grappling with similar issues elsewhere.

Acknowledgments

Over the decade that we have been engaged with this project, we have generated more debts than we can ever repay and from more people and institutions than we can possibly name here. Nevertheless, we shall try, beginning with the institutions that have generously funded our surveys and time over the years: the Mershon Center at The Ohio State University; the National Science Foundation; the Robert Wood Johnson Foundation; and the Community Engagement and Experiments Laboratory (CEEL) at the University of Oklahoma. Sara Doskow and John Haslam at Cambridge University Press believed in this project from the beginning, and Mamta Jha of the American Society of Indexers provided quality assistance at very short notice. We gratefully acknowledge the Public Religion Research Initiative (PRRI) for sharing its survey data with us; they are an exemplar of public goods creation. Finally, our ideas benefited from presentations at the University of California, San Diego, the University of Notre Dame, and the University of Michigan.

PERSONAL ACKNOWLEDGMENTS

Allyson F. Shortle

I thank my colleagues at the University of Oklahoma, in particular Andrea Benjamin, Alisa Fryar, Tyler Johnson, Allen Hertzke, Ann Marie Szymanski, and Kathleen Tipler, for their support. I am indebted to the University of Oklahoma Political Science department's office managers, Cathy Brister and Rhonda Hill, for their patience and expertise in navigating numerous survey data collections and lab co-founding activities. I thank Ana Bracic and Mackenzie Israel-Trummel for their friendship and support.

I would additionally like to thank the friends and family who have encouraged me along the way: Stephanie Conklin, Scott Drew, Andrea Doenges Martin, Peter Forshay, David Rudd Ross, Georgina Serroukas Smith, and John Stupak. This includes the educators who have made a true impact on me personally, Mary Fregosi, John Peterson, and Terry Weiner. I am eternally grateful to my mother, sister, brother, sister-in-law, niece, and nephew, and partner for their love and constant entertainment. Most of all, I would like to thank Eric and Irfan.

Eric L. McDaniel

I thank my colleagues at the University of Texas (UT), in particular Daron Shaw, Bryan Jones, Christopher Wlezien, Robert Moser, Paula Newberg, and Reuben McDaniel, for their feedback. I am grateful to the Population Research Center and the Provost's Mid-Career Writing Fellowship for critical support that allowed completion of the manuscript. Outside of UT, I thank J. Jionni Palmer, Errol Henderson, and Andrea Benjamin for their steadfast support. A Robert Wood Johnson fellowship at the University of California at Berkeley brought me into the orbit of Laura Stoker, Jack Citrin, and Taeku Lee, and I thank each for their continued mentorship and advice.

Writing a book requires far more than just academic help. On the personal front, I thank my Alpha Phi Alpha Fraternity, Inc. brothers, especially Keylan G. Morgan, Ahmos Zu-Bolton III, DeQuincy L. Adamson, Y. Sekou Bermiss, Gregory Parks, and Jay Augustine. I am eternally grateful to my wife, daughters, dogs, and existing and new extended family for their love. I do not deserve such great people in my life, but I thank God that I have them.

Irfan Nooruddin

I was born and raised in Bombay, but my family was always global with off-shoots – that sprang new roots – in Hong Kong, Switzerland, England, Singapore, Saudi Arabia, the UAE, Canada, and America, and who knows where else. My parents spent almost four decades in Manama and Dubai. My brother lives in Japan, resuming a journey begun by our paternal grandparents who went there in the 1930s. What a gift it was to understand young that human connections unite us in spite of the political borders that divide us. I dedicate this book to my peripatetic family, and especially to Heidi, Esme, and Emil, in whose company I am always home.

Introduction

If you would be a true patriot, then become a Christian. If you would be a loyal American, then become a loyal Christian.

Billy Graham (1953)

On Interstate 65, in Alabama between Montgomery and Birmingham, a landowner posts two large signs along the roadside. The first warns, "America, love it or leave it," the other demands greater respect for the Bible. In Effingham, Illinois, where I-57 meets I-70, a cross towers 198 feet over the intersection. In locations spread out across ten states, Whataburger franchise windows display an American flag proclaiming "One Nation Under God Indivisible." Throughout the nation there are monuments and signs extolling religion's importance in American society. It may be more overt in certain sections of the nation, but it is an ever-present force in American life. National pride is even more aggressively on display from sea to shining sea. American flags fly on homes, office buildings, and churches; in school gymnasiums, classrooms, and athletic fields; and on lapels of aspiring politicians everywhere. And, indeed, some of the most overt expressions of national pride are coupled with religious language. This became most evident in the wake of the attacks on September 11, 2001, the military response that followed, and the omnipresent fears of another attack. American flags proliferated as anxious citizens waved them from their car antennas and front porches and wore hats and shirts emblazoned with them – and with this outpouring of national affection, overt, public expressions of religious piety also increased. These religious expressions highlighted the connection, obvious in many Americans' minds, between the nation and a higher power. The American proclivity to conflate nation and God is on full display during American sporting events where crowds sing "God Bless America," an incantation every American politician now reflexively uses to punctuate any public appearance.

That the divine and the nation are connected is not simply folk wisdom; it is an idea advanced by political leaders who argue this is the way the nation was intended. David Barton, former vice chair of the Republican Party in Texas and founder of the religious nationalist organization Wall Builders, has written several books arguing the Founders were highly devout individuals, justifying the conflation of religion and patriotism (Barton 1992, 2012, 2016). Michael O'Fallon, the CEO of Sovereign Nations and the owner of Sovereign Cruises and Events LLC, has created a set of cruise packages that promise customers the beauty of nature, which they can enjoy while attending conferences to "Honor the Lord" and reclaiming "our national heritage" (Jenkins 2019). These occurrences are part of a larger culture, including books, movies, and television networks, built around the belief the nation is divinely inspired (Stewart 2019; Du Mez 2020; Keddie 2020).

The leaders of this cultural movement are actively working to codify the connection between America and the divine. The phrase "God Bless America" is now the official slogan on Alabama license plates and is an option for license plates in a variety of other states. The Texas State Board of Education redesigned its curriculum to increase the prominence of religion in its telling of nation's founding (Chancey 2014). In 2015, a group of White Christian conservatives launched Project Blitz, a package of state and national bills designed to reaffirm conservative Christian values in American public life. The bills would compel a range of "divine interventions," from expanding the placement of "In God We Trust" to public spaces, such as schools and police vehicles, to offering classes on the Bible in schools. It also calls for greater recognition of Christianity through the creation of a "Christian Heritage Week" and proclamations recognizing the role of the Bible throughout history (Clarkson 2018; Stewart 2018). Project Blitz has found allies at the federal and state level, suggesting their hope for a national religious revival may not be far-fetched. Their efforts found an unlikely advocate in Donald Trump, who, lacking a sense of irony, urged the nation to reclaim its religious heritage and endorsed biblical literacy classes (Chancey 2019). As of mid-2020, six states – Alabama, Arizona, Arkansas, Florida, Louisiana, and Tennessee – had enacted legislation *mandating* public schools to display "In God We Trust."

Tempting as it is to attribute such trends to "Trumpism" and some new viral strain of right-wing populism, the fact is that Donald Trump did not invent the intermingling of religious pride and national pride. He along with Barton and O'Fallon and others driving this agenda are simply the latest expression of deep-seated beliefs among Americans that have been fostered since the nation's founding. White Americans' visceral reactions to the September 11 attacks, to the nation's changing demography, and to perceived increases in secularism and multiculturalism, have made this conflation more noticeable, but linking God with nation has always been a part of American social and political culture (Jones 2016). Rev. Billy Graham, who provides our epigraph, resonated with the nation because he touched on a belief system rarely discussed but commonly understood. Because it is generally accepted, Americans barely notice the religious nature of their national motto "In God We Trust," the overt public expectation that political leaders end their messages with "God Bless America," or the incongruence of "patriotic pulpits" festooned with American flags. They take for granted the piety associated with national holidays and the patriotism associated with religious holidays. One only need look at the rhetoric surrounding the "War on Christmas" to see how celebrating this Christian holiday has been linked to patriotism. Such instances, whether overt or subtle, are the manifestation of a national myth that has been reproduced for more than two centuries. The myth contends that the United States' creation and purpose are part of a divine plan. The nation was not created by chance; it was created by a Supreme Being to stand above all others and to lead them to a higher form of being. This is the myth of American religious exceptionalism, and it has been a critical component of American thinking since the colonies and provides a wellspring to which every generation of American citizens can return to define themselves and their nation.

We do not use the word myth as an insult to its adherents. We realize that for many, the word myth connotes an entertaining story or at worst the example of the primitive or savage mind run wild (Lévi-Strauss 1981; Vernant 1988; Overing 1997). Where *logos* is the establishment of truth through logical and rigorous thought, *mythos* is based upon rhetorical skills and the ability to impress (Overing 1997). Myth believers are caricatured as childlike – believing in Santa Claus or the Tooth Fairy, or imbecilic – believing Lebron James is better than Michael Jordan. To the contrary, we understand myths as crucial to identity formation and providing structure to how one perceives the world (Green 2015). As such, myths are important clues into how people interpret their world and the subsequent actions they take (Geertz 1973). We believe the myth of American religious exceptionalism buttresses many Americans' sense of a complicated world. The purpose of this book is to understand how these "disciples" of the myth of American religious exceptionalism use it to understand themselves, their nation, and its place in the world.

Claude Lévi-Strauss viewed myths as scientific emptiness, but also acknowledged their immense social power (1981). Their social utility comes from their ability to provide pleasure and emotional appeal to their audiences. The myth captures people's attention and convinces them that this is how the world works (Vernant 1988; Overing 1997). Myths become the bedrock of a community. In Bronislaw Malinowski's words, myth is "a vital ingredient of human civilization; it is not an idle tale, but a hard-worked active force; it is not an intellectual explanation or an artistic imagery, but a pragmatic charter of primitive faith and moral wisdom" (Malinowski 1954, p. 82). Robert Segal states: "to label a belief as a myth is to elevate, not denigrate, it by noting the hold it has on those who accept it, no matter what the evidence" (Segal 2001, p. 173). Robert Bellah contends that myths demonstrate the power of an event to provide "moral and spiritual meaning to individuals and society" (1975, p. 3), while Richard Hughes describes myth as "a story that speaks of meaning and purpose, and for that reason it speaks truth to those who take it seriously" (Hughes 2004, p. 2). Some scholars go further to argue myths reveal the truth of a nation or group better than "accurate" historical accounts (Schöpflin 1997; Berger 2009). Acknowledging the difficulty of separating myth from "true" history, William H. McNeill titled his American Historical Association presidential essay, "Mythistory, or Truth, Myth, History, and Historians." In it, he argued:

Myth and history are close kin inasmuch as both explain how things got to be the way they are by telling some sort of story. But our common parlance reckons myth to be false while history is, or aspired to be, true. Accordingly, a historian who rejects someone else's conclusion calls them mythical, while claiming that his own views are true. But what seems true to one historian will seem false to another, so one historian's truth becomes another's myth, even at the moment of utterance. (McNeill 1986, p. 3)

In other words, that we label a belief a "myth" should not be understood as a judgment about its reality or "truthiness."

Myths are the shared stories that shape the culture, politics, institutions, communication, method of coping, and identity of a community. Critically, myths are shared; they are public. They are "a cultural force" (Malinowski 1954, p. 143). Robert Doty argues that myths cannot be private, they must be socialized and examined among the public (1980). Once a myth has taken a hold, it alters the culture of the people. Historical complexity is shaped by human reaction to the adoption of myth: "any theory of human life, if widely believed, will alter actual behavior, usually by inducing people to act as if the theory were true" (McNeill 1986, p. 4). As "self-validating" beliefs, myths become core aspects of the culture and shape all aspects of society. As a way of providing a definitive understanding of how the world works and how it should be structured, myths also serve as ideology (Doty 1980; Segal 2001). Bruce Lincoln put it beautifully when he wrote myth is "ideology in narrative form" (Lincoln 1999, p. xii). As a force for structuring values and norms, myths generate support for institutions and induce group members to adhere to the social order (Bruner 1959; Segal 2001). Consider Lauri Honko on this point:

Myths give support to accepted patterns of behavior by placing present-day situations in a meaningful perspective with regard to the precedents of the past. Myths provide a valid justification for obligations and privileges. Myths act as safety valves by making it possible for people to ventilate their emotions without socially disruptive effects. (1984, p. 47)

For nations, myth unifies disparate interests and legitimizes institutions and policies. A good example are the myths that underpin the self-enforcing nature of successful constitutions (Elkins, Ginsburg and Melton 2009). People must accept a constitution's legitimacy for it to carry weight. Imagining constitutions and political institutions as sacred – courts become "temples" to justice and parliaments are "temples" of democracy – shames those susceptible to defection into contributing to the collective body. Thinking of the nine people who serve on the Supreme Court as the ultimate arbiters of the US Constitution, as being impartial guardians of "justice" rather than political appointees inclined to interpret the law as benefits their ideological preferences, is part of the necessary mythology that allows us to accept their rulings and to keep the faith in the constitutional process.

How Myths Are Reproduced and Communicated

The reproduction of myths by elites, institutions, rhetoric, symbols, rituals, and ceremonies enhances their accessibility (Doty 1980; Honko 1984; Schöpflin 1997). The reproduction of the community myth reinforces the core values of the community and encourages solidarity (Overing 1997; Schöpflin 1997). Even those who believe themselves to be objective, scientific historiographers of a community are influenced by the power of the myth as they attempt to provide meaning to historical events (McNeill 1986; Lorenz 2008). Historians are core players in the reproduction of myth (Zelinsky 1988; Lorenz 2008; Berger 2009). McNeill's term "mythistory" is incisive, revealing that because historians weave facts together into a story that has meaning, they allow myths to guide the meaning of historical events. Further, because groups like to be flattered, historians have an incentive to describe the group the way they see themselves. This leads to an amalgamation of facts and fiction, whether intentional or not, that reproduces the established myth (McNeill 1986, p. 8).

Group Cohesion

The accessibility of myths provides groups the assurance they will prosper, even during trying times (Malinowski 1954; Bruner 1959; Segal 2001). George Schöpflin contends that communities that express intense beliefs in their myths are more likely "to withstand much greater stress and turbulence" (Schöpflin 1997, p. 22). In his trenchant analysis of the race problem in America, Gunnar Myrdal argued the lack of group myth stymied Blacks' sense of self-respect and their ability to fight back against America's caste system. As he states: "It is more difficult for them to answer prejudice with prejudice and, as the Orientals may do, to consider themselves and their history superior to the White Americans" (Myrdal 1944, p. 54). Myths offer psychological and emotional resources community members can draw upon to sustain group cohesion in the most troubling of circumstances (Schöpflin 1997). Jerome Bruner contends that communities will fall into disarray when their myths no longer help members cope with the world they experience (Bruner 1959).

Identity

Myths bind communities; they also tell us who we are, providing a source of identity. Scott Leonard and Michael McClure's definition of myth highlights its role as source of identity:

Myths are ancient narrative that attempt to answer the enduring and fundamental human questions: How did the universe and the world come to be? How did we come to be here? Who are we? What are our proper, necessary, or inescapable roles as we relate to one another and to the world at large? What should our values be? How should we behave? How should we *not* behave? What are the consequences of behaving and not behaving in such ways?

(Leonard and McClure 2004, p. 1)

The importance of the role of myth in identity formation is stressed by other seminal accounts too. Bruner asserts that myths provide group members with a "library of scripts" that they can use to comprehend their multiple identities and serve as the "criterion for the self-critic" (Bruner 1959, p. 353). He further argues that "the myths that are the treasure of an instructed community provide the models and the programs in terms of which the growth of the internal cast of identities is molded and inspirited" (p. 357). Schöpflin contends that myths are "an instrument of self-definition" and provide individuals and communities with an identity that establishes their "special qualities" and boundaries (1997, p. 22). He also argues that "myth can be an instrument of identity transfer," meaning it provides the community with the ability to adapt to major upheaval – circumstances might change, but the shared answer to "who we are" provides a north star that does not waver. And, as illustrated throughout America's history, the preeminence of well-established myths of national identity accelerates the assimilation of outsider groups – anyone can be an American as long as they believe in freedom and apple pie (1997, p. 22). And that is perhaps the key American myth itself.

The Role of Power Justification

The fact-basis of a myth can be debated, but its power cannot. Myths serve as a basis for a community and provide its members with an understanding of their role in the world. Even though these aspects of myths are praised, scholars also acknowledge the inherent dangers in myths. Because myths emphasize the "virtue and righteousness" of a group, McNeill cautions of the power they grant those who would use them to denigrate outsiders and to increase resistance to intergroup cooperation. These myths can lead to intense ideological clashes, such as the Cold War, and were used to justify the genocidal bloodlust of the Nazis, who built their Third Reich using popular myths that dehumanized minority ethnic and racial groups (1986, p. 9). Schöpflin contends that the political and ideological nature of myths can enhance division in multiethnic societies (1997). Also, the emotional nature of myths makes them cognitively delimiting, leading societies to make suboptimal, even inhumane decisions. Furthermore, when a society is faced with competing myths, it faces a higher probability of imploding upon itself. Some of the greatest internal crises that a group faces stem from having to reconcile competing narratives about itself (Bruner 1959; Lorenz 2008).

A NOTE ON METHODS AND APPROACH

Students of nationalism have no shortage of source materials. The origin stories nations tell of themselves, the collective moments of pride (to some) that tell others – and ourselves – of how we came to be where we are today, and the dreams and ambitions of our collective future that animate us into action are repeated in classrooms and churches, around dining tables and campfires, and in movies, plays, art, and dance. We can read these stories in our daily newspapers and glossy magazines, see them whiz past on Twitter, TikTok, and Instagram, and in each other's Facebook feeds. And we see them, often barely noticing, when we drive down the streets and boulevards that connect and divide our communities, named for our national heroes, whose statues and monuments form the centers of our public spaces. Maps, museums, libraries, and oral history archives capture the voices and thoughts that form the master narrative of a nation.

In this book, we contribute to our understanding of what, who, and why America is by asking those who live here for their answers to these questions. Ours is a study of public opinion. We deploy the powerful methodology of random sample surveys to interview everyday residents of the United States. By carefully adhering to the best practices of sampling, we are able to generalize from these slices of survey respondents to the American public at large. Starting in 2008, and throughout the decade that followed, we implemented seven original national surveys and two original state-level surveys. Where feasible, we supplemented these original data with surveys conducted independently by the Public Religion Research Institute (PRRI). We provide details for all the surveys we analyze in the appendix. Any one of these surveys would have been adequate for academic purposes; to have nine original surveys spanning three presidential administrations, including that of the first Black president and the first openly White nationalist one (at least in the modern era), is an embarrassment of riches.

To analyze these data, we rely on a technique called regression analysis. Widely used across the social and physical sciences, this technique allows us to estimate the prevalence and determinants of the American religious exceptionalism worldview in the public. Armed with a valid measure of this multidimensional concept, we can then use the same techniques to estimate its relationship with the concepts of interest that motivate this book: how people define what it means to be American, how they evaluate their leaders and the policies they enact when in power, and how they wish America to engage with the world. Importantly, we can account for a host of factors relevant to these relationships, such as a respondent's political ideology and partisanship; their race, age, income, and education; and their religious affiliation and practice. This bolsters our confidence that we are uncovering meaningful relationships rather than spurious ones. And, importantly, because the statistical models are based on large quantities of data, we can calculate measures of uncertainty for our estimates that allow us to be transparent about which findings are statistically reliable and which are not.

If you have ever wondered what the equivalent of kids let loose in a candy store is for academics, it is three political scientists with a decade's worth of surveys. Engaged in this project for almost thirteen years, there is no shortage of research questions we have generated and sought to answer. Literally hundreds of statistical models, refined and honed over years of sustained inquiry, form the spine of this book. All the results are available in the appendices, but it is our job to distill the results of this research to make our findings as easily digestible as possible for you, our readers, while honoring the integrity and rigor of the scholarly enterprise. To that end, we present all our results graphically and focus the textual discussion of our results on the core relationships only so that we do not get distracted. Furthermore, we focus on the differences in attitudes that result from varying levels of adherence to the American religious exceptionalism worldview, seeking to convey the relative impact of greater fealty to this founding myth on how citizens understand the United States and its politics today. Our hope is that these authorial choices make our research more accessible to those interested in these aspects of American public opinion, while convincing our fellow academics that we have cut no corners in our pursuit of reliable answers to critical questions.

PLAN OF THE BOOK

Given the recent events in the United States, many would see this book as a reaction to the rise of the Tea Party, Donald Trump, and other groups that have overtly mixed religion with their view of the nation. Such a reading would be incorrect. The phenomenon of Trumpism and its many acolytes motivate us to explain the larger phenomenon at work. As we will explain, the Tea Party and Trump were able to gain prominence because they tapped into a cultural reservoir filled by the myth of American religious exceptionalism. We uncover the role of religious belief systems in shaping the political attitudes and actions of citizens.

Much like other scholars who examine religious belief systems, we believe the most important differences are in religious thought, not religious tradition and denomination. In establishing this, we hope to expand our understanding about what people believe their religion calls upon them to be and to do.

To address the role of American religious exceptionalism in public opinion we report an expansive set of empirical tests to examine how adherence to this myth generates difference in the American public along a range of issues. We begin Chapter 1 by documenting the importance of myths in nation-making. Further, we examine how the myth of American exceptionalism became integral to American nationalism and subsequently American identity. Specifically, we pay attention to how religious institutions helped disseminate the myth and how religious language made it palatable for citizens. The reliance of religious institutions and religious language on American exceptionalism gave it a holiness that morphed into American religious exceptionalism. Using historical analysis, we conceptualize American religious exceptionalism and demonstrate its power throughout American history. With the core concept defined, Chapter 2 empirically establishes the unique role of religion in the United States and demonstrates why religious exceptionalism is such an important factor in American social and political thought. Most importantly, this chapter validates a measurement of American religious exceptionalism and provides an image of its adherents, whom we refer to as disciples, and those who reject it, whom we refer to as dissidents, by examining the relationships between religious exceptionalism, prominent American values, religious demographics, social demographics, and political leanings. Chapter 3 provides the first examination of how American religious exceptionalism influences Americans' definitions about what it means to be American. Building upon the national attachment and identity literatures, we exploit multiple surveys to understand how the dissidents and disciples differ in their feelings of oneness with the nation and feelings of national superiority, as well as how they envision the ideal American. Whereas Chapter 3 establishes the American public's response to the question "who are we?," Chapter 4 addresses the question, "who can become one of us?" Specifically, it identifies those the disciples believe should be allowed to gain admission to the nation versus those they perceive as threats to it by examining immigration attitudes. Chapter 5 investigates the role of the nation on the global stage. It begins with a discussion of how the disciples of American religious exceptionalism have influenced American grand strategy, followed by a discussion of how religious exceptionalism's tenets help structure foreign policy attitudes. Focusing specifically on cooperative internationalism, militarism, and isolationism, this chapter demonstrates how religious exceptionalism serves as a core value that helps structure American foreign policy attitudes. Chapter 6 provides an examination of the domestic arena with a focus on attitudes toward political candidates and domestic public policies, by analyzing who the disciples consider to be the heroes and villains in American politics and further examining their political behavior. Chapter 7 examines how marginalized groups link American religious exceptionalism to their social and political beliefs. White Christians have been the primary focus of historical and empirical discussions; however, history has demonstrated that the language of religious exceptionalism has often been co-opted by marginalized groups to challenge the dominant system. Focusing on religious and racial minorities, we examine the extent to which adherence to American religious exceptionalism produces results like their White and Christian counterparts. The Conclusion chapter offers valedictory remarks, summarizing our core findings and discussing the implications of American religious exceptionalism for our understanding of public opinion and the modern American political landscape. Additionally, we explore how the myth of religious exceptionalism can be applied outside the context of the United States. Americans are not unique in their belief in the myth they are divinely favored. Groups in other nations also see their nation as the representatives of a divine mission, though those myths are not backed with the might of American military hegemony. This chapter concludes with a consideration of how religious exceptionalism in other nations influences prospects for international cooperation and conflict.

The United States is the most powerful state the world has ever known. It has used its might to advance its interests around the globe and justified its actions under the guise of being the champion of democracy and freedom. Critics are quick to point out the myriad ways in which the language of liberty has been a fig-leaf for the pursuit of naked self-interest, and one might reasonably wonder if its use was a cynical ploy to justify America's military goals. Perhaps. But as we document in this book, Americans have long believed they have a special duty to promote a set of values. This stems from a deep sense of America as an exceptional, indispensable nation bound to answer the clarion call of liberty anywhere it is imperiled. Yet this idea of the nation sits uneasily with another hallmark of American political thought: that America is a city on a hill that must be protected against intruders and from entanglements abroad that might corrupt and distract it from its divine mission. This book is about how those who live in that blessed city understand themselves and their place in the world.

I

Myths, Gods, and Nations

Blessed is the nation whose God is the LORD; and the people whom he hath chosen for his own inheritance.

Psalm 33:12

Benedict Anderson's popular conceptualization of a nation as "an imagined political community" that is "imagined as both inherently limited and sovereign" (1983, p. 6) is a useful pedagogical device for explicating how myths underpin the formation of nations and nationalism. The national community is *imagined* because its members need not know the actual behaviors or even existence of other members to believe they are in communion. *Limited* indicates that national members see the nation's population as finite, and draw clear boundaries between who is and who is not a member. Finally, *sovereign* signifies that national members understand the nation as self-determined.[1] Communities embrace national myths to explain to themselves that they are bound together for a purpose as opposed to happenstance (Lorenz 2008; Clement 2014). Myths connect us to each other, give us a sense of self-determination, and establish boundaries that separate us from those who are not us.

Myths are the bedrock of nationalism (Zelinsky 1988; Clement 2014). Nationalism is the building block for national identity (Gellner 1983; Smith 1991), though like the myths on which it is based, nationalism is linked to exclusionary policies and violence (Allport 1927; de Figueiredo and Elkins 2003). Just as myths possess an affective aspect and legitimize group structures, nationalism "gives legitimacy to the state, and inspires

13

its citizens to feel an emotional attachment towards it" (Kellas 1998, p. 1). The basis of nationalism can be claimed to be civic ideals or ethnic connections depending on the myths to which the nation's members ascribe. Like those myths, nationalism plays different roles. It has served as the source of liberation for oppressed groups as well as a source of justification for those who would oppress them. For the groups it motivates, nationalism is a force for political, economic, and cultural action (Kohn 1944; Snyder 2000; Henderson 2019).

1.1 NATIONALISM AS AN ELITE TOOL

Scholars of state-building view nationalism as an ideology used by elites to generate a singular understanding of the nation, to achieve specific goals. Ernest Gellner defines it as "primarily a political principle, which holds the political and national unit should be congruent" (1983, p. 1). John Breuilly comes to a similar conclusion arguing "there exists a nation with an explicit and peculiar character; the interests and values of this nation take priority over all other interests and values; the nation must be as independent as possible" (1985, p. 3). Jack Snyder points directly to the role of elites in fostering nationalism, defining it "as the doctrine that a people who see themselves as distinct in their culture, history, institutions, or principles should rule themselves in a political system that expresses and protects those distinctive characteristics" (2000, p. 13). Taking this political understanding of nationalism further, James Kellas argues nationalist ideology provides a justification for elites to pursue their self-interests (1998, p. 31). Elites use nationalist frames to advance their interests and alter the considerations citizens bring to bear in their decision-making (Riker 1996; Chong 2000; Druckman 2011; Stone 2012). Much as any successful frame is constrained by local culture and customs (Chong 2000), nationalist rhetoric is constrained by local norms and traditions (Geertz 1973). After all, as Hans Kohn puts it, "nationalism is not a natural phenomenon ... it is a product of the growth of social and intellectual factors at a certain stage of history" (1944, p. 6). While the love of family and community is "natural" because the individual routinely interacts with its members, a love of nation requires the "identification with the life and aspirations of uncounted millions who we shall never know, with a territory which we shall never visit in its entirety" (Kohn 1944, p. 9). Because elites need individuals to contribute to the goals of a large group, they need to create a sense of common fate that motivates people to contribute to the larger good (Snyder 2000). Clifford Geertz argues the first stage of nationalism requires a "deliberately constructed" concept of the nation. Further, he contends nationalism is not the reflection, cause, expression, or engine of the development of new states, "but the thing itself" (1973, p. 252). In line with this understanding, Eric Hobsbawm argues "nationalism comes before nations" (Hobsbawm 1992, p. 10). Myth-making about the nation is how elites craft an idea of a nation that resonates (Edsman 1972; Lorenz 2008; Clement 2014). It is how, to borrow from Anderson (1983) again, nations come to think of themselves as old.

1.1.1 Cultural Reproduction of Nationalistic Myths

Using myths as the basis for a nationalist ideology provides elites with a more effective way of justifying their nationalism, and this works to the extent that their ideologies resonate with citizens through rituals, symbols, and communication (Edsman 1972). Eric Hobsbawm frames this effectively: While the idea of a nation is "constructed essentially from above," it "cannot be understood unless also analyzed from below" (1992, p. 10). Similarly, for Rogers Brubaker, nationalism is a set of "nation-oriented idioms, practices, and possibilities that are continuously available or 'endemic' in modern cultural and political life" (1996, p. 10). Nationalism is thus not just a private good for elites but a potent political force because it is constantly transferred, socialized, and internalized among the masses.

In a famous 1882 lecture at the Sorbonne, Ernest Renan argued that nations are not the consequences of dynasties, language, religion, race, or geography, but that they are a "soul" based on two facets: the common possession of "a rich legacy of memories" and "the desire to continue to invest" in that heritage (1990, p. 19). Benedict Anderson urges scholars to move from analyzing nationalism from a political standpoint to analyzing it as part of a "large cultural system" (1983, p. 12). Michael Billig argues our constant focus on "hot" nationalism in developing nations ignores the "banal" nationalism in western developed nations. In those "older" nations, such as the United States or the United Kingdom, the idea of nationhood is a constant backdrop shaping politics, culture, and even the media (1995). Anthony Smith also emphasizes the cultural role of nationalism but goes further, arguing it "is the secular, modern equivalent of the pre-modern, sacred myth of ethnic election" (1991, p. 84). As a "civic religion," it inspires intellectuals and serves as the foundation for language, rituals, symbols, and practices, which continually reproduce the idea of the nation among its people. Smith also argues the ideological manifestation of nationalism through social movements can only emerge after "the gestation of nationalism as language-and-symbolism, and as consciousness-and-aspiration" (1991, p. 85).

1.1.2 Nationalism as Shaper of Attitudes and Behavior

Routinely exposed to the language, symbols, and rituals of nationalism, citizens internalize this meaning of the nation. Nationality's main criteria, Floyd Allport recognized almost a century ago, "are psychological" (1927, p. 292). Elites and cultural institutions are critical in fostering national attachment through the telling of national stories and repeated rituals; however, at the end of the day, the idea of a nation exists only in the mind of the individual. So, when individuals no longer believe in the nation, elite and institutional efforts and desires notwithstanding, it ceases to exist, or, less dramatically, its power to direct collective behavior is weakened. It is through institutions that individuals actualize their idea of the nation and act. Those who adhere to nationalist perspectives view the nation as an "overperson" possessing emotions and purpose requiring loyalty and devotion (Allport 1927, pp. 293–94). The nation embodies the person, and the nation's honor is linked to the individual's honor. Kohn describes it well: "nationalism is first and foremost a state of mind, an act of consciousness" (1944, p. 10). From this foundation, contemporary psychological studies of nationalism examine how it joins a person's consciousness and shapes their understanding of the world. In their discussion of American nationalism, Bart Bonikowski and Paul DiMaggio define nationalism as "the complex of ideas, sentiments, and representations by which Americans understand the United States and their relationship to it" (2016, p. 949). In contrast to this neutral definition, other scholars view nationalism as an emotional, even irrational, psychological phenomenon. Wilbur Zelinsky characterizes nationalism as an "intense devotion to the nation, that real or supposed community of individuals who are convinced they share a common set of traditions, beliefs, and cultural characteristics" (1988, p. 17). Other definitions not only emphasize this strong link to the nation but also include beliefs of national superiority (Citrin, Wong, and Duff 2001; de Figueiredo and Elkins 2003; McDaniel, Nooruddin, and Shortle 2016). Like religion, nationalism provides a way of understanding how the world works. Nationalism helps individuals understand their world and their role in it. Like religious teachings and folk myths, it answers common questions, such as who am

I, why am I here, how should I behave, and who are my people? As a psychological resource, it simplifies the world and gives individuals a structure for processing information that can be applied to various decisions, from political choices to supermarket purchases (Allport 1927; Citrin, Wong, and Duff 2001; de Figueiredo and Elkins 2003; Bonikowski and DiMaggio 2016).

The discussion of nationalism thus far reflects a bias toward its virtues for building communities and providing the basis for functioning, legitimate nation-states. But the darker side of nationalism has been equally the object of scholarly inquiry. Expressing his disdain for nationalism, George Steiner wrote:

Nationalism is the venom of our age. It has brought Europe to the edge of ruin. It drives the new states of Asian and Africa like crazed lemmings ... Every mob impulse in modern politics, every totalitarian design, feeds on nationalism, on the drug of hatred which makes human beings bare their teeth across a wall, across ten yards of waste ground ... If the potential of civilization is not destroyed, we shall have to develop more complex, more provisional loyalties. (1998, p. 152)

George Kellas is less strident but acknowledges that nationalism is double-edged, that it can "protect or destroy freedom, establish peace or lead to war" (1998, p. 41). Such grappling with nationalism's many effects is reflected by Geertz, who argues nationalism deserves its negative image, as it has wrought "havoc upon humanity," even as he posits it "has been a driving force in some of the most creative changes in history" (Geertz 1973, pp. 253–54).

Why is this? Well, by identifying the community members who belong (the in-group), nationalism necessarily must exclude others (the out-group). Further, the emotional and shallow thinking produced by nationalism encourages beliefs in zero-sum relations with outsiders (Sidanius et al. 1997; de Figueiredo and Elkins 2003; Parker and Barreto 2013). Allport views the idea of the nation as noble; however, he acknowledges its emotional aspect makes it easy to "fall prey to the clever manipulations of the jingoist" (1927, pp. 299–300). The centrality of the emotional aspect of nationalism requires us to understand the myths a community adopts that dictate the content of its nationalism. To this task, we now turn.

1.2 THE MYTH OF AMERICAN EXCEPTIONALISM

The myths a nation adopts influence how it defines itself and how its members understand themselves and their role in the nation and world

(Zelinsky 1988; Lorenz 2008). The American case is unique because its nationalism is rooted in the belief that its ideals are transcendent. A central myth of America is that its nationalism is not founded on the basis of territory, religion, or language. Susan-Mary Grant argues the uniqueness of the American case provides one of the best examples for demonstrating how myths shaped a nation and its nationalism. She states these myths were a way to "produce unity from disunity, consensus from conflict" (1997, p. 90). The distinctiveness of the colonies, along with their conflicts with each other, made it imperative that the nation generated national myths quickly to forge an American identity that brought them together and distinguished them from the British (Zelinsky 1988; Grant 1997).

Numerous myths were created to help unify the young nation, but the myth of American exceptionalism – the idea that the United States has something special other countries wish to achieve – was the one that was most effective in capturing the public's attention. Kohn argues Americans see themselves as different from all other nations because they share the belief they had developed a nation that is "the greatest possible approximation to perfection" (1944, p. 291). Many Americans believe America overcame the corruptions plaguing Europe to create a form of government that recognized rights as nature intended. Thomas Paine's *Common Sense* vehemently argues for the separation of the colonies from England because the monarchies throughout Europe perverted natural governance of humanity (Paine 1776). Hector St. John de Crèvecoeur's thoughts on the new men of America, qualitatively different from their European brethren, are worth reading at length:

What then is the American, this new man? He is either an European, or the descendant of an European, hence that strange mixture of blood, which you will find in no other country. I could point out to you a family whose grandfather was an Englishman, whose wife was Dutch, whose son married a French woman, and whose present four sons have now four wives of different nations. He is an American, who, leaving behind him all his ancient prejudices and manners, receives new ones from the new mode of life he has embraced, the new government he obeys, and the new rank he holds. He becomes an American by being received in the broad lap of our great Alma Mater. Here individuals of all nations are melted into a new race of men, whose labours and posterity will one day cause great changes in the world. Americans are the western pilgrims, who are carrying along with them that great mass of arts, sciences, vigour, and industry which began long since in the east; they will finish the great circle. (1782, p. 33)

De Crèvecoeur's is an evocative proclamation of American exceptionalism, which Wilbur Zelinsky more prosaically describes as the belief the nation embodies "the materialization of novel ideas that had been smoldering among the intellectually and religiously disaffected ..., but were first to reach criticality and burst into flames in such places as Boston and Philadelphia in the 1770s" (1988, p. 27). Seymour Martin Lipset noted the American claim that it was the first "new" nation, where membership is "creedal" or "civic," rooted in shared political and civic ideals, such as equality and the right to liberty, rather than "ethnic" or "sanguinal," based in premodern notions such as ethnicity, language, or religion (1979). This idea has been reaffirmed so often, from Alexis de Tocqueville to Louis Hartz, that Gunnar Myrdal referred to American nationalism as the American Creed (Myrdal 1944; Tocqueville 1945; Hartz 1991).[2] Writing at the same time as Myrdal, Hans Kohn argued,

the American nation has not been determined by "natural" factors of blood and soil, nor by common memories of a long history. It was formed by an idea, a universal idea. Loyalty to America meant therefore loyalty to that idea, and as the idea was universal, everyone could be included. (1944, p. 324)

Further, scholars note that because Americans see themselves as the group that perfected society, their nationalism is one that looks forward, not backward; that celebrates not only its past, but what its goodness and ideals will yet accomplish (Kohn 1944; Tuveson 1968; Zelinsky 1988). However, the conviction that America is a model to the world implies that any nation which does not meet its standards is deficient, even corrupt, and a threat to the ideals upon which Americans believe their nation was uniquely founded (Kohn 1944; Hughes 2004).

Celebrations of national documents and monuments dedicated to national heroes are all part of the myth of American exceptionalism. Americans revel in grand displays celebrating their history through festivities, rituals, and reenactments (Adam 1937; Zelinsky 1988). These events are supposed to serve as reminders that throwing off the yoke of British oppression and European corruption allowed Americans to create a nation that left men to live as they truly should (Grant 1997). Beyond these overt events, the myth of exceptionalism pervades all aspects of American life. Myrdal again: "All means of intellectual communication are utilized to stamp [ideas of American exceptionalism] into everybody's mind. The schools teach them, the churches preach them" (1944, p. 8). The symbols of American nationalism are deeply embedded in mainstream American culture. The daily reciting of the pledge of allegiance in school, the singing of the national anthem before sporting events, the placement of American flags in private businesses, and the incorporation of national symbols in commercials are all ways American nationalism sustains itself (Billig 1995).

The constant reification of American exceptionalism, its heroes, and its symbols fuels intense outpourings of national affection. Data from the International Social Survey Programme's 2013 National Identity Survey reveal that US citizens express higher levels of pride than those in other developed nations (see Figure 1.1). More than two-thirds of American respondents say they are very proud of being a member of their nation. The next highest proportion are the Irish (56 percent), followed by respondents from Iceland (47.3 percent). National pride is measured using two scales. The first captures pride in the nation's *actions* ($\alpha = .83$), such as how its democracy works, its political influence in the world, economic achievement, security system, and fair treatment of groups within its borders.[3] The second focuses on pride in the nation's purported *achievements* ($\alpha = .59$), whether in scientific, technological, athletic, or artistic domains, both historical and in the present day. As Figure 1.1 demonstrates, American citizens express relatively higher levels of pride. On the action scale, only the Norwegians and Swiss score significantly higher. Americans are on par with Danes and Germans, and score significantly higher than all the remaining nations surveyed. Regarding achievements, Americans score significantly higher than ten of the nations studied and are statistically tied with the others. Americans might not be alone in feeling great pride in their nation, but they certainly are second to none in the level of the pride they express.

Along with generating a sense of pride, the exceptionalism myth also implies a comparison between the greatness of the United States and shortcomings of other nations (Meyer and Royer 2001). Scholars have routinely characterized American nationalism as narcissistic or chauvinistic (Kohn 1944; Savelle 1962; Zelinsky 1988; Citrin, Wong, and Duff 2001). Other surveys document that members of other nations – and many Americans too – associate narcissism and arrogance with being American (Terracciano and McCrae 2007; Miller et al. 2015). To assess the extent to which Americans distinguish themselves from other nations regarding a sense of national superiority, we created a measure of national hubris. *Hubris* ($\alpha = .69$) is measured by agreement with statements about only wanting to be a member of their country, the belief that the world would be better if more countries were like their own, and the belief that their country is better than most other countries. Our analysis confirms Americans' distinctive hubris. They score significantly higher on the hubris scale than all other nations except for the Japanese. Another aspect of this sense of superiority is a denial of national transgressions since the narcissism bred by the myth of American

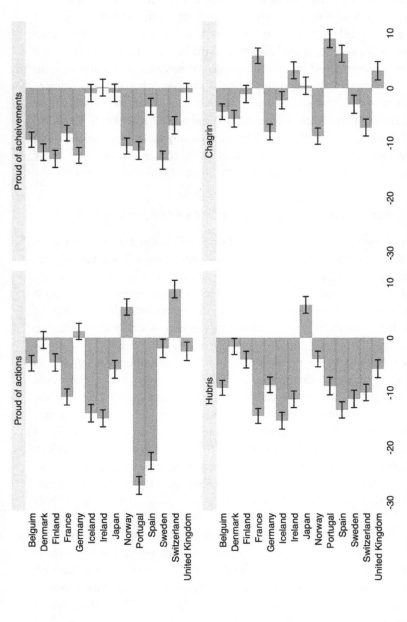

FIGURE 1.1 Difference between citizens of other developed nations and the United States regarding feelings toward the nation

exceptionalism also fosters a sense of national innocence that makes it difficult for Americans to acknowledge their failures and misdeeds. We measure this with what we call the national chagrin scale. *National chagrin* ($\alpha = .57$) is measured through agreement with statements about whether one ever feels ashamed by her country's actions, whether one feels less proud than she would like to be, or if she believes the world would be a better place if the country acknowledged its shortcomings. A revealing comparison is to France, Portugal, Spain, and the United Kingdom, who were the primary colonizers of the Americas and were heavily engaged in the Atlantic slave trade. The populations of all four states reveal much higher levels of chagrin than do Americans. But the United States is equally guilty of colonialism and slavery; thus, its significantly lower level of chagrin reveals the consistency with which Americans cling tightly to the myth of national innocence.

1.3 RELIGION AND AMERICAN EXCEPTIONALISM

Scholars have often compared nationalism to religion or argued nationalism is a modern replacement for religion (Anderson 1983; Smith 2000). John Armstrong contends religion and religious institutions were central in establishing American nationalism (1982). The religious networks developed through the revivals of the eighteenth and nineteenth centuries provided the most effective method for communicating the idea of a national identity to the masses. George Thomas argues the Great Awakenings that swept through America in the 1730s and again in the 1790s played a key role in establishing the myths that formed an American identity (1989). Consistent with Benedict Anderson's assertion that print capitalism accelerated the spread of nationalism, access to mass printing provided religious groups the ability to distribute sermons and pamphlets that imagined America as a nation, not just a political collective (Haselby 2015). Early American nationalists were not merely religious zealots; their nationalism and religiosity were tightly intertwined (Lieven 2004; Blum 2005). Fueled by millennialist beliefs, they saw America as "the triumph of Christian principles," a "holy utopia" (Tuveson 1968, p. 34). Millennialism is a product of the Protestant Reformation, which reinterpreted the end-of-times story in the book of Revelations. This reinterpretation altered it from being a cosmic battle waged between God and Satan to a battle in which humanity would partake. God would work through nations to accomplish victory over the forces of evil, and in doing so, a divine nation that properly reflected God's laws would be formed. Prominent biblical scholar David Austin's *The Downfall of*

Mystical Babylon, published in 1794, articulates the faith that the young United States is God's hero to the world:

Behold the regnum montis, the kingdom of the mountain, begun on the Fourth of July, 1776, when the *birth* of the MAN-CHILD—the hero of civil and religious liberty took place in these United States. Let them read the predictions of heaven respecting the increase in his dominion – that he was *to rule all nations with a rod of iron*; that is, bring them into complete and absolute subjection; and that the young hero might be equal to this mighty conquest, he is supported by an omnipotent arm; he is *caught up unto God, and to this throne.* (1794, p. 392)

To exemplify this millennialist belief about the connection between their new nation and divine prophecy, the Founders chose the eagle as its national symbol. The eagle plays a prominent role in the book of Revelations, offering a warning to the world's inhabitants of impending judgment, and its wings are used to carry people to safety. From this, loyalty to God and to the nation became synonymous (Tuveson 1968; Beam 1976).

These nationalists held that the success of the American experiment was because of divine selection. Americans were better than other nations because they were conducting themselves the way God had intended (Hughes 2004). The ability for a disparate group of colonies to come together with an untrained army to defeat British forces, and its endurance of faith to overcome the challenges posed by the Civil War, were signs that Americans were the new chosen people and the United States was divinely favored (Tuveson 1968; Grant 1997). A common belief was that much like God protected David in his battle against Goliath, America would over-come insurmountable evils because it held God's favor. This faith in an ordained connection between divine will and national success has persisted undimmed over the nation's almost 250-year history.

There has been much discussion by commentators about the decline of religion in the United States; however, personal religiosity is still relatively stronger in the United States compared to other industrialized nations (Putnam and Campbell 2010). Political scientists have often nodded to the religious nature of American nationalism, but rigorous research examining the religious dimension of American nationalism is limited. Most of our knowledge of the connection between American religion and national-ism has come from sociologists, historians, and theologians. When political scientists have examined these ideas, it has mainly been to explain US foreign policy. Further, previous examinations have operated at the national level. By focusing on an ideology, which we refer to as American religious exceptionalism, this book documents its prevalence at the individual level and demonstrates how it influences public opinion in a variety of realms.

1.4 AMERICAN RELIGIOUS EXCEPTIONALISM

American religious exceptionalism is an ideology that perceives the nation as divinely inspired, favored, and called upon to carry out a divine mission. It is a fusion of religious identity and national pride. The nation is integral to the fulfillment of a divine plan. American religious exceptionalism reflects what Mark Juergensmeyer defines as ideological religious nationalism. This is in contrast with ethnic religious nationalism, which refers to contexts in which groups seek greater political authority over a region, which often involves the fusion of religion with a "culture of domination or liberation" (1996, p. 4). Examples of this would be the struggle of both Protestants and Catholics in Ireland to gain greater political power or that of the *Hindutva* movement in India that seeks to establish India as a Hindu nation. In contrast, ideological religious nationalism is based on ideas. In this instance, politics has been religionized and "compatibility with religious goals becomes the criterion for an acceptable political platform" (Juergensmeyer 1996, p. 5). Furthermore, "national aspirations become fused with religious quests for purity and redemption" (Juergensmeyer 1996, p. 6). Secular leaders are reviled as being part of a conspiracy to undermine the nation. Examples of ideological religious nationalism would include the Islamic Revolution in Iran and Christian nationalism in the United States (Whitehead and Perry 2020).

As an ideology that politicizes religion and religionizes politics, religious nationalism melds the two, rendering piety and patriotism indistinguishable. Adherence to American religious exceptionalism betrays the image of civic nationalism the nation has promoted. Instead, it reflects primordialism, the belief that a nation should be constructed based on a common ethnicity, culture, or history (Smith 2001). It is exclusionary in identifying who and why individuals are national heroes, as well as the importance of certain documents. It makes the nation a "sacred communion," one that combines religious and political traditions together and often confounds religious leaders with political leaders and vice versa. The result of the widespread adherence to a religious exceptionalism ideology is that the legitimacy of the nation is no longer based on political principles but religious doctrine. Religious miracles become national celebrations, and Holy Scriptures "are reinterpreted as national epics" (Smith 2000, p. 799).

While scholars have long noted the similarities between nationalism and religion, specifically their abilities to create communities and norms, and to stir intense emotions, the concepts are more often than not treated as mutually exclusive (Kohn 1944; Armstrong 1982). Nationalism has often been framed as the secular replacement of religion, with Anthony Smith characterizing it as a "political religion" (Smith 2001). However, some scholars have noted the role religious traditions and symbolism have played in advancing nationalist ideologies. This is especially the case in the United States, where religious practices and symbols have been co-opted to represent the nation's purpose and provide guidance to its citizens (Smith 2000; Herzog 2011; Whitehead and Perry 2020). The best example of this is what Robert Bellah famously refers to as American civil religion, which is the interweaving of religion into American social and political life through "a collection of beliefs, symbols, and rituals with respect to sacred things and institutionalized in a collectivity" (1967, p. 7). The American civil religion "reaffirms, among other things, the religious legitimation of the lightest political authority" (p. 3). The American civil religion calls on Americans individually and collectively to fulfill the obligation of carrying "out God's will on earth" (p. 4).

We build on Bellah's foundational insight by incorporating several components scholars have highlighted since he introduced the concept of civil religion. Bellah recognized the negative consequences of a civil religion – think Manifest Destiny and American Imperialism, but overall, he viewed it as a positive or at least benign force. Other scholars portray it as a dichotomy, either encouraging a narcissism and superiority to other nations or encouraging humility and a brotherhood of nations (Marty 1974; Bulman 1991; Kent and Spickard 1994). Robert Wuthnow discusses American civil religion as having both liberal and conservative dimensions (1988). The liberal dimension argues the nation is blessed, not chosen. It views the United States as part of a global brotherhood with other nations. In this brotherhood, America's duty is to work with other nations to achieve global peace and human advancement. The conservative dimension emphasizes the idea of the United States as a divinely chosen nation, reveres the Founding Fathers as almost sacred figures, and regards the Declaration of Independence and the Constitution as quasi-sacred texts. It emphasizes exceptionalism and evangelizes the need for other nations to emulate the United States. In addition to the liberal–conservative typology of civil religion, others contend it indicates a type of divinely inspired mission. This mission compels the nation to lead all other nations and bring about a higher state of living (Tiryakian 1982; Pierard and Linder 1988; Coles 2002). This mission-oriented understanding of American civil religion is a reflection of what Wilson Moses refers to a "hard-line messianism," which "developed into the doctrine of white racial supremacy, ruthless expansionism, religious intolerance, and economic insensitivity" (Moses 1982, p. 8). Philip Gorski (2017) contends that civil religion is a mixture of secular and religious thought that draws on civic republicanism and prophetic religion. In recognizing the importance of both secular and religious thoughts, it calls for both to be a part of the public space, while also enforcing borders on them. Gorski's civil religion exists between two diametrically opposed poles. At one end is radical secularism, which calls for taking religion out of the public discourse and making it a purely private phenomenon. On the other end is religious nationalism, which seeks to shut out secular thought and reasoning. Emulating some of the characteristics of Wuthnow's conservative civil religion, Gorski refers to religious nationalism as "the dark side of civil religion" (p. 35). It is fueled by two narratives – conquest and the apocalypse – that breed hubris, separation, and violence. The narrative of conquest calls on followers to seek "vengeance on the unrighteous" (p. 21). The apocalyptic narrative emphasizes an eventual war between good and evil, where the good will reign supreme for eternity.

Our definition and conceptualization of American religious exceptionalism is based upon these definitions of the darker conservative aspects of civil religion. We argue that religious exceptionalism functions as a buttress for beliefs about American exceptionalism and its messianic approach to global politics. Further, religious exceptionalism serves as an undergirding belief system explaining how to define the nation as well as shaping governmental and individual behavioral norms. In our analysis, American religious exceptionalism uses civil religion as a way to legitimize itself, while in actuality being antagonistic toward it.

Religious exceptionalism structures citizen beliefs by establishing three core aspects of identity: position, purpose, and origin. The disciples of American religious exceptionalism believe that a higher power played a role in the creation of the nation by setting aside a territory for a specific group to inhabit. They believe the nation's successes and failures are linked to divine judgment. They interpret times of struggle as divine tests or punishments. This belief system is exemplified by the tradition of issuing jeremiads, religious explanations for why a "chosen" people face tragedies (Bercovitch 1978; Moses 1982). Before landing in America, Puritan leaders, such as John Winthrop and John Cotton, issued warnings of God's swift and harsh punishment if they went astray. Thomas

Jefferson offered his own jeremiad in his lament about God's punishment for slavery:

And can the liberties of a nation be thought secure when we have removed their only firm basis, a conviction in the minds of the people that these liberties are of the gift of God? That they are not to be violated but with his wrath? Indeed I tremble for my country when I reflect that God is just: that his justice cannot sleep forever: that considering numbers, nature and natural means only, a revolution of the wheel of fortune, an exchange of situation, is among possible events: that it may become probable by supernatural interference! The Almighty has no attribute which can take side with us in such a contest. (Jefferson 1999, pp. 174–75)

Actual abolitionists, both Black and White, issued their own jeremiads warning the nation of divine punishment for allowing the atrocity of slavery to continue (Bercovitch 1978; Moses 1982; Walker 1995). In his second inaugural address, President Lincoln offered his own jeremiad:

If we shall suppose that American slavery is one of those offenses which, in the providence of God, must needs come, but which, having continued through His appointed time, He now wills to remove, and that He gives to both North and South this terrible war as the woe due to those by whom the offense came.

(Lincoln 1865)

Prominent disciples of American religious exceptionalism have also issued their own jeremiads. Under the specter of a war with the USSR, evangelist Billy Graham came to national prominence, issuing warnings of how America's divine protection would be removed if the nation did not correct its immoral ways. In response to the September 11, 2001, attacks, Jerry Falwell ranted that the tragedy was caused because Americans had taken God out of society:

The ACLU has got to take a lot of blame for this. And I know I'll hear from them for this, but throwing God ... successfully with the help of the federal court system ... out of the public square, out of the schools, the abortionists have got to bear some burden for this because God will not be mocked and when we destroy 40 million little innocent babies, we make God mad. ... I really believe that the pagans and the abortionists and the feminists and the gays and the lesbians who are actively trying to make that an alternative lifestyle, the ACLU, People for the American Way, all of them who try to secularize America ... I point the finger in their face and say you helped this happen.[4]

In response to the devastation caused to New Orleans by Hurricane Katrina, Franklin Graham, Billy Graham's son, argued it was divine punishment for it being a "wicked city."[5] In response to the 2012 Sandy Hook elementary school shooting that left twenty-six dead, including twenty children, James Dobson, the founder of Focus on the Family, stated: "I think we have turned our back on the Scripture and on God Almighty and I think he has allowed judgment to fall upon us. I think that's what's going on."[6] And, more recently, in April 2020, Pat Robertson opined that the coronavirus pandemic would only end if Americans ended their "wicked ways."[7]

Disciples of American religious exceptionalism also believe the Almighty has defined their purpose through an enduring and unquestioned national mission. While certain aspects of a nation's purpose are malleable, its central mission, handed down by the Supreme Being, cannot be changed. Because of this, its disciples hold a narrow view of who is part of their nation or who can lead it. Here's Pat Robertson again:

> The Constitution of the United States, for instance, is a marvelous document for self-government by Christian people. But the minute you turn the document into the hands of non-Christian and atheistic people they can use it to destroy the very foundation of our society.[8]

Nor are such ideas limited to the lunatic fringe of American society. In 2019, then US Attorney General William Barr warned that the waning influence of Judeo-Christian values relative to other religions and secularism constituted a major threat to the nation and its ability to uphold the Constitution (2019).

1.5 THE CULTURE AND POLITICS OF AMERICAN RELIGIOUS EXCEPTIONALISM

American religious exceptionalism has cultural and political functions that are steeped in a long-held American tradition of supporting religious institutions. Culturally speaking, it is inculcated through everyday practices. To many, the American use of religious language and symbols seems innocuous, but they serve as repeated practices and behaviors that allow religious exceptionalism to remain an enduring aspect of American social and political life. Politically, elites often invoke the language of God and nation to justify their policy goals and justify their ideological stances (Domke and Coe 2008; Haselby 2015). As a result, God and nation are ever present in America's political proceedings, on the campaign trail, as well as deeply entrenched in its political institutions.

American religious exceptionalism is continually reproduced through rituals and practices that are routinely embedded in daily life to the extent that many people do not even recognize them as religious. Others choose to ignore them. Obvious examples of the reproduction of religious exceptionalism are arguments over prayer in school or the display of the Ten Commandments on government property. However, there are several practices that may go unnoticed, such as the words "under God" in the pledge of allegiance, which American children regularly recite in school. The national motto is "In God We Trust." The back of the national seal displays the Eye of Providence, also referred to as the "All Seeing Eye of God," and the Latin phrase *Annuit cœptis*, which translates to Providence (or God) "favors our undertakings." Further, the display of the American flag in church sanctuaries extends the sacredness of the place of worship to the sacred nation. After the September 11, 2001, terrorist attacks, Americans began singing "God Bless America," as opposed to other patriotic songs such as "America the Beautiful" or "My Country, 'Tis of Thee." Such cultural practices may appear benign, but together they constitute a process that reinforces the linkage between the nation and the divine and reaffirms the spirit of American religious exceptionalism in the national psyche.

Political leaders have used religious imagery to shape the nation from its founding. James Byrd argues that many of those who chose to fight in the American Revolution had a limited understanding of the philosophical and ideological reasoning behind American independence, but through the work of pastors, they understood the theological reasoning for independence (2013). Religion served as their basis for understanding their world. Ideas about the declaration of rights and representative government did not have the same emotional impact as a sermon. Because of this, clergy played a central role in making the revolution meaningful to the average colonist. These clergy linked the ideological arguments and the fight for independence to divine will (Wood 1998; Byrd 2013). Recognizing the power of religion, Thomas Paine, who elsewhere openly questioned the truth of the Bible (Byrd 2013), used scripture and Biblical imagery to justify his call for American independence in *Common Sense* (Paine 1776). The success of *Common Sense* has been attributed to the fact that it mimicked the meter of a sermon (Stout 1977).

The idea of divine favoritism toward nations was embedded in the minds of the British colonists long before the Puritans arrived in New England (Hudson 1970). However, the Puritans served as the impetus for American religious exceptionalism. The Puritans viewed Britain as corrupt and unworthy of God's favor and saw the colonies as a place to start anew and fulfill their divine destiny (Hudson 1970; Hughes 2004). Puritans referred to America as "New Jerusalem," a place chosen for God's people. "God had led the Jews out of Egypt, through the Red Sea, and into the Promised Land. Now God led the Puritans out of England, across the Atlantic Ocean, and into another promised land" (Hughes 2004, p. 30). Escaping the corruption of Europe allowed colonists to establish a "New Israel" where they could properly practice their religion and governance as God intended. The Puritans, who found significant financial success in the new land, saw America as the pinnacle of civilization. John Winthrop's "Model of Christian Charity" memorably articulates this view: "For we must consider that we shall be as a city upon a hill. The eyes of all people are upon us" (1630). This view of America and its residents as part of divine plan spread through the First Great Awakening in which the colonies were swept up in a decade-long religious revival. These revivals embedded the idea that colonists were a distinct group created by a divine force and commissioned to save the world from its degradation (Hudson 1970; Hughes 2004; Prothero 2012). In *White Jacket*, novelist Herman Melville articulates this missionary aspect of America's purpose: "We Americans are the peculiar, chosen people – the Israel of our time, we bear the ark of the liberties of the world" (Melville 1988, p. 150). He continues:

God has predestined, mankind expects, great things from our race; and great things we feel in our souls. The rest of the nations must soon be in our rear. We are the pioneers of the world; the advance-guard, sent on through the wilderness of untried things, to break a new path in the New World that is ours. In our youth is our strength; in our inexperience, our wisdom. At a period when other nations have but lisped, our deep voice is heard afar. Long enough, have we been skeptics with regard to ourselves, and doubted whether, indeed, the political Messiah had come. But he has come in us. (Melville 1988, p. 151)

The Founding Fathers understood the implementation of democracy as honoring divine will. By establishing a democracy, they had returned the world to the order God intended (Hughes 2004). Because of the success of the "great experiment," many saw the spread of democracy as their divinely commanded duty (Hughes 2004; Monten 2005). As the world's "political Messiah," it was the duty of the United States to spread its way of life through all means possible. The nation's constitutional design reflects the Founders' beliefs; even though it established a separation of church and state, it encouraged religious practice and proselytization. This compromise of religion's role in the national identity embodied a free enterprise spirit of religiosity that only encouraged the myth of a divine global mission to spread the nation's democratic values. While sometimes interpreted as constitutional moderation of religion's role in the nation, the resulting religiosity of the American model rivals most religious states, especially in the widely held ideology of the nation's inherently religious purpose.

Even with the success of the new nation and its alignment with the divine vision, many members were concerned about the future of religion in America. At the beginning of the American Revolution, most Americans were unchurched. One estimate is that only 10–15 percent of Americans belonged to a church (Kramnick and Moore 2005). Further, many of the Founding Fathers, including the nation's first four presidents, ranged from being nontraditional Christians to Deists. Thomas Jefferson, who had made his skepticisms about Christianity well-known and championed religious liberty, was the target of repeated attacks as religious leaders viewed him as the enemy of a religious nation. During Jefferson's 1800 presidential campaign, a minister printed the following in the *New England Palladium*:

Should the infidel Jefferson be elected to the Presidency, the seal of death is that moment set on our holy religion, our churches will be prostrated, and some infamous prostitute, under the title of Reason, will preside the sanctuaries now devoted to the worship of the Most High.

(quoted in Kramnick and Moore 2005, p. 89)

Additionally, the ideological similarities between the American and French Revolutions, combined with excessive violence and rejection of religion among the French, increased colonial anxiety about an American "terror." Economic changes and expansion into the western territories sparked fear that without structured Christian instruction the nation would not realize civilization. The Second Great Awakening developed in response to these fears (Hughes 2004; Lacorne 2011; Haselby 2015). Led by individuals such as Lyman Beecher, Evangelical preachers swept through the nation, arguing that America was founded to be a Christian nation and seeking to enforce long-forgotten blasphemy laws. Tapping into the heritage of the Puritans, they campaigned for laws protecting the Sabbath, such as the end of Sunday mail delivery (Kramnick and Moore 2005; Stone 2010). By the end of the Second Great Awakening, a third of Americans were church members and the myth of a Christian nation was imprinted on the American imagination (Johnson 2004; Howe 2007).

The establishment of a Christian nation in the minds of Americans helped bring about the period of Manifest Destiny, during which elites argued God ordained the United States to spread westward and consume the entire continent. Manifest destiny is the rhetorical zenith of American religious exceptionalism. Arguing it was their religious duty to expand the nation, religious and political elites convinced ordinary Americans that westward expansion was heavenly ordained (Hudson 1970; Hughes 2004). When the mission of extending the nation to the Pacific Ocean was completed, many began to call for overseas expansion. Consuming the continent was not enough to fulfill divine wishes. The imperial era of American foreign policy, as with any nation's quest for imperialism, was fueled by the ideological belief that as God's chosen people they had a responsibility to spread their knowledge to the world (Hughes 2004). No longer satisfied to serve merely as a beacon, it was now their responsibility to proselytize their way of life (Moses 1982). Progressives, such as Josiah Strong and Senator Albert J. Beveridge, saw this as a duty of servitude to help their brothers and sisters in less developed areas (Hudson 1970; Monten 2005; Moore 2017). While Strong argued for a servant role in colonizing the Philippines and Cuba, Beveridge took a more patronizing tone:

The dominant notes in American life henceforth will be not only self-government and internal development, but also administration and world improvement. It is the arduous but splendid mission of our race. It is ours to govern in the name of civilized liberty. It is ours to administer order and law in the name of human progress. It is ours to chasten, that we may be kind. It is ours to cleanse, that we may save. It is ours to build, that free institutions may finally enter and abide. It is ours to bear the torch of Christianity where midnight has reigned a thousand years. It is ours to reinforce that thin red line which constitutes the outposts of civilization all around the world. (1970, pp. 117–18)

Such rhetoric fueled support for the Spanish–American War and the annexation of Pacific territories.

The use of this rhetoric declined in the late nineteenth and early twentieth centuries but revived in the latter half of the twentieth century. Figure 1.2 charts overt references to God in presidential inaugural addresses, visualizing their dramatic increase during the twentieth century. Furthermore, the use of other religious language, terms such as Almighty, Providence, prayer, or the Bible, also increased.

We can normalize the number of religious mentions per 1,000 words. Lincoln's second inaugural address, given during the Civil War, outpaces all the others with a rate of 17.1 religious mentions per 1,000 words. There is a steep decline after Lincoln, followed by a sustained resurgence near the end of World War II and the beginning of the Cold War. During World War II and the Cold War, American religious

Frequency of the use of god and other religious language in presidential inaugural addresses

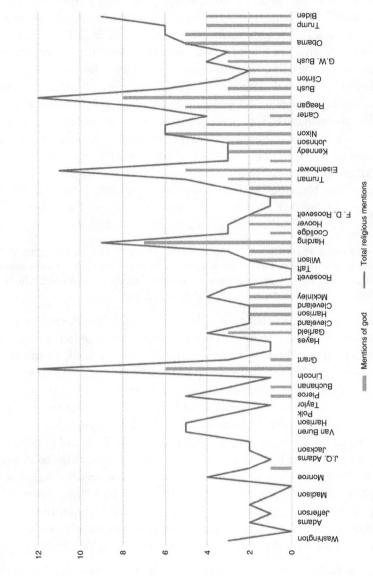

FIGURE 1.2 Frequency of the use of God and other religious language in presidential inaugural addresses
Source: The American Presidency Project (www.presidency.ucsb.edu/index.php) (Peters and Woolley 2017)

Legend: Mentions of god — Total religious mentions

exceptionalism was used as a call to action. In his 1942 State of the Union Address, a month after the Pearl Harbor attacks, President Franklin Delano Roosevelt invoked a divine imperative when he stated: "The world is too small to provide adequate 'living room' for both Hitler and God."[9] He warned failure would cause the Nazis to impose their own "pagan" religion on the world, and the Bible and Cross would be replaced with *Mein Kampf* and the swastika. After the war effort, the expansion of "godless" communism in Eastern Europe and Asia demanded a national religious revival in response (Wuthnow 1988; Wald 1994; Putnam and Campbell 2010). Church attendance grew rapidly as religious and national teachings coincided. In 1954, Presbyterian minister George MacPherson Docherty, who drove the addition of "under God" to the US Pledge of Allegiance, stated that "an atheistic American is a contradiction in terms" (quoted in Bates 2004, p. 29). Religious leaders worked to establish a biblical justification for free market systems and a strong military. Evangelist Billy Graham, a fervent anti-communist hawk, thundered about communism:

[It] has decided against God, against Christ, against the Bible, and against all religion. Communism is not only an economic interpretation of life – Communism is a religion that is inspired, directed and motivated by the Devil himself who has declared war against Almighty God. (1988, pp. 54–55)

Senior government officials agreed. FBI Director J. Edgar Hoover encouraged parents to fight communism by sending their children to church (Bates 2004). In a briefing to newspaper editors, President Eisenhower shared his "unshakeable belief that it is only through religion that we can lick this thing called communism" (New York Times 1953). The US Congress instituted a National Day of Prayer to emphasize the nation's connection to the divine (Wuthnow 1988; Wald 1994; Bates 2004; Prothero 2012). In response to the continuing Cold War, and to growing racial and social justice movements in the United States, religious leaders such as Pat Robertson and Jerry Falwell extolled the need for Americans to remain religiously and politically vigilant. President Reagan's famous 1983 "Evil Empire" speech was made to the Annual Convention of the National Association of Evangelicals. In it, Reagan exemplifies the intermingling of nation, religion, and foreign policy during this time:

While America's military strength is important, let me add here that I've always maintained that the struggle now going on for the world will never be decided by bombs or rockets, by armies or military might. The real crisis we face today is a spiritual one; at root, it is a test of moral will and faith.[10]

With the fall of communism, religious exceptionalism's foreign policy influence appeared set to wane. However, the events of September 11, 2001, changed this trajectory. The Bush Doctrine, which underpinned America's formal response to the terror acts, proclaimed the renewed role of the nation as the world's divinely appointed savior (Bacevich and Prodromou 2004; McCartney 2004; Monten 2005). As a policy arguing that the best way to sustain national security was to expand US influence, it fit with earlier expansionary themes in American history, such as *Manifest Destiny* and America's dominance of the Pacific (Green 2017). The overtly moralistic tone of the Bush Doctrine demonstrated the renewed value of religion in foreign policy decisions. By framing the War on Terror as a war between good and evil, President Bush invoked religious imagery to convince the public that his plan was noble and divinely inspired (McCartney 2004; Maoz and Henderson 2020).

The religious zeal underpinning the Bush administration's prosecution of the War on Terror was evident in the rhetoric and actions of members and supporters of the administration. General William Boykin, at the time serving as Deputy Undersecretary for Defense Intelligence, repeatedly framed this as a battle between American and Satan (Cooper 2003). In 2009, reports surfaced that in the early years of the war effort, military briefings included cover pages with biblical passages and images (Sanger 2009). In early 2010, it was reported that a military arms supplier was inscribing biblical references on rifle sights (Eckholm 2010).[11] Bob Woodward's account of President Bush's decision-making provides an understanding of how religious exceptionalism influenced the president in developing his course of action. Woodward notes how Bush's faith directed his policy agenda and that he truly felt that the invasions of Iraq and Afghanistan were part of a great divine purpose. Thus compelled, there was no need for multilateral legitimation of American action (2004). Many within the administration subscribed to the belief that once other nations saw that the United States was on the side of good and that good would prevail, they would join the fight – a coalition of the willing, inspired to battle evil by the City on the Hill (Monten 2005).

1.6 REBUTTALS TO AMERICAN RELIGIOUS EXCEPTIONALISM

The narrative of American religious exceptionalism as a line through American intellectual history and policy-thinking is not without its challengers. As with any mythology, there are those who refute it or want to replace it with another. Many are skeptical of the sincerity of the messianic narrative of American foreign policy, which they describe as a rhetorical technique advanced by nonreligious neoconservatives (Bacevich and Prodromou 2004). Critics, such as Gregory Boyd (2005), challenge the Christian nation myth, citing the first sentence from Article 11 of the Treaty of Tripoli as *prima facie* evidence:

As the government of the United States of America is not in any sense founded on the Christian Religion, as it has in itself no character of enmity against the laws, religion or tranquility of Musselmen (*sic*), and as the said States never have entered into any war or act of hostility against any Mehomitan (*sic*) nation, it is declared by the parties that no pretext arising from religious opinions shall ever produce an interruption of the harmony existing between the two countries. (Miller 1931, p. 365)

Critics also emphasize that there is no mention of God in the Constitution, and that any mention of religion limits government intervention, thus allowing people to be religious or nonreligious. To some, the very existence of the First Amendment confirms America's credentials as a secular nation (Hughes 2004). Such skeptics are joined by religious scholars and leaders in their rejection of the tenets of American religious exceptionalism. During the Cold War, theologian Reinhold Niebuhr cautioned against myths envisioning the nation as God's chosen because they promote false understandings of the world and had the potential to generate great harm to humanity (Niebuhr 2008). More recently, progressive Christians such as Jim Wallis have vociferously criticized the connections between religious groups and American nationalism, often referring to this connection as a form of idolatry (Wallis 2019).

Some of the harshest critiques of American religious exceptionalism have come from those discussing the lives of marginalized groups. They argue that a nation inspired by God would not commit atrocities, such as slavery and decimation of the Native American population (Hughes 2004; Boyd 2005). As Wilson Moses points out, Blacks have accepted the idea of a divine connection to the nation and have used it to issue jeremiads of their own that criticize and demand change of the nation's actions (1982). In 1829, David Walker condemned the nation to divine punishment for allowing slavery and the mistreatment of Blacks (Walker 1995). Following Walker's path, Maria Stewart compared the United States to Babylon because it was "a seller of slaves and the souls of men." She continues:

I believe that the oppression of injured Africa has come up before the Majesty of Heaven; and when our cries have reached the ears of the Most High, it will be a tremendous day for the people of this land; for strong is the arm of the Lord God Almighty. (2001, p. 127)

In his 1968 address at the National Cathedral, Dr Martin Luther King, Jr. offered his own jeremiad against his nation's failure to protect those with the greatest need:[12]

One day we will have to stand before the God of history and we will talk in terms of things we have done. Yes, we will be able to say we built gargantuan bridges to span the seas, we built gigantic buildings to kiss the skies. Yes, we made our submarines to penetrate oceanic depths. We brought into being many other things with our scientific and technological power.

It seems that I can hear the God of history saying, "That was not enough! But I was hungry, and ye fed me not. I was naked, and ye clothed me not. I was devoid of a decent sanitary house to live in, and ye provided no shelter for me. And consequently, you cannot enter the kingdom of greatness. If ye do it unto the least of these, my brethren, ye do it unto me." That's the question facing America today.

He continues his last Sunday sermon by directly invoking the image of an ever present and judgmental deity as he offers his critique of the war in Vietnam:[13]

The judgment of God is upon us today. And we could go right down the line and see that something must be done – and something must be done quickly. We have alienated ourselves from other nations so we end up morally and politically isolated in the world. There is not a single major ally of the United States of America that would dare send a troop to Vietnam, and so the only friends that we have now are a few client-nations like Taiwan, Thailand, South Korea, and a few others.

Forty years later, during the 2008 Democratic primaries, Rev. Jeremiah Wright shocked White America with his fiery condemnation of the nation's foreign and domestic policy, which ended in a call for divine retribution against America (McKenzie 2011). As we have sought to make clear in this chapter, far from being un-American as his critics accused him, Wright's language could not have been more squarely in the American rhetorical tradition.

1.7 CONCLUSION

Even with its critics, the myth of American religious exceptionalism has shaped and animated the nation's consciousness. While often used as a tool by elites to achieve political outcomes, America's unique religious brand of nationalism reflects an ideology steeped in an enduring history of embedding a divine mission into national myths. In this manner, American religious exceptionalism has played an important role in shaping the psychology of Americans and subsequently directed their attitudes about what the nation is, what it is not, and how it ought to behave. Nor is this myth of American religious exceptionalism the stuff of yore; it is as prevalent today as ever, and will continue to influence attitudes and behaviors for many decades to come. We will seek to convince that contemporary Americans' attitudes and behaviors are well explained by the politicization of a commonplace ideology of American religious exceptionalism that has guided American public opinion since the country's formation. The remainder of this book explicates who adheres to this myth and how these adherents think about what it means to be an American and therefore who can be an American, and what this understanding means for how the nation should interact with the rest of the world.

2

Who Are the Believers?

"You are my witnesses," declares the LORD, "and my servant whom I have chosen, so that you may know and believe me and understand that I am he. Before me no god was formed, nor will there be one after me.

Isaiah 43:10

If America is exceptional, it has less to do with the nature of its politics than it has to do with its brand of religiosity (Tocqueville 1945; Wuthnow 1988; Putnam and Campbell 2010). America is a nation of believers and a nation of unique beliefs. These two factors help explain how American religious exceptionalism was adopted, refined, and retained. This chapter's focus shifts from elite rhetoric to the beliefs and behavior of everyday citizens. We discuss first the nature of American piety, demonstrating the uniqueness of the American religious experience and the continued importance of religion among Americans. From that vantage, we can examine the historical and contemporary connections ordinary American citizens make between a Supreme Being and the nation. Our approach is unapologetically empirical and centers on an original survey-based measure of adherence to American religious exceptionalism, which we use to uncover how factors like one's religious denomination, personality, and values predict one's affinity to this ideological framework.

2.1 AMERICAN PIETY

The secularization or modernization hypothesis in social science posits that as societies increase their economic development, they become less religious (Norris and Inglehart 2011). For example, European nations have witnessed a decline in religious service attendance and beliefs as they have grown wealthier since World War II. However, among its wealthy peers, the United States is an outlier. Even though the United States boasts the richest economy in the world, it is also one of the most religious countries in the industrialized world. Data taken from Wave Seven of the World Values Survey show that the United States outpaced other developed nations (other than Greece) on belief in God and matters of religious importance. Americans also report a relatively higher level of weekly worship attendance and daily prayer.

Data from the 2018 International Social Survey Programme confirm Americans express higher rates of religiosity compared to citizens in other developed nations. More than a quarter (28.1 percent) of Americans describe themselves as "extremely" or "very religious," whereas only 15.0 percent of Italians, the second-most religious group of citizens in these data, describe themselves as such.

The uniqueness of American piety is even more evident when examining specific religious beliefs. As Figure 2.2 demonstrates, close to three-fourths of Americans report always believing in God without any doubts.

Further, close to a third of Americans express a great deal or complete confidence in religious institutions. Finally, Americans are more likely to believe God is actively involved in their lives, with more than two-thirds holding an image of a God who is concerned with human beings and more than half believing in religious miracles (ISSP Research Group 2020).

Figure 2.3, using data from the 2015 Pew Global Attitudes Survey, demonstrates the level of importance citizens of select developed countries place on different freedoms, such as freedom of religion, free speech, and honest elections. Americans view all freedoms as very important, but Americans are much more likely than citizens of other countries to emphasize the importance of the freedom to practice religion.

Despite studies continually showing Americans are more religiously devout than their counterparts in other economically developed nations, internally there have been concerns about the decreasing role of religion in American society. There has been a decline but it is not as sharp as some have speculated and as some bemoan. One Gallup study found that between 1944 and 2016 the proportion of Americans who believed in God dropped from 96 percent to 89 percent, a marginal decrease. The 2016 study also found that 72 percent believed in angels, 71 percent believed in heaven, and over three-fifths of the sample still believed in hell and the devil (Newport 2016).

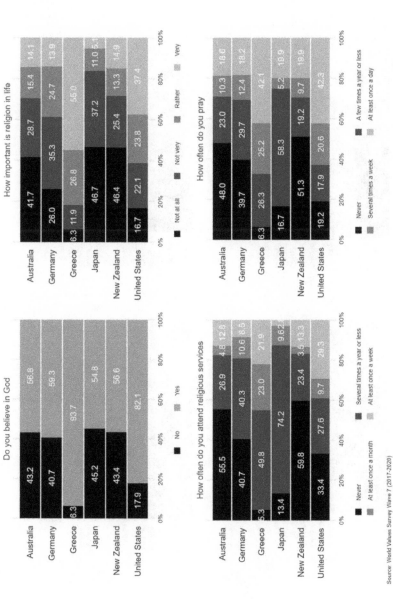

Source World Values Survey Wave 7 (2017-2020)

FIGURE 2.1 Belief in God, importance of religion, and religious activity among select developed nations (Haerpfer 2020)

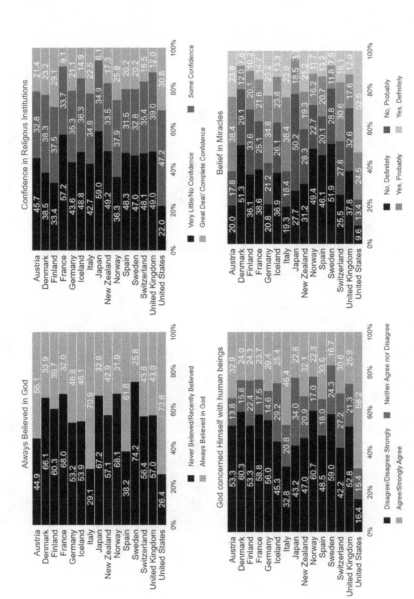

FIGURE 2.2 Religious beliefs and practices across developed countries

Very Important to have in our country

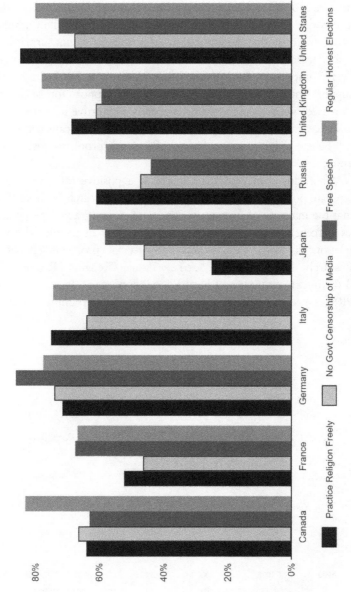

FIGURE 2.3 Freedoms deemed as very important to have in nation

Practice Religion Freely   No Govt Censorship of Media   Free Speech   Regular Honest Elections

Figure 2.4 explores the nature of Americans' diminishing religiosity over the past three decades. Some declines are sharper than others. For instance, in 1993, a majority 53 percent of Americans reported having either a great deal or quite a lot of confidence in organized religion; by 2020, this had dropped to a minority 42 percent. Given scandals associated with the Catholic Church and numerous other denominations, this is probably not surprising. There is a similar 10-point drop in the share of Americans stating that religion was "very" important. But, on the other hand, there has been an increase in support for religion in the public square: support for prayer in school increased, with 45 percent of Americans supportive in 2018 compared to 40 percent in 1990. Finally, more than half of Americans surveyed in 2020 still believe religion answers many of society's problems, just as they did in 1993.

Americans clearly regard religion as a positive force in society. Three separate polls, fielded by the Public Religion Research Institute (PRRI), find that the majority of Americans (2010: 56 percent; 2012: 56 percent; 2013: 55 percent) agree that increasing the number of people with a personal relationship with God would solve social problems (Public Religion Research Institute 2010, 2012; Public Religion Research Institute, Brookings Institution and Ford Foundation 2013). In 2012 and 2013, the PRRI asked respondents to indicate the most important action needed to

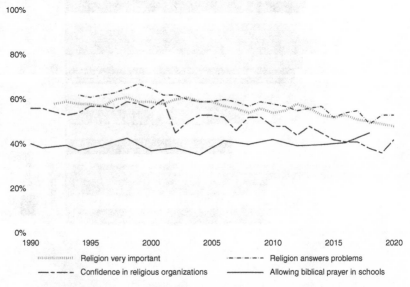

FIGURE 2.4 Attitudes toward religion, religious organizations, and religion and society (1990–2020)

prevent mass shootings. In both years, stricter gun control laws and better mental health screenings were the top two responses. However, in both years one in five respondents chose "Put more emphasis on God and morality in school and society" (Public Religion Research Institute and Religon News Service 2012; Public Religion Research Institute 2013).

Religion's central role in American society also becomes apparent once we examine how the American public feels about the nation's nonreligious persons. Much of America's growing fear about the diminishing of religion is fueled by the belief atheists have overtaken American society and pushed out religion. Surveys suggest that somewhere between 10 percent and 15 percent of the population identifies as atheists. But their small numbers notwithstanding, the mere notion of atheism causes great angst and stress among those who are most committed to protecting and promoting religion's role in American society. Over the past half-century, public opinion polls indicate that Americans have become slightly more tolerant of atheists, but overall significant distrust of atheism persists. A 1984 poll found that more than a third of Americans (38 percent) attributed the Soviet Union's enemy status to its atheism (Public Agenda Foundation 1984). Another poll found that a fifth of Americans (22 percent) believed atheists could not be patriotic, while a third (32 percent) believed that atheists could not be moral (CBS News/New York Times 1984). Three decades later, little has changed: a 2011 Pew Global Attitudes Survey found that more than half of Americans (53.6 percent) still assert that a person must believe in God to be moral. In 1992, 40 percent of Americans indicated that believing in God was extremely important to making someone a true American (Center for Political Studies and University of Michigan 1992). When asked about how they would react to a member of their family marrying an atheist, 46 percent of Americans were comfortable saying they would be unhappy, compared to only 11 percent admitting being unhappy if the family member married someone of a different race (National Opinion Research Center and University of Chicago 2014).

A most telling indicator of reliable American animus toward atheists comes from the public's willingness to vote for one as president. Between 1999 and 2015, Gallup investigated how citizens' willingness to support their party's candidate varied based on the candidate's personal characteristics, such as being Black, Catholic, homosexual, or an atheist. Figure 2.5 displays the results of this investigation.

Even though more people say they'd be comfortable voting for an atheist in 2015 than in 1999, atheists continue to trail other groups in acceptability as a possible presidential candidate by a considerable

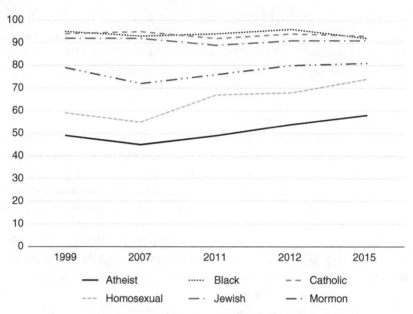

FIGURE 2.5 If your party nominated a generally well-qualified person for president who happened to be . . ., would you vote for that person?

amount, lagging behind even members of historically marginalized and discriminated groups who are still actively fighting for civil rights protections on a daily basis. As a further comparison, in 2012 and 2015, Gallup asked about Muslim candidates. In these years, respondents expressed marginally more comfort in voting for a Muslim in 2012 (58 percent) and 2015 (60 percent) than an atheist (2012: 54 percent; 2015: 58 percent). We suspect this has much to do with social desirability bias and attests the fact that atheists remain one group in American society with which it is still permissible to express publicly one's discomfort.

2.2 GOD AND NATION: PERSONAL SUCCESSES AND FAILURES

Along with the distinctiveness of religion's place in American social life relative to other advanced industrial democracies, Americans hold unique views of their relationship with God. For example, they are more likely to view God as active in their lives compared to citizens in other developed nations. This idea of a God who is actively involved in human lives and who influences personal successes and failures is a strong component of the American religious sentiment. The General Social Survey (GSS) asked respondents the extent to which they agreed with the following statement: "There is a God who concerns Himself with every human being personally." In 1991, 45 percent of the respondents indicated they strongly agree with the statement, while in both 1998 and 2008, 40 percent of the respondents strongly agreed with the statement. A 1997 poll found 58 percent of Americans believed God answered prayers often. When prayers were not answered, 54 percent of the respondents explained this by saying answering the prayer must not have been in God's will as opposed to 11 percent who stated God did not hear the prayer. The same survey found Americans see God's hand in a variety of areas, such as politics, employment, and marriage. A third of Americans (36 percent) believe God sometimes answers prayers about electing a candidate. Almost three-fourths (73 percent) believe God sometimes answers prayers about employment and 57 percent believe God sometimes answers prayers about marriage (Newsweek 1997). Between 2013 and 2017, the PRRI asked if God played a role in determining who won a sporting event. Their data show that a quarter of Americans believe God has a rooting interest in the outcomes of sporting events. In 1997, 79 percent of Americans believed God sometimes answered prayers to help heal "someone with a disease considered incurable by medical science" (Newsweek 1997). The 2017 Pew American Trends Panel Poll finds most Americans believe God or some higher power or spiritual force determines what happens in their life all the time (30 percent) or most of the time (25 percent). The same poll reports that three-fourths of Americans (74 percent) believe they have been rewarded by God (higher power) or a spiritual force.

A significant segment of Americans also attributes hardships to a higher power. In 1993, the GSS asked for reasons why a person's life might turn out poorly: a quarter of the respondents (23 percent) indicated "the decision of God" was a very important factor. The 2017 Pew American Trends Panel Poll finds that close to half of Americans (44 percent) believe they had been punished by a higher power. When asked how often a higher power determines what happens in their life, a third stated, "all the time," and a quarter said, "most of the time." A specific example of the belief in God's punishment is how Americans interpret the AIDS crisis. In 1987, 43 percent of respondents agreed with the statement that "AIDS might be God's punishment for immoral sexual behavior." By 2013, this proportion had dropped to 14 percent. Even though this change can be attributed to increased information about the disease along with decreasing animus toward LGBTQIA+ persons, it demonstrates the extent to which Americans view God as both a rewarding and punishing force in people's lives.

2.3 NATIONAL SUCCESS AND FAILURES

Attitudes about the role of a higher power influencing the lives of individuals also extend to the belief that a higher power plays a role in the successes and failures of nations. A sizable share of Americans believes a higher power endows the nation with special protection. In a 1984 poll, 27 percent of Americans agreed that "[i]n a nuclear war with the communists, our faith in God would ensure our survival" (Public Agenda Foundation 1984). Contemplating success over a more contemporary enemy, more than a third of Americans (39 percent) agreed that "God had a hand in helping the U.S. find and kill Osama bin Laden" (Religion News Service 2011). The 2002 Pew Religion and Public Life Survey finds 48 percent of Americans agree that "The U.S. has had special protection from God."[1]

One popular opinion illustrates the enduring belief among Americans that their nation has a special God-given purpose. Between 2010 and 2020, the PRRI asked respondents the extent to which they agreed with the statement, "God has granted America a special role in human history." Over that period more than half of all respondents on average agree. White evangelicals were the most likely to agree with the statement, often generating greater than 80 percent agreement with the statement. Black Protestants are also very likely to agree, though one sees a marked drop in their support for this idea during the Trump presidency. Agreement among other groups hovers closer to the half-way mark, except for the religiously unaffiliated who generally do not buy into the notion. But the key takeaway is that half of adult Americans believe firmly that their nation is charged with a special role by God.

America's complex and special relationship with God is also evidenced by the high degree to which PRRI's respondents also believe that natural disasters and other calamities are evidence of divine retribution for people's sins on earth. Such fatalism is surprising in a developed economy that has arguably the most highly advanced scientific research community in the world, but support for the notion of a vengeful God is high in America, especially among religiously conservative White evangelicals, and Black and Brown Protestants (see Figure 2.6).

Such views of divine retribution contribute to Americans' personal and national sense of self. Many of the disciples of American religious exceptionalism described the connection between God and the nation as a covenant, in which the nation would receive God's blessings as long as the nation stayed committed to God (Bellah 1975; Bercovitch 1978). This belief in a divine covenant has contributed to a divine logic attributed to national tragedies.

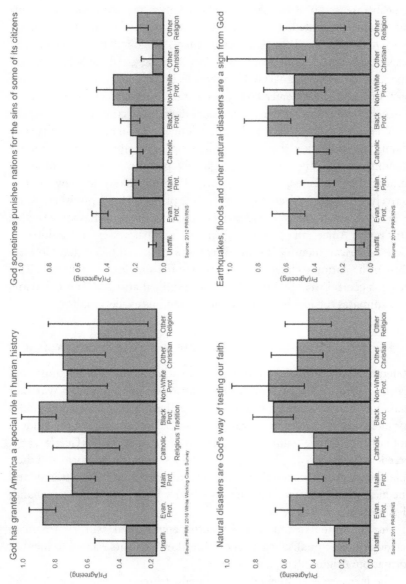

FIGURE 2.6 Percentage of people who agree God granted America a special role in human history and that national tragedies are divine punishments by religious tradition

A 2005 poll found that 23 percent of Americans attributed hurricanes Katrina and Rita, which battered the Gulf Coast and are attributed with causing close to 2,000 deaths and $91 billion in economic damage, to a deliberate act of God. After the September 11, 2001, attacks, some Americans attributed that horrific event to divine intervention. In November 2001, a Pew Research Center Poll found that 8 percent of respondents agreed with religious leaders who suggested the September 11, 2001, attacks were a signal God is not protecting the nation as much as in the past. In a 2002 Pew Center Poll, 5 percent of Americans saw the attacks as a sign the nation no longer enjoys the same divine protection it had in the past.

A decade of survey data and a much longer textual history confirm our claim that America is distinctive in its religious commitment and understanding of the divine: More religiously pious than citizens of other industrialized nations, Americans are also more likely to view God as actively involved in their lives as both a protector and punisher. Their belief in divine involvement extends to their nation as well, with a sizable portion of Americans attributing the nation's successes and failures to God. American identity is shaped by the widespread belief that God has chosen the nation to have a critical role in the shaping of humanity. This belief is central to explaining American political attitudes and behaviors and animates the ideology of American religious exceptionalism.

2.4 MEASURING AMERICAN RELIGIOUS EXCEPTIONALISM

Religious exceptionalism is an ideology that combines religious and national pride. As a result, piety and patriotism are linked in a way that makes demarcation difficult. Ideologies are best conceptualized as guides for understanding how to operate in society. The accuracy of the guide is not critical, but the willingness of the group to accept it is (Geertz 1973; Freeden 1998). Ideology helps people make sense of their world and their role in it by providing guidelines for behavior and establishing friends and enemies, which ultimately influences identity formation and maintenance (Festenstein and Kenny 2005).

Our conceptual definition and resulting empirical measure of American religious exceptionalism focuses on three key elements related to identity formation: origin, place, and purpose.

The measure is comprised of four items (three positively worded and one negatively worded), reflecting the belief that the nation was divinely created, divinely favored, and is crucial to the divine plan. The first two items capture the notion of divine favor, while the latter two items address beliefs regarding the origin and purpose of the nation. The items are: (a) America holds a special place in God's plan; (b) the success of the United States is not a reflection of divine will;[2] (c) the United States is spiritually predestined to lead the world; and (d) the vast resources of the United States indicate that God has chosen it to lead other nations. The concept of American religious exceptionalism is broader than what these items capture; however, as we demonstrate later in the chapter, this measure not only meets the criteria for internal validity, it also meets the criteria for external validity.

In all, we applied a form of the American religious exceptionalism measure to nine surveys: seven national and two state. The surveys use different sampling procedures which limits our ability to make assertions about how time has influenced the level of adherence or the nature of the relationships; however, they do allow us to examine the reliability of the measure and the consistency of its relationships. An analysis of the reliability of the measure in the national surveys finds the alpha scores for the surveys, including all four items ranged between 0.79 and 0.84. In the surveys with only three of the items, the score ranged between 0.61 and 0.73. Finally, the survey with only two of the items had an alpha score of 0.68. A description of each survey can be found in the Appendix.

For interpretative convenience, we rescaled the measure to run from 0 to 1 and have assigned all our respondents to one of three different groups: disciples, dissidents, and laity. We categorize those who score below 0.35 as the dissidents, those who score above 0.65 as the disciples, and those who fall in between 0.35 and 0.65 the laity. The disciples represent those individuals who wholeheartedly believe the nation is divinely favored and has a divine mission. The disciples are the individuals highlighted in books, such as Kristin Kobes Du Mez's *Jesus and John Wayne* and Katherine Stewart's *The Power Worshippers*. The dissidents, on the other hand, are those individuals who reject the idea of a special connection between the nation and a higher power. They are not necessarily atheist or nonreligious; they may also be members of religious traditions who reject the idea that God plays favorites with nations and view this belief system as dangerous; Reinhold Niebuhr's *The Irony of American History* provides a nice example of such thinking. The laity are those who neither reject American religious exceptionalism nor tightly embrace it. They embrace some elements but reject others. Figure 2.7 provides a distribution of these groups for the four surveys that used a nationally representative probability sampling frame. The results show that the disciples are a small yet significant group; they make up 13.9–20.7 percent of the respondents in these samples. The

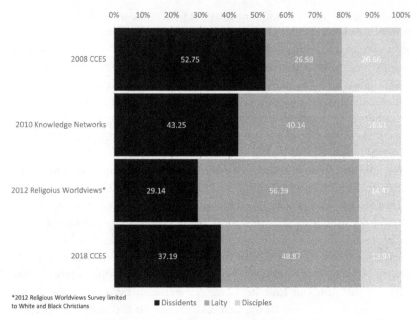

FIGURE 2.7 Distribution of dissidents, laity, and disciples of American religious
exceptionalism

dissidents comprise between 29.1 percent and 52.8 percent across our
surveys, and the laity constitute the majority (56.4 percent) in one and the
plurality (26.6 percent) in another.

To gauge how well the American religious exceptionalism scale predicts
attitudes consistent with our discussion of the concept, we examined its
relationship with the belief that national tragedies are a form of divine
punishment. American history is replete with examples of disciples of
American religious exceptionalism preaching sermons, proclaiming that
national crises were brought about as punishment for immoral actions.
Our analysis has already documented that a significant number of
Americans believe that God punishes nations for its citizens' sins, but they
are less likely to attribute specific crises to divine punishment. Figure 2.8
depicts the extent to which Americans support for the belief that national
crises are divine punishment given their categorical placement.

Overall, our survey respondents strongly disagree with the idea of
divine punishment, with the dissidents being most opposed. The dissidents
are nearly unanimous in expressing strong disagreement with the belief
that the September 11 attacks were the act of God, punishing the nation

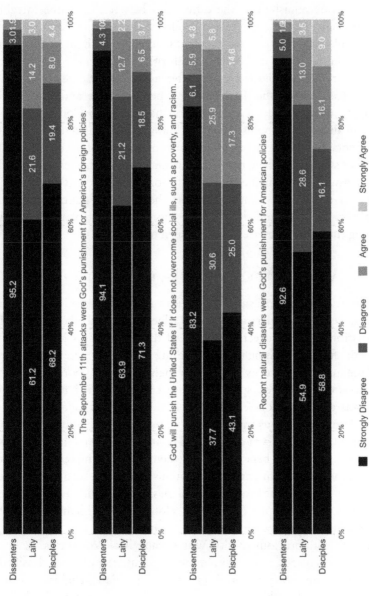

The September 11th attacks were God's punishment for America's domestic policies.

Dissenters	95.2		3.0 1.9
Laity	61.2	21.6	14.2	3.0
Disciples	68.2	19.4	8.0	4.4

0%   20%   40%   60%   80%   100%

The September 11th attacks were God's punishment for America's foreign policies.

Dissenters	94.1		4.3 10
Laity	63.9	21.2	12.7	2.2
Disciples	71.3	18.5	6.5	3.7

0%   20%   40%   60%   80%   100%

God will punish the United States if it does not overcome social ills, such as poverty, and racism.

Dissenters	83.2	6.1	5.9	4.8
Laity	37.7	30.6	25.9	5.8
Disciples	43.1	25.0	17.3	14.6

0%   20%   40%   60%   80%   100%

Recent natural disasters were God's punishment for American policies

Dissenters	92.6		5.0 1.9
Laity	54.9	28.6	13.0	3.5
Disciples	58.8	16.1	16.1	9.0

0%   20%   40%   60%   80%   100%

■ Strongly Disagree   ■ Disagree   ■ Agree   ■ Strongly Agree

FIGURE 2.8 Agreement with the idea that national tragedies are God's punishment given placement on the American religious exceptionalism scale

for foreign or domestic policies. Among the laity, fewer than two-thirds strongly disagree with these statements, while one-fifth disagree, and the same is true for the disciples. However, as we move to more general ideas about divine punishment, the differences between the three categories becomes clearer. As in the earlier results, there is near-unanimity among the dissidents in rejecting the idea that God will punish the nation for not addressing its social ills. Only a tenth of the dissidents agree with this statement. Among the laity, a quarter agree and 7.3 percent strongly agree; and, among the disciples, 17.3 percent agree and 14.6 percent strongly agree. Finally, the analysis of the belief that God brings about natural disasters as punishment for human sins finds almost all of the dissidents. But, one-fifth of the laity and one-quarter of the disciples either agree or strongly agree with the sentiment. These results demonstrate that the measure behaves in the expected fashion. The dissidents strongly reject the idea that divine punishment was the cause of national tragedies; however, the laity and disciples are more accepting of this idea. And among them, disciples are the most open to it.

2.5 WHO ARE THE DISSIDENTS, LAITY, AND DISCIPLES?

With a functioning measure of American religious exceptionalism established, we turn to understanding who adheres to it and who rejects it. The discussion of the intellectual history of the concept in Chapter 1 along with the findings relating to God granting the United States a special role in human history lead us to expect a high level of support for it among religious conservatives, specifically conservative Christians, such as the Puritans of the past or White evangelical Protestants today. Beyond the attachment to religious traditions, other aspects of religious life may also be important. Scholars of religion and politics have noted the three "B's of religion": belonging, believing, and behaving. Belonging refers to identification; membership in particular religious traditions, such as evangelical Protestant or mainline Protestant; and message exposure. Figure 2.9 demonstrates the importance of religious belonging by highlighting the differences in adherence between religious traditions.

Fitting with previous results, White evangelical Protestants are one of the highest scoring groups, with more than a quarter of them classified as disciples. Interestingly, those in other Christian religions, such as Mormons or Jehovah's Witnesses, are highly committed to this belief as more than half are in the disciple category and the rest are in the laity category. This relationship is most likely being driven by the Mormon

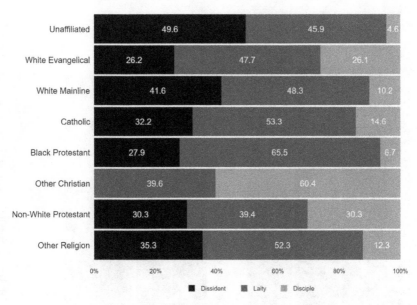

FIGURE 2.9 Percent of members in religious traditions who are classified as dissidents, laity, and disciples of American religious exceptionalism

respondents whose spiritual canon, specifically Doctrine and Covenants of the Church of the Latter-Day Saints, views America and its institutions as divinely inspired (Tuveson 1968; Smith and Church of Jesus Christ of Latter-Day Saints 1971). Regarding the other traditions, we find that 14.6 percent of Catholics fall into the disciple category, while a tenth of mainline Protestants are disciples. Finally, half of the religiously unaffiliated are classified as dissidents. Moving next to behaving and believing, the results in Figure 2.10 demonstrate that almost a quarter of those who attend church at least once a week are classified as disciples, and close to half of those who report never or seldom attending worship services are in the dissident category. Regarding beliefs, specifically biblical inerrancy, we find the expected pattern as two-thirds of those who reject the usefulness of the Bible are categorized as dissidents. In comparison, 17.7 percent of those who believe the Bible is the word of God are categorized as dissidents, while a quarter are disciples.

To understand this relationship, we statistically examine how belonging, behaving, and believing are related to adherence to American religious exceptionalism, while also accounting for sociodemographic factors. Figures 2.11 and 2.12 present the results from these analyses. Beginning

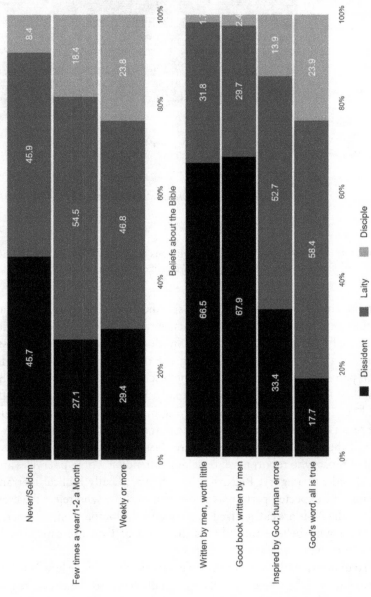

FIGURE 2.10 Percentage of people who are dissidents, laity, or disciples of American religious exceptionalism given worship attendance and biblical inerrancy beliefs

with belonging, we find that the differences between the traditions become increasingly muted when accounting for behaving, believing, and socio-demographic attributes. This lack of difference between the traditions is consistent with what Andrew Whitehead and Samuel Perry found in their analysis of Christian nationalism (Whitehead and Perry 2020). Once we account for other religious and social demographics, we see that adherence to this belief is not concentrated in a specific religious tradition but is spread out among them.

As additional analysis of how behaving may relate to adherence, we also investigate the relationship between sermon exposure and personal religious identification. Sermons are one of the key methods religious elites communicate what their religions mean in the real world. It allows religious elites to draw comparisons between examples in religious text and examples in the real world. In congregational settings, the sermon provides the religious leader the opportunity to set the culture of the religious body and shape how members interact with each other and the world (Harris-Lacewell 2004; McDaniel 2008; Djupe and Gilbert 2009). Because of this, the type of sermon a person is exposed to can influence their outlook on the world and how they fit in it. Using data from the 2012 Religious Worldviews Survey, we find that the disciples are less likely to report exposure to sermons about protecting the poor and more likely to report exposure to sermons about national defense. If the modal respondent reported never hearing a sermon about protecting the poor, she would have a 23 percent chance of being a dissident and a 11 percent chance of being a disciple. However, if she were exposed to these sermons very often, the odds for being a dissident increase to 55 percent, while the odds of being a disciple drops to 3 percent. For sermons about national defense, the results show that if the modal respondent were to report never hearing these sermons, she would have a 47 percent chance of being a dissident, but if she reported hearing them very often, the probability is just 9 percent. Exposure to other types of sermons, such as those focusing on racial equality and equality for homosexuals, do not differentiate the categories from each other.

Personal religious identification is measured by whether the respondent identifies as a religious fundamentalist. Fundamentalism is crucial to understanding religious identity, because it indicates an extremely high level of commitment to one's religion that dismisses other religions and draws clear boundaries on what is and what is not part of the religion (Kellstedt and Smidt 1991). Unsurprisingly, scholars have compared nationalism to religious fundamentalism. Fitting with these arguments, our analysis of the 2008 CCES finds that if the modal respondent

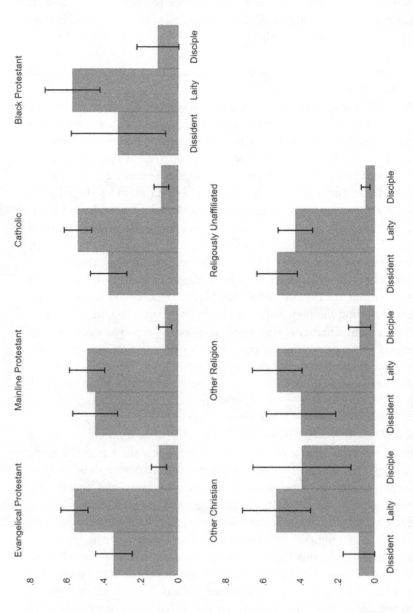

FIGURE 2.11 Predicted probability of being a dissident, laity, or disciple of American religious exceptionalism given religious tradition

Note: Predicted probabilities were generated using coefficient estimates from ordered logit regression models that control for religious tradition, practices, beliefs, personal demographics, and political ideology. Capped lines indicate estimated 95 percent confidence intervals.

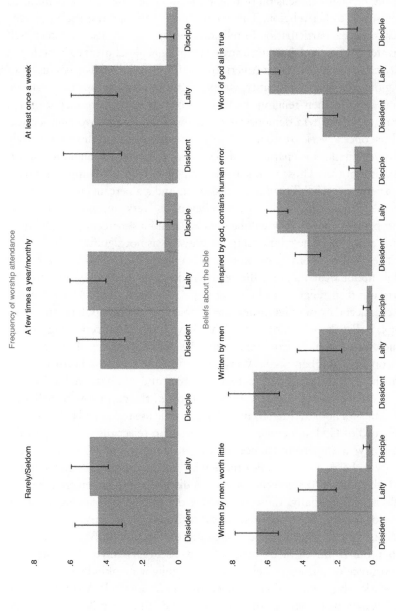

FIGURE 2.12 Predicted probability of being a dissident, laity, or disciple of American religious exceptionalism given worship service attendance and biblical inerrancy

Note: Predicted values were generated using coefficient estimates from ordered logit regression models that control for religious tradition, practices, beliefs, personal demographics, and political ideology. Capped lines indicate estimated 95 percent confidence intervals.

identified as a fundamentalist, she would have a 24 percent chance of being a disciple. If she did not identify as a fundamentalist, her odds are 11 percent.

The behaving dimension of religion is an indication of how committed a person is to her religion. This commitment can manifest itself publicly, such as active participation in religious services; it can also manifest itself privately by a person holding a strong emotional attachment to her religion (Layman 1997). Given that American religious exceptionalism is a fusion of religious and national identity, we expect those who demonstrate a strong connection to their religion, publicly or privately, to score higher on the measure. Figure 2.12 demonstrates that those who attend worship services at least once a week are no more likely to be disciples than those who rarely or never attend. In separate analyses, we also examined religious import-ance and prayer. Those who state that religion is not at all important have a 70 percent probability of being dissidents and a 2 percent chance of being disciples. For those who view religion as very important, there is a 37 percent chance they will be dissidents and a 9 percent probability of being a disciple. The relationship for prayer was not significant.[3]

The final religious dimension is believing, which reflects how people think about their religion, the relationship with the divine, and how to carry out their religious calling properly. Classically scholars have focused on the inerrancy of religious texts as a measure of beliefs (Glock and Stark 1965; Kellstedt and Smidt 1993). They have found that accounting for this belief was better at explaining attitudes than belonging and behaving (Olson and Warber 2008; Wuthnow and Lewis 2008). Further, those who believe the texts are factually correct and unquestionable express more ardent beliefs. Figure 2.12 demonstrates the gap between believing the Bible is a book written by men that has little use today and believing it is the word of God and entirely true. Those who reject the inerrancy of the Bible have a 66 percent chance of being a dissident and a 3 percent prob-ability of being a disciple. For those who fully accept the inerrancy of the text, the odds are 28 percent for being a dissident and 14 percent for being a disciple. Essentially, those who reject the role of a divine actor in the creation of the Bible score significantly lower than those who believe a divine power played a role in creating the document. Beyond attitudes about the truthfulness of religious texts, scholars have also noted the importance of purposive beliefs, which highlight mankind's purpose and its relationship with the divine (Glock and Stark 1965; Glock 1972). Several studies have demonstrated that images of God influence political and social beliefs. Those who view the divine as active in people's lives and as judgmental are more conservative, while those who view the divine as distant and nonjudgmental are more likely to take liberal stances (Froese and Bader 2010). As the earlier results demonstrated, the disciples of American religious exceptionalism are more likely to attribute national tragedies to God's wrath, indicating they view God as active and judgmental. Using the 2012 Religious Worldviews Study, we find that beliefs about how God operates at the personal level, such as personal affairs or being angered by personal sins, are not significantly correlated with adherence, but beliefs about how God operates at the global level are correlated. Those who believe God is directly involved in worldly affairs are more likely to identify as disciples. An individual who strongly disagrees with the idea that God has a hand in worldly affairs has a 65 percent probability of being a dissident, while one who strongly agrees with this idea has a 16 percent. For the probability of being a disciple, if the modal respondent strongly disagrees, it is 2 percent, but it is 15 percent if she strongly agrees.

Along with purposive beliefs, scholars have highlighted implementing beliefs. These types of beliefs establish "the proper conduct of man toward God and toward his fellow man for the realization of divine purpose" (Glock and Stark 1965, p. 25). Two implementing beliefs currently receiving attention are the social and prosperity gospels. The social gospel emphasizes humility and argues Christians have a religious responsibility to protect the weak and marginalized (Rauschenbusch 1918). In contrast, the prosperity gospel emphasizes divine favoritism and contends those who express high levels of faith will be favored by God (Coleman 1993; Bowler 2013; McDaniel 2016). Our analyses of these two implementing beliefs find a significant relationship for both. If the modal respondent does not adhere to the social gospel measure, she would have a 16 percent chance of being a disciple. If she were in strong agreement with the social gospel tenets, the odds are 3 percent she is a disciple.[4] The reverse is true for the prosperity gospel, where disagreement yields a 2 percent chance of being a disciple, while adherence to the prosperity gospel results in a 52 percent probability when one is categorized as a disciple.[5]

We now shift our perspective away from religious demographics and toward social demographics, such as age, sex, education, income, and race. It is not clear how age will factor into support for American religious exceptionalism. Given that many disciples reminisce about a glorious past, one might expect older Americans to score higher than younger Americans. Also, the age gap in religiosity may also factor into differences. Regarding sex, several studies have linked nationalist and masculine beliefs, and so we might expect men to score higher than women (Nagel 1998; Du Mez 2020).

However, our analyses show no systematic relationship between age cohorts or sex with the probability a respondent is classified as a disciple on our measure.

Moving to education and income, we expect higher levels of both to be associated with lower levels of adherence to American religious exceptionalism. Research has shown that higher levels of education are associated with lower levels of both religiosity and nationalism. People with higher levels of education are less likely to view religion as salient in their lives and are less likely to adhere to religious traditionalism (Albrecht and Heaton 1984; Schwadel 2015). Furthermore, those with higher levels of education are exposed to more information about the world, making them less likely to express nationalist attitudes (Hjerm 2001; Hainmueller and Hiscox 2006). We expect income to be negatively associated with adherence because those with higher levels of income have greater security, making them less likely to draw on religion and nationalism for comfort (Oliver and Wood 2018). The results fit this expectation for education, but it is less clear for income. The results for the analyses show that a person with less than a high school education has a 35 percent chance of being a dissident and a 10 percent chance of being a disciple. For those with postgraduate training, the odds of being a dissident are 60 percent and for a disciple 4 percent. For income, those in the highest income category, $150,000 or more, are more likely to be dissidents and less likely to be disciples. For all of the other income categories, the odds of being a dissident range from 36 percent to 48 percent; however, for those making above $150,000, it is 67 percent. Regarding being a disciple, the other income categories range between a probability of 6–9 percent, while those in the highest income category have a 3 percent probability.

We do not have clear expectations about how one's race might affect one's acceptance of American religious exceptionalism. On the one hand, the tumultuous relationship between the nation and racial minorities has led racial minorities to be less exuberant in their expressions of pride in America. While they are attached to the nation and will defend it, they are more likely to view the nation through a critical lens and focus on ways to improve (Du Bois 1990; Shaw 2004; Parker 2009). This runs contrary to the exaltation of the nation associated with American religious exceptionalism. However, racial minorities have used the idea of a special connection between God and the nation to challenge the nation to do better regarding race religions. Because of these conflicting aspects, we are not sure if racial minorities will differentiate themselves from their White counterparts. Indeed, our data reveal no significant differences between racial groups.

We also need to account for political ideology. Given that American religious exceptionalism places the nation at the forefront of other nations and emphasizes a strictly positive version of the nation's history, we expect more conservative respondents to have higher levels of adherence. Our data demonstrate that the more politically conservative a person is, the less likely she is a dissident and the more likely she is a disciple. The odds for being a dissident are 65 percent for someone who identifies as extremely liberal, 45 percent for someone who is middle of the road, and 30 percent for someone who identifies as extremely conservative. Contrariwise, someone classified as a disciple is three times more likely to identify as extremely conservative than as extremely liberal.

The final set of analyses examines how values and personality traits may factor into adherence. Using surveys of undergraduates at the University of Texas at Austin, we examine how value frameworks, narcissism, and social dominance orientation relate to commitment to American religious exceptionalism. Values should be understood as abstract beliefs about desirable ends and how to achieve those ends. As such, values guide behavior, how others are evaluated, and how issues are prioritized (Rokeach 1973; Schwartz 1992; Kinder 1998). Shalom Schwartz's universal model of values provides a systematic approach to understanding values (1992, 1994). His model identifies ten value types: benevolence, universalism, self-direction, stimulation, hedonism, achievement, power, security, conformity, and tradition. From these ten value types, Schwartz developed four superordinate values: self-transcendence, conservation, self-enhancement, and openness to change. *Self-transcendence* (α = .82), comprised of universalism and benevolence, represents concern for others and the world at large. *Conservation* (α = .85), comprised of conformity, tradition, and security, represents restraint and a resistance to change. *Self-enhancement* (α = .61), comprised of power and achievement, emphasizes pursuit of self-interests and dominance. Finally, *openness to change* (α = .77), comprised of hedonism, stimulation, and self-direction, emphasizes independence and creativity (Rathbun, et al. 2016).

As figure 2.13 demonstrates, there are no significant relationships between adherence to American religious exceptionalism and the superordinate values of openness to change and self-enhancement; however, there are strong relationships between adherence, conservationism, and self-transcendence. Beginning with the conservationism scale, we see that if the modal respondent were at the bottom of the scale, she would have a virtually 0 percent chance of being classified a disciple, but if she were at the top of the measure, it would be 21 percent. For self-transcendence, we find the opposite: if the

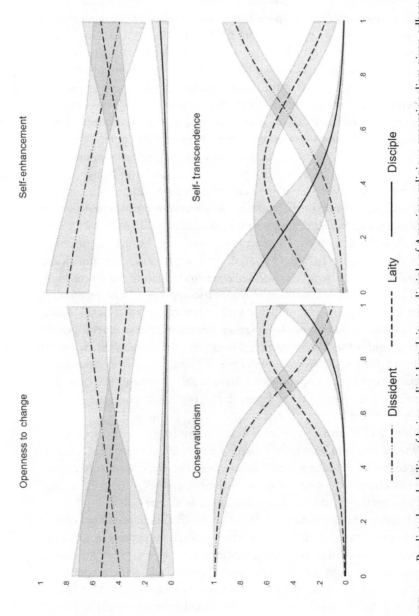

FIGURE 2.13 Predicted probability of being a dissident, laity, or disciple of American religious exceptionalism given adherence to Schwarz's superordinate values

Note: Predicted values were generated using coefficient estimates from ordered logit models that control for religious tradition, practices, beliefs, personal demographics, and political ideology. Shaded areas indicate 95 percent confidence intervals.

modal respondent is at the bottom of this scale, she has a 75 percent chance of being a disciple. If she was at the top of it, the probability would be 1 percent. Given that American religious exceptionalism is a form of religious nationalism and is associated with both religious and political conservativism, it is not surprising to see it associated with values emphasizing conformity and tradition and negatively correlated with values associated with universalism and benevolence.

We next focus on two personality characteristics: narcissism and social dominance orientation. Narcissism is a personality trait developed early in life, which is related to a person's level of self-absorption, beliefs of superiority and entitlement, and exhibitions of grandiosity. While scholars argue that moderate levels of narcissism are needed to be psychologically healthy, an overabundance of it is a sign of mental illness (Emmons 1987; Millon 1996; Ackerman, et al. 2011). Individual narcissism can be validated at the group level through racism, sexism, and nationalism (Emmons 1987). Since the core components of American religious exceptionalism emphasize the divinely established superiority of the nation, we expect those who express higher levels of narcissism also to express higher levels of adherence. We examined *narcissism* using three different measures of the concept. The first is a four-item measure (α = .81) that captures the core elements of the concept, such as wanting to be admired by others and expecting special favors (Jonason and Webster 2010). The other two measures seek to capture specific dimensions of narcissism, such as leadership/authority and superiority (Emmons 1984; Ackerman, et al. 2011). The *leadership/authority* dimension (α = .88) represents an individual's perception of how effective she is as a leader to the extent the person desires to take on a position of authority. The *superiority* dimension (α = .72) measures the respondent's belief that she is more capable than others, not dependent upon others, and possesses visions of greatness for herself. Figure 2.14 demonstrates that all three measures of narcissism are related to an increase in adherence. Beginning with the traditional four-item narcissism measure, we find that the percentage point difference in being a dissident if the modal respondent were at the bottom of the scale compared to the top of it is 47 percentage points. Moving to the superiority and leadership dimensions of narcissism, we find a similar pattern. For the superiority dimension, an individual at the bottom of scale has a 63 percent chance of being a dissident, while one at the high end of the measure has a 24 percent chance. On the leadership dimension we find a 42-percentage point difference in the odds of being dissident. Finally, we examine the relationship

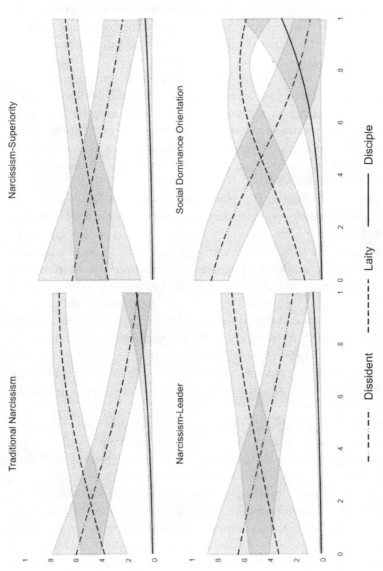

FIGURE 2.14 Predicted probability of being a dissident, laity, or disciple of American religious exceptionalism given personality traits

Note: Predicted values were generated using coefficient estimates from ordered logit regression models that control for religious tradition, practices, beliefs, personal demographics, and political ideology. Shaded areas indicate 95 percent confidence intervals.

between adherence and social dominance orientation. Social dominance orientation is a personality trait that encourages individuals to create and maintain social hierarchies that benefit their in-group. Those who possess this trait will seek inter-group relations that are hierarchical as opposed to equal. Social dominance orientation offers an explanation for ethnic and religious prejudice, as well as nationalism (Pratto, et al. 1994; Sidanius, et al. 1997; Sidanius and Pratto 1999). The analysis of *social dominance orientation* ($\alpha = .91$) demonstrates a much stronger relationship. If the modal respondent were at the bottom of the scale, she would have an 85 percent chance of being a dissident and a 1 percent chance of being a disciple. If she were at the high of the social dominance measure, she would have a 9 percent probability of being a dissident and a 32 percent probability of being a disciple.

2.6 CONCLUSION

This chapter outlines the theoretical motivation behind the book's central concept of American religious exceptionalism, which is steeped in notions of America's origin, purpose, and place in the world. We situate the basis of this ideology in the nation's higher levels of religiosity than other economically privileged countries, as well as the public's tendency to justify America's dominant global position using religious myths. Finally, we answer the question of who comprises the nation's disciples and dissidents of the ideology of American religious exceptionalism.

We find that disciples are a small but significant part of the American population. Further, it is clear they are highly distinct from the dissidents. For instance, we find that disciples express higher levels of religious importance and orthodoxy. Further, they are more likely to perceive God's influence in worldly affairs and are more likely to adopt purposive beliefs that are more individualized than communal. Importantly, disciples do not fall predominantly within one racial or religious category and are not explained by any one demographic, such as income or educational group. In keeping with their beliefs about the nation's supremacy, they tend to have higher levels of narcissism and social dominance orientation, but overall we could find no evidence that any one of the factors we analyzed explained religious exceptionalism adherence more than the mechanisms we have theorized. We therefore must examine how this ideology manifests in other attachments, which is where we turn next in our chapter on its connection to national identity.

3

Who Dwells in His House?

Behold, how good and how pleasant it is for brothers to dwell together in unity!

Psalm 133:1

I appeal to you, brothers, by the name of our Lord Jesus Christ, that all of you agree, and that there be no divisions among you, but that you be united in the same mind and the same judgment.

1 Corinthians 1:10

Surely, to be a Christian and an Anglo-Saxon and an American in this generation is to stand on the very mountain-top of privilege.

Strong 1893, p. 354

National identity has two key meanings. One refers to the identification or positive affective response an individual has toward her nation, while the other refers to the criteria of understanding who belongs to said nation, or literally, what constitutes a nation's identity (Anderson 1983; Smith 1991; Citrin, Wong and Duff 2001; Huntington 2004; Citrin and Sears 2009; Theiss-Morse 2009; McDaniel, Nooruddin and Shortle 2011, 2016; Citrin, Johnston and Wright 2012). The affective aspect emphasizes the strength of attachment to the nation. Political psychologists Jack Citrin and David Sears describe it as "the emotional significance" of identifying with a nation (2009, p. 147), while Benedict Anderson describes it as inspiring a "profoundly self-sacrificing love" (1983, p. 141). These intense positive emotional responses inspire explicit demonstrations of love for the nation through poetry, art, and songs. Further, it contributes to a willingness to sacrifice personal gains to protect or advance the group's interests. This feeling contributes to a person's willingness to die and, if needed, to harm others on behalf of the nation.

National identity also concerns defining what the nation is. Anthony Smith contends: "nations must have a measure of common culture and civic ideology, a set of common understandings and aspirations, sentiments and ideas that bind the population together" (1991, p. 11). This is the "content" of national identity (Citrin, Wong and Duff 2001, p. 141). The content of national identity details what is and what is not of the nation. It establishes the features, beliefs, and behaviors of national members. Those who exhibit proper attributes, attitudes, and actions will be accorded the full rights of citizenship, while those deemed deficient on these criteria are subject to diminished rights or even the revocation of citizenship (Smith 1997; Theiss-Morse 2009). The criteria or content of group identity is fluid and multiple sets of criteria can and do exist at any given time, and are in conflict with each other. These divisions become the basis for political battles.

How groups and nations define themselves shapes their responses to problems and who can make demands on the group. For example, Cathy Cohen attributes the reluctance of many Black organizations to respond to the AIDS crisis to their use of heterosexuality as a criterion for establishing Blackness (1999). Because of this, Black leaders refused to respond to a disease that then and now ravages the Black community. In sum, the content of group identity refers to the perception of who belongs in the group, and these perceptions have observable consequences for how the group behaves.

In this chapter, we survey existing scholarships about these two aspects of national identity as they relate to American religious exceptionalism. By explicating the multidimensional nature of American national attachment, this chapter reveals how beliefs about American religious exceptionalism relate to each dimension. Further, even though national rhetoric stresses civic principles as the sole membership criterion for being American, the historical record demonstrates that ascriptive criteria have been consistently used for establishing membership. We expect the disciples to express a high level of attachment to the nation and to have a stringently defined set of criteria for what it means to be an American. Our surveys of the American public show the disciples express high levels of national attachment, especially regarding beliefs about unquestioned loyalty and national superiority. Further, disciples endorse strict criteria for being a true American. They are more likely to stress certain principles and practices as being "truly" American and are also more likely to reject a culturally pluralistic definition of being American and are more likely to believe that "true" Americans have a specific race, heritage, and religion. Finally, disciples are more likely to derogate groups in American society that do not fit or challenge these criteria, while expressing support for groups that view themselves as defending the "authentic traditions" of the nation.

3.1 NATIONAL ATTACHMENT

National attachment is multidimensional (Allport 1927; Kosterman and Feshbach 1989; Citrin, Wong and Duff 2001; de Figueiredo and Elkins 2003). Two principal dimensions of national attachment have been identified. The first dimension refers to a sense of connection and pride derived from national consciousness resulting from a deep, affective attachment to one's nation (Citrin, Wong and Duff 2001; de Figueiredo and Elkins 2003; Huddy and Khatib 2007). This dimension is theoretically associated with the noble aspects of national attachment, such as contributing to civic life, artistic expressions, and being a positive representation of the nation (Allport 1927; Hurwitz and Peffley 1987). The second dimension expresses many of the same sentiments but deems the nation as superior or infallible (Feshbach 1987; de Figueiredo and Elkins 2003; Huddy and Khatib 2007; Parker 2010). The second dimension is associated with expressions of dominance, violence, and an unapologetic global presence.[1]

Christopher Parker contends the first dimension dominated early American understanding of national attachment (Parker 2010). During this time, he suggests, national attachment was open to critical assessments of government along with commitment to principles. The second dimension and its emphasis on superiority arose during the nineteenth century as part of the Redemption Period after the Civil War and the rise of American Imperialism. Finally, the reaction to the rise of communism shifted national attachment to an emphasis on loyalty. The feeling of national superiority and the emphasis on loyalty led to restricting the citizenship rights of perceived outsiders as well as promoting the exile of those deemed disloyal (Shklar 1993).

Such beliefs are not benign. Support for either of these dimensions of national identity has political ramifications. Studies of national pride, such as pride in the nation's political system, history, and scientific achievements, find that it is not associated with xenophobic and ethnocultural attitudes (Citrin, Wong and Duff 2001; de Figueiredo and Elkins 2003; Citrin, Johnston and Wright 2012). Parker finds that those who express pride in national symbols, such as the American flag, are less supportive of extending civil liberties to those accused of betraying the nation. However, they express more positive views of ethnic and religious outgroups, specifically Blacks and Jews (2010). Using Social Identity Theory as their intellectual foundation, Leonie Huddy and Nadia Khatib find that those who express a personal connection and embodiment of the nation are more civically engaged (2007).

In contrast to this pragmatic commitment to the nation, there are those whose sense of national attachment is associated with chauvinism, intolerance, and authoritarianism. Floyd Allport compared this form of national attachment to religious fundamentalism as those who embrace it assume their nation is above reproach, emphasize blind obedience, and view all other nations as fundamentally flawed. He further argues that their undying devotion to the nation and the protection of its symbols creates a "nationalistic fallacy," which contributes to aggressive behavior against out-groups, such as support for wars (1927). Others confirm that those who express this form of national attachment are more supportive of aggressive behavior, such as nuclear armament (Feshbach 1987; Hurwitz and Peffley 1987). Still others show that this form of national attachment is more likely to generate xenophobic attitudes (Kosterman and Feshbach 1989; Hjerm 2001; de Figueiredo and Elkins 2003). In line with this form of national attachment, John Somerville contends that some individuals adopt an uncritical understanding of their nation, which generates support for actions that may be of great cost to humanity. Further, he contends, numerous institutions, such as schools, the media, the arts, and churches, have embedded this belief in the national consciousness (Somerville 1981). Another study argues that those who adhere to this belief system are opposed to the rhetoric "that challenges the righteousness and magnificence of the country as a whole" (Schatz, Staub and Lavine 1999, p. 170). This study finds that people who adhere to this belief are more likely to express feelings of national superiority, but are less likely to be civically engaged.[2] They are also more likely to support a racially and religiously homogenous society (Spry and Hornsey 2007; Parker 2010).

While existing scholarship has stressed the differences between these two types of national attachment, our own previous work questions whether they are as different as theorists might wish them to be (McDaniel, Nooruddin and Shortle 2016). Using two different waves of the General Social Survey, we show that the alleged difference between the two concepts is attenuated markedly in 2004 compared to 1996. In 2004, the United States was at war in Afghanistan and in Iraq and had embarked on a global "War on Terror"; popular fears about terrorist threat were high; and anti-Muslim prejudice was rampant. We found that the purported difference between the two dimensions of national attachment identified by previous scholars using a survey from 1996 disappeared when their analysis was replicated using a survey from 2004, raising serious doubts about whether the earlier analysis was simply picking up social desirability effects among self-identified liberals.

The theoretical distinction between these two aspects of national attachment would have seemed strange at the nation's founding. The early colonists along with the nation's Founding Fathers characterized America and the United States as a "New Israel." It was to serve as a new beginning for the world, and the Almighty had given it His blessing. This reinforced the belief in their new nation's innocence, the faith that this nation was purer than all the other nations. Reinhold Niebuhr argues that when nations perceive themselves as innocent, they have the potential to cause great harms to humanity (Niebuhr 2008). Innocent nations perceive their actions as righteous and perceive any critique of their actions as stemming from malice. Further, the image of innocence and purity contributes to Manichean thinking, which frames the nation's activities as a battle between good and evil. In these strict dichotomies, any critique of the good must stem from malice and an evil source. Niebuhr's insight leads us to expect that the disciples of religious exceptionalism will be highly supportive of a form of national attachment that is uncritical and demands unquestioned loyalty. This sense of innocence and a special connection to the Divine also contributes to beliefs of national superiority. If a person believes God has ordained her nation to lead all others, she will be more likely to express national chauvinism. This national hubris is not justified by technological, economic, or political advancements, but a mandate from a higher power. The favor of a higher power justifies members of the nation to condescend toward other nations and demand they be more like them. Because disciples believe the nation is divinely inspired and favored, we expect them to express a high level of pride in the nation's accomplishments and to express a stronger emotional connection to its symbols. Along with this connection to the "nobler" dimension of national attachment, we also expect disciples to express support for more worrisome forms of national attachment. Most importantly, we expect the relationship between religious exceptionalism and the chauvinist dimension of national attachment to be stronger than with the affective pride dimension. In other words, we expect supporters of American religious exceptionalism to be more distinguishable from nonsupporters in their support for uncritical loyalty and beliefs of national superiority. This ideology's emphasis on the nation being divinely inspired and favored strongly contributes to viewing the nation as infallible and supreme.

To examine the connection between religion and national attachment, we analyze the differences in expressions of national attachment between religious traditions. The predicted probabilities in Figure 3.1 demonstrate that overall Americans, regardless of religious tradition, express high levels of national attachment.

In this sample, 55 percent of respondents report being extremely proud of the United States. Those who are religiously unaffiliated have the lowest probability of stating they are extremely proud, while White evangelical Protestants have the highest probability of expressing extreme pride in being citizens of the United States. White evangelicals are also significantly more likely to express extreme pride than mainline Protestants, Catholics, and non-White Protestants. A different perspective on this question comes from an item asking respondents if they have ever experienced a moment in which they did not feel proud to be an American. When the question is posed this way, the religiously unaffiliated and non-White Protestants have the highest probability of admitting to ever feeling this way. The religiously unaffiliated have a significantly higher probability of expressing this than White evangelical Protestants, White mainline Protestants, and Catholics. Non-White Protestants are significantly more likely to express a period of not being proud than White evangelicals, Catholics, Black Protestants, and those in other Christian religions. The results summarized in Figure 3.1 also document how race and religion shape how one feels about her place in the nation. We find that Black Protestants, non-White Protestants, and those in non-Christian religions are least likely to state that they think of themselves as a typical American. Being a member of a racial or religious minority appears to diminish the perception she fits the American mold or, framed more provocatively, our results reveal the extent to which racial and religious American minorities feel alienated. Finally, our examination of attitudes toward public displays of national pride, such as displaying a flag, finds strikingly and uniformly high agreement across all groups, even the religiously unaffiliated, that such overt demonstrations of pride are important. Indeed, the absence of any meaningful variation across groups in how they answer this question is perhaps the most telling part of this analysis.

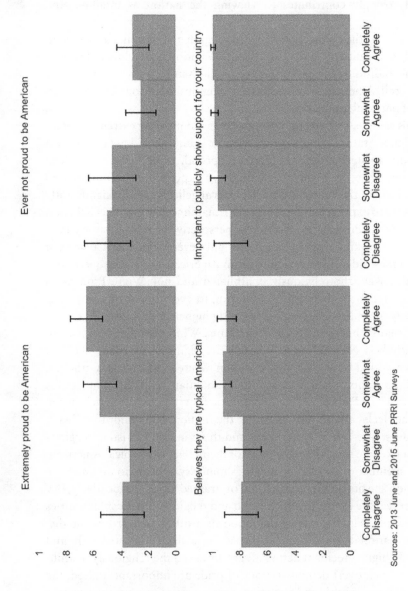

FIGURE 3.1 Predicted probability of national attachment as predicted by religious tradition

Note: Predicted probabilities were estimated from logit regression models that control for personal demographics and political ideology. Capped lines indicate 95 percent confidence intervals.

Sources: 2013 June and 2015 June PRRI Surveys

Moving next to measures of national pride, which ask respondents to make implicit and explicit comparisons of America to other nations, we find White Christians are the most likely to express beliefs that the United States is an exemplar to other nations (Figure 3.2).

White evangelical Protestants, White mainline Protestants, and Catholics are the most likely to express belief in the innocence and goodwill of the American nation. Black Protestants, non-White Protestants, and the unaffiliated are less likely to agree with this statement, though members of this group also have high baseline probabilities of agreeing. Interestingly, when asked, respondents across the board are less likely to think that America today sets a good moral example for the world. This disjuncture is consistent with our sense that many Americans, especially those who are religiously observant, simultaneously believe in the promise of America while bemoaning the extent to which it does not live up to its promise or divine covenant. Finally, we note that White evangelical Protestants, White mainline Protestants, and Catholics are the most likely to agree the world would be much better off if other countries adopted American values and way of life.

We get at the question of how Americans understand the idea of loyalty to the nation by asking citizens if anti-government protests are useful or not (Figure 3.3). Protests are time-tested effective methods for signaling political leadership about the content and intensity of citizen concerns (Gillion 2013). Further, those who are supportive of a critical assessment of the nation should view protest as an expression of citizen commitment to the ideals of the nation, while those who adopt an uncritical national attachment will view protests as harmful. A survey conducted by the PRRI in their 2020 American Values Survey provides the opportunity to assess how citizens perceive protests, and under two instructively different conditions. The sample was randomly split in half, with one half responding to the statement, "When Americans speak up and protest unfair treatment by the government it always makes our country better." The other half of the sample was provided the same prompt, but the investigators identified the protesting group as "Black Americans." Comparing the probability of agreement among respondents demonstrates that the positives associated with protesting are contingent upon who is protesting. Among those exposed to the unspecified "American protestors" prompt, 63 percent were of the opinion that such protests against unfair government action strengthen America. But when the protesting group was identified as "Black Americans," the proportion in favor dropped to 54 percent. This difference is statistically significant and suggests two substantive

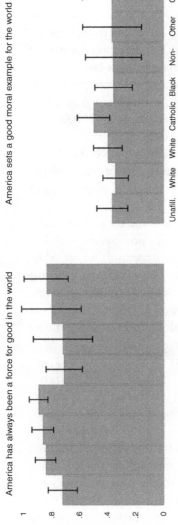

America has always been a force for good in the world

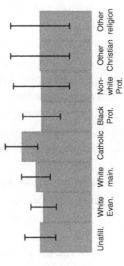

America sets a good moral example for the world

If more countries had american values, world would be better

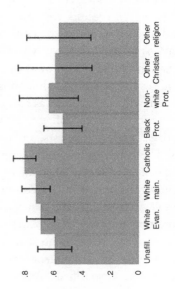

FIGURE 3.2 Predicted probability of expressing national pride and hubris as predicted by religious tradition

Note: Predicted probabilities were estimated from logit regression models that control for personal demographics and political ideology. Capped lines indicate 95 percent confidence intervals.

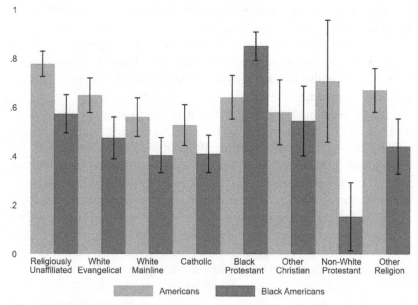

Source: 2020 PRRI American Values Survey

FIGURE 3.3 Predicted probability of viewing protests as positive given the protester, by religious tradition
Note: Predicted probabilities were estimated from logit regression models that control for personal demographics and political ideology. Capped lines indicate 95 percent confidence intervals.

conclusions. First, the respondents to this survey are less supportive of Black Americans exercising their right to protest than they are of some generic American protesting; and second, this is likely because the survey respondents understood the "generic American" to be White, indicating the extent to which ordinary citizens internalize a racialized view of who is a prototypical American. One could argue that the results are a consequence of the Black Lives Matter protests that gripped a polarized nation during the summer of 2020. However, a comparison of the same items asked in 2015 found the same significant difference.

When we examined how religious tradition was associated with responses to these statements, we find differences within and across the statements. The analysis of the generic "Americans" prompt finds that the probability of agreeing with this statement is greater than 50 percent for all the groups, with the religiously unaffiliated being the highest at 78 percent followed by Non-White Protestants at 71 percent. When asked about "Black Americans" protesting, there is a significant reduction in support for all groups except for those in other Christian religions and Black Protestants. This decline ranges from 12 percentage points for Catholics to 55 for non-White Protestants. In contrast to these groups, for Black Protestants there is an increase. The odds for a Black Protestant in the "American" condition is 64 percent, but in the "Black American" condition, it is 85 percent.

Clearly, religious tradition matters when discussing national attachment, with White Christians consistently expressing higher levels of national pride than other groups. While these results are helpful for understanding the connection between religion, national identification, and pride, they are limited in explaining how a belief in a special connection with the divine and the nation influences national attachment. To assess the belief that the nation has a unique relationship with God, we examine how agreement with the statement "God has granted the United States a special place in human history" corresponds with these measures of national attachment. Those who express higher levels of support for this belief also express higher levels of national identity (Figure 3.4). Beginning with the probability of stating they are extremely proud to be American, we find a respondent who completely disagrees with the notion that the United States has a divinely ordained place in human history has a 38 percent probability of expressing extreme pride in being American. By contrast, someone who completely agrees with the statement has a 65 percent probability. Likewise, a respondent who completely agrees has a 31 percent chance of stating that there was a time when she was not proud to be an American, while the odds for one who completely disagrees is 49 percent. Particularly interesting is whether respondents think of themselves as "typical Americans." Even though the probability of a respondent agreeing she is a typical American is high across the board, those who completely agree with the nation's divine placement have an 89 percent chance of believing this compared to 78 percent for those who completely disagree with the idea of divine placement. Likewise, while all respondents agree it is important to display national support publicly, those who completely disagree with the nation's divine role support this at a significantly lower level than the others.

Moving from national identification to national pride, we find that those who believe the nation was granted a special place by God are more likely to agree with expressions of national pride and hubris that emphasize the nation's moral superiority. Beginning with a sense of national innocence, the analysis of the 2013 survey finds that Americans overwhelmingly (82 percent) agree the nation has always been a force for

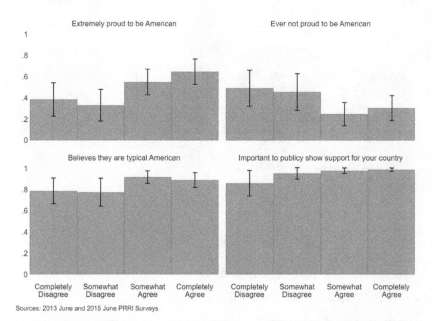

Sources: 2013 June and 2015 June PRRI Surveys

FIGURE 3.4 Predicted probability of national identity given agreement with the belief that God has granted the United States a special role in human history
Note: Predicted probabilities were estimated from logit regression models that control for religious tradition, personal demographics, and political ideology. Capped lines indicate 95 percent confidence intervals.

good. When comparing those at the polar ends of the special place in history statement, we find the difference is between a high probability of agreeing with this statement (68 percent) and an extremely high probability (93 percent). Moving to questions regarding the nation's status as a role model, we find that two-thirds of respondents agreed with the sentiment that "If more countries adopted American values and way of life, the world would be much better off." Agreement with this view is especially high among those who believe America has been ordained with a special place in history. Interestingly, in 2015, this sense of innocence had receded; when asked if the nation was a moral exemplar for the world, only 43 percent of the respondents agree with this statement. Even with this lower level of overall support, there is a significant difference between those at the ends of the measure. A respondent who completely disagrees with the idea that God has ordained a special role for America has an 18 percent probability of agreeing that the United States is a moral exemplar for the world, while one who completely agrees has a 48 percent probability.

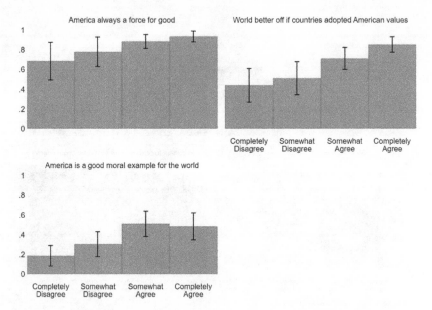

FIGURE 3.5 Predicted probability of expressing national hubris given agreement with the belief that God has granted the United States a special role in human history
Note: Predicted probabilities were estimated from logit regression models that control for religious tradition, personal demographics, and political ideology. Capped lines indicate 95 percent confidence intervals.
Source: Author analysis of the PRRI/Brookings 2013 Economic Values Survey and PRRI/RNS June 2015 Survey.

Finally, we conclude our analysis of the PRRI data by examining the belief that protests have a positive impact on the nation. When asked about "Americans" who protest, the relationship between support for protesting's effects and American religious exceptionalism is not statistically significant. If the modal respondent completely disagrees with the nation having a divine role, she has a 51 percent chance of agreeing that protesting has a positive impact. If she completely agrees with this idea, the odds rise to 63 percent. Switching gears to the question of whether the same modal respondent holds a positive view of "Black Americans" protesting, the relationship becomes negative and significant. The odds of viewing Black protests as positive for the nation are 65 percent for someone who rejects a divine hand in the nation's actions compared to 47 percent for someone who embraces it. This suggests believing the nation has a divinely specified role does explain attitudes toward protesters of different races.

The PRRI data are extremely useful for establishing a baseline under-standing of how beliefs about the nation's special connection with a higher power are linked to identification and admiration of the nation. To test this connection further, we turn to our own surveys that contain measures of American religious exceptionalism along with other measures of national attachment that allow us to measure directly different forms of national attachment. For these analyses, we utilize four measures of national attach-ment: national identity, national pride, national hubris, and uncritical patriotism. The *national identity* scale (α = .60), adapted from Huddy and Khatib (2007), measures the extent to which an individual feels psychically attached to the nation and internalizes a sense of belonging. The *national pride* (α = .82) and *national hubris* (α = .78) measures are adopted from research by Citrin, Wong, and Duff (2001). The pride measure assesses positive affective responses to the nation's accomplishments, while the hubris measure captures a sense of superiority of the nation over others. The *uncritical patriotism* measure (α = .78) is adopted from Schatz, Staub, and Lavine (1999)'s blind patriotism scale, which measures an inflexible and unquestioning positive attachment to the nation that is intolerant of criticism. As highlighted earlier, national identity and pride are viewed by some scholars as the nobler aspects of national attachment as they express an admiration and connection to the nation. In contrast, hubris and uncrit-ical patriotism are considered the darker forms of national attachment as they encourage the diminution of other nations and demand unquestioned loyalty to the nation. A comparison of the mean scores on these measures finds that the respondents score highest on the American national identity measure (average score of 0.81 on a scale of 0–1, followed by national hubris (average = 0.71), national pride (average = 0.67), and uncritical patriotism (average = 0.49).

Figure 3.6 displays the results from the analysis of the relationship between our American religious exceptionalism measure and these meas-ures of national attachment. Americans demonstrate a high level of national identity and pride. However, the results also show a stepwise increase in the predicted values when comparing the categories. In the case of both national identity and pride, a respondent in the laity scores significantly higher than a dissident and a disciple scores significantly higher than a respondent in either of these groups. Moving to the darker forms of national attachment, the same relationship is present, as a modal respondent in each group scores significantly higher as we move up the exceptionalism scale. However, the gap between a dissident and a disciple is larger. The gap between a dissident and a disciple on predicted values of

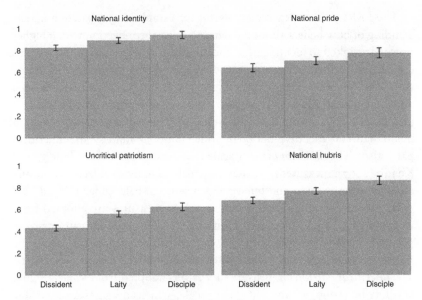

FIGURE 3.6 Predicted values of national attachment given adherence to American
religious exceptionalism
*Note: Predicted values were generated using coefficient estimates from OLS
regression models that control for biblical literalism, religious tradition, religious
behaviors, personal demographics, and political ideology. Capped lines mark the
estimated 95 percent confidence intervals.*

national identity attachment and national pride is 12 and 13 points,
respectively. For uncritical patriotism and national hubris, the difference
is 19 and 18 points, respectively.

Public opinion data from nine original surveys we generated and fielded
over the past decade, corroborated by our analysis of independent surveys
by leading research institutes, confirm our expectation that American
religious exceptionalism promotes an unyielding identification, with the
nation fostering a distrust and arrogance toward other nations and an
unquestioned commitment to all the nation's endeavors. These darker
forms of national attachment are associated with highly restrictive ideas
of what it means to be an American. We delve into this second aspect of
national identity – its content – next.

3.2 NATIONAL CONTENT

Whereas national attachment refers to how one feels about the nation,
national content establishes the criteria for being a part of the nation. If we

adhere to Benedict Anderson's (1983) logic that nations are "imagined communities," content establishes what or whom a person is imagining (Abdelal, et al. 2006; Schildkraut 2011). These criteria establish boundaries of who can rightfully claim citizenship. By being able to assert a legitimate claim to citizenship, an individual can make demands of the nation as well as take on leadership roles (Theiss-Morse 2009). The ability to be viewed as legitimate or rightful members of the national community grants individuals more than the formal rights of citizens, such as due process and the right to vote. For instance, supporters of felony disenfranchisement argue that those who are convicted of certain crimes have forfeited their full citizenship rights and should be prohibited from voting. Beyond these formal rights, "legitimate" citizens have the freedom to have their interests respected and taken seriously (Theiss-Morse 2009; Schildkraut 2011). Major social movements by women, racial minorities, and the LGBTQIA+ community have sought not only formal rights, such as voting, employment, and marriage, but also full acceptance as part of the nation. These movements argue that gender, race, or sexuality should not be used as criteria for citizenship. The criteria a nation uses to develop its formal and informal citizenship boundaries have large ramifications for understanding the direction of policy. As Anne Schneider and Helen Ingram demonstrate, how we perceive other citizens dictates how we respond to their problems (1997). Numerous other studies have demonstrated how we define the ideal citizen influences our policy preferences; the ideal citizen is rewarded or empowered, whereas the deviant is punished or marginalized (Smith 1997; Morone 2003; Weaver 2007). Debates over "English-only" language policy as well as multiculturalism in education are responses to how Americans define the content of being American (Huntington 2004; Schildkraut 2011).

Given the importance of such boundaries in shaping who is considered a "legitimate" or "rightful" citizen, we must pay attention to the various criteria used to establish these boundaries. Some citizens might claim to stress value adoption and activities as criteria for admitting someone to US citizenship; others rely on ancestry and religion. Americans' public rhetoric emphasizes values and activities as the criteria for citizenship. However, in practice ancestry and faith play a prominent role. Because of the numerous ways Americans have defined the content of being American, several traditions have emerged (Smith 1997). Deborah Schildkraut highlights four traditions in her analysis of the content of national identity: liberalism, ethnoculturalism, civic republicanism, and incorporationism (Schildkraut 2011).

Liberalism has taken on many forms throughout American history, but its main argument contends that people should be able to live their lives to the fullest with little interference. Those who embrace liberalism view people as being reasonable and agreeable by nature and view various social, economic, cultural, and political constraints as unnatural (Hartz 1991; Gerstle 1994). This emphasis on the reduction of constraints on individuals has been championed as the primary criteria for the uniqueness of the American nation (Lipset 1979) and the success of American democracy (Dahl 1989; Gutmann 2003; Huntington 2004). The Declaration of Independence's emphasis on "inalienable rights," along with the US Constitution containing a Bill of Rights, demonstrates the commitment of the nation to the liberal tradition. Many of the major political fights in American history have been around whether or not the nation has lived up to this ideology, specifically around economic and political rights. Arguments about the regulation and deregulation of businesses surround the concern about whether or not people will receive benefits from their hard work or if economic constraints will strip them of these benefits. Arguments over freedom of speech and expression are concerned with the ability for groups to be able to express and defend their political and social interests without repercussions. Both progressive and conservative movements have used liberalism to frame their cause (Gerstle 1994).

Whereas the liberal tradition speaks to thoughts and beliefs, the civic republicanism tradition speaks to actions. Civic republicanism emphasizes the need for people to be actively involved in civic and political life to be considered Americans (Banning 1986; Held 2006). It builds upon the liberal tradition's emphasis on political freedoms, by calling on citizens to use these freedoms actively. This tradition invokes Alexis de Tocqueville's observation that Americans were politically knowledgeable and engaged in civic and political life (1945). Essential to extending citizens' political freedoms is that they will actively use them to learn, dialogue with each other, and engage the political system (Crick 2016). At the extreme, supporters of civic republicanism take the stance of Athenian statesman Pericles who stated: "we do not say that a man who takes no interest in politics is a man who minds his own business; we say that he has no business here at all" (Thucydides, Warner and Finley 1972). While few people take this stance, most civic republicans hold that political freedoms likely turn people toward engagement with political and civic acts. In their minds, a properly functioning democracy has an active civil society (Crick 2016). The concerns of political scientists regarding the degradation of

American civil society (Putnam 1995) and with low levels of political interest and information (Verba, Schlozman and Brady 1995; Delli Carpini and Keeter 1996; Prior 2010) reflect this line of thought.

Incorporationism, sometimes referred to as cultural pluralism or multi-culturalism, urges newcomers to embrace certain "American" social and political customs while expecting existing citizens to allow newcomers to retain their heritage and acknowledge its relevance to the nation (Kymlicka 1995; Schildkraut 2011). This approach is distinct from the ideology of assimilationism, which enforces conformity in the name of unity. Throughout much of the nation's history, groups were encouraged or coerced to cast aside their cultural heritage in order to mirror an American prototype, which was White, English-speaking, Protestant, and middle class. Groups viewed as nonassimilable, such as the Chinese or Blacks, were excluded or regulated to lower-class citizenship (Takaki 1989; Fox 2012). Over time, due to the hard work of activists and leadership of these "new American" communities, greater efforts have been made to embrace cultural differences by allowing these groups to express their heritage through public institutions, including in schools (Alba and Nee 2003). Whereas assimilationism placed little burden on the "hosts," incorporationism demands more of them. These added responsibilities have generated significant backlash as demands for the recognition of multiple languages and multicultural education have forced Americans to ask themselves the extent to which they are willing to accept this responsibility (Citrin, Wong and Duff 2001; Schildkraut 2005; Citrin and Sears 2009).

Liberalism, Civic Republicanism, and Incorporationism are the "progressive" dimensions of how Americans like to define who they are. Ethnoculturalism, on the other hand, is viewed as an unsavory relic of America's past and something the nation has attempted to move away from. Unlike liberalism and civic republicanism, which emphasize political values and behaviors, ethnoculturalism emphasizes heredity and religion in defining who is an American.[3] Furthermore, it is viewed as the antithesis of incorporationism as it rejects the idea any other culture can be compatible with the American nation. Some Americans have attempted to move away from this tradition, but its consistent reemergence reveals how deeply it resonates with many others (Smith 1997; Devos and Banaji 2005; Schildkraut 2005; Phillips 2018; Butler 2021). Samuel Huntington praised the liberal tradition as the reason for American superiority, while also emphasizing religion and language as a criterion for being American (2004). The reaction to the terrorist attacks on September 11, 2001, along with the rise of the Tea Party and Donald Trump, have further pushed this tradition forward (Schildkraut 2002; Davis and Silver 2004; Parker and Barreto 2013; McDaniel 2016). Recent works have demonstrated how the belief that race and religion were vital aspects of an American is not an issue of the past, but an important issue of the present (Jones 2020; Whitehead and Perry 2020; Butler 2021). Evidence suggests that perceived threats to the United States' status as a White Christian nation explained much of the support among White Americans for Donald Trump's presidential campaign (Mutz 2018; Whitehead, Perry, and Baker 2018).

Along with these racial and religious restrictions on who is "truly" American, scholars have also noted the role of gender in making an American. Throughout much of the nation's history, women were regulated to private life. Because most women were limited in the social, economic, and political rights, they were reliant on a husband or father to have their rights recognized (Marston 1990). Furthermore, women were viewed as emotional and illogical, and therefore incompatible with the new rational political system the founders created (Pateman 1980). Because of these biases, the prototypical American remains a White Protestant man (Smith 1997; Alba and Nee 2003; Ritter 2006). These concerns drastically limit who is considered American, who can become American, and who can make demands on the nation. Furthermore, as opposed to the other traditions that require greater inspection to see if a person is living up to their ideals, ethnoculturalism uses easily identifiable markers.

The nature of American religious exceptionalism leads to several expectations regarding the willingness of Americans to embrace certain content traditions. The rhetoric of liberalism and civic republicanism invokes the supposed genius of America. This appeal to American superiority should make such rhetoric appealing to those who subscribe to the idea of American exceptionalism. But disciples should be just as likely to find attractive the ideas of ethnoculturalists. American religious exceptionalism is not a political nationalism, it is an ethnic nationalism; its understanding of the nation is not rooted in political ideologies, but in ethnic ties. Furthermore, we also expect disciples to reject any tradition expressing support for a pluralistic society. This raises a difficult point that bears greater scrutiny: While scholars have long posed liberalism and civic republicanism as "strangers" to ethnoculturalism, our framework leads us to expect these ideas to be more like "first cousins," joined by a core appeal to a shared American understanding of their nation as exceptional.

To test the relationship between religious exceptionalism and these traditions, we utilize measures developed by Deborah Schildkraut that capture commitment to each of these traditions (Schildkraut 2011). We asked a random sample of Americans to indicate how important certain traits *should* be to be considered truly American. Other surveys have asked how important these traits *are*. We worried that phrasing may lead the respondent to respond based upon what they believe society views as important. By asking how important these traits *should* be, we provide a respondent with greater freedom to imagine her ideal American. As Schildkraut's analysis pointed out, these traditions do exist in the minds of Americans, but some are more concrete than others. Traditions such as *ethnoculturalism* (α = .82) and *civic republicanism* (α = .78) are well-formed constructs in the minds of Americans. However, liberalism and incorporationism are more elusive ideas. We measure *liberalism* not through a single index, but by capturing agreement with the principles of the importance of free speech and of pursuing economic success through hard work. *Incorporationism* is measured using two indices that capture the two sides of tradition: *assimilation* (α = .67) and *cultural pluralism* (α = .53) The assimilation scale measures the importance of immigrants making changes to fit into a specific version of contemporary American society, such as speaking English, adopting certain values, respecting existing laws, and blending into larger society. The cultural pluralism scale measures the importance respondents ascribe to Americans accepting and welcoming immigrants. This scale includes items such as seeing people of all backgrounds as American, respecting other cultures, and allowing immigrants to retain their cultural traditions.

Our analysis of the relationship between religious exceptionalism and belief in these traditions reveals nuanced relationships. Beginning with the two items used to measure liberalism, the most prominent of the nation's traditions, we find a familiar stepwise pattern regarding support for the bootstrap philosophy as a dissident is predicted to score 0.81, a laity 0.85, and a disciple 0.94. When we turn to commitment to freedom of speech, we find no significant difference between disciples and dissidents, but both score significantly higher than laity. These results suggest that dissidents and disciples agree regarding freedom of speech. We find the same stepwise pattern in civic republicanism as in the other analyses, with an 11-point gap between a dissident and a disciple. Likewise a disciple has greater expectations that newcomers assimilate compared to a laity or dissident. However, adherence to cultural pluralism, which requires current Americans to make accommodations for newcomers, is not associated with differences in adherence to religious exceptionalism. Finally, explicit commitment to ethnocultural- ism generates the largest gap, as the disciples score 26 points higher than the dissidents and 12 points higher than laity. Furthermore, consistent with our expectations, American religious exceptionalism has a significantly stronger relationship with this tradition than with any of the others. As theorized, there exists a strong bond between beliefs about a divinely created nation and ethnic ascriptions of citizenship (see Figure 3.7).

The results thus far tell how dissidents, laity, and disciples differ in defining the nation. The next set of analyses provides more detailed analysis of how they view various policies and groups that challenge our understanding of what it means to be an American. The positive and negative views of members of the community are critical in understanding their support for the sharing of resources and the protection of rights.

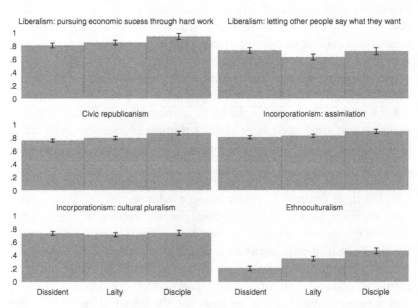

FIGURE 3.7 Predicted values of support for national content traditions given adherence to American religious exceptionalism

Note: Predicted values were generated using coefficient estimates from OLS regression models that control for biblical literalism, religious tradition, religious behaviors, personal demographics, and political ideology. Capped lines mark the estimated 95 percent confidence intervals.

Members of the community viewed with suspicion or believed to violate norms face greater difficulty in requesting resources, having their grievances heard, and guaranteeing their freedoms are protected (Schneider and Ingram 1997; Morone 2003). Scholars demonstrate that even if members are objectively part of a group, some members of the group may reject or minimize their membership (Cohen 1999). Social identity scholars note the "black-sheep effect" whereby individuals derogate in-group members because they believe they violate the group's norms (Marques and Paez 1994; Lewis and Sherman 2010). In the American context, historians and scholars have long noted groups that challenge religious, racial, and gender norms have been viewed as the "black-sheep" of the American family (Smith 1991).

As highlighted earlier, the United States has emphasized political and economic beliefs as critical to what it means to be an American. We have shown already that the American public claims to support more abstract values-based criteria of what it means to be an American over racial and religious criteria. However, the nation has historically relied on ethnocultural criteria for defining the content of American national identity. This has created obstacles for religious and racial minorities who have had to use a multitude of tactics to ensure full citizenship. Americans' history of discrimination against non-Protestants forced Catholics and Jews to have to overcome suspicion and their marginalized status, and, even today, anti-Semitism remains a potent force in American politics (Wilcox 1989; Berinsky and Mendelberg 2005). After the September 11, 2001, attacks, bigotry against Muslim Americans was heightened and their loyalty to the nation openly questioned (Zolberg and Woon 1999; Smidt 2005; Kalkan, Layman and Uslaner 2009; Creighton and Jamal 2015). Racial minorities have also gained the ire of the American public for a host of perceived violations. Ronald Takaki demonstrates that the consistent perception of Asian Americans as outsiders contributed to the creation of Japanese internment camps during World War II, as well as continued suspicions about the group's loyalties (1989). Historically, the nation's reluctance to accept Black Americans was rooted in biological and explicitly racist language. As that language became taboo, new arguments emphasized how Blacks violated American values, specifically individualism (Kinder and Sanders 1996; Sears, Sidanius and Bobo 2000). Finally, scholars, such as Rogers Smith and Gretchen Ritter, contend that because American citizenship is understood as masculine, women were long excluded from numerous economic and political rights (Dietz 1987; Smith 1997; Ritter 2006). The praise of masculinity as an American ideal allows feminist groups and causes to be framed as symbolic violations or attacks on the nation (Hurwitz and Peffley 1987). More recently, the rise of the Tea Party and Donald Trump's ascension to the presidency has been linked to the rise in overt expressions of ethnoculturalism (Parker and Barreto 2013; Cox, Lienesch and Jones 2017; Mutz 2018). Emboldened by a president sympathetic to White nationalist views, White Americans are increasingly comfortable affirming the quiet parts of American identity out loud.

These patterns in American history along with contemporary concerns indicate the importance of deeper investigation into national content to see how adherence to American religious exceptionalism shapes attitudes toward groups historically associated with being the desired citizens and those associated with being the deviant citizens. Given the results from analyses of national attachment and traditions of American citizenship, we expect the disciples of religious exceptionalism to enforce racial, religious, and gender hierarchies.

Figure 3.8 demonstrates that adherence to American religious exceptionalism is associated with downplaying racism and supporting the idea of a racial hierarchy.

We begin with a survey question asking Americans their assessment of the pervasiveness of racism in American society. Specifically, we ask respondents whether they agree with the statement that racial problems in America are rare, isolated events. A disciple of American religious exceptionalism has a 25 percent chance of agreeing racial problems are rare, the odds for laity and dissidents are lower at 9 percent and 11 percent, respectively. When asked whether they think White Americans have an advantage because of their skin, a dissident is significantly more likely to agree than laity or disciples. Taken together, these two items indicate that dissidents are most likely to recognize there is a race problem in the United States, while the laity and disciples are more resistant to acknowledging this issue.

Indeed, when asked about what the nation should look like and their attitudes toward other racial groups, those who score higher on American religious exceptionalism express higher support for a racial hierarchy where White Americans are on top. For instance, a disciple has a 24 percent probability and a laity a 13 percent probability of being bothered by the prospect of a future United States that is no longer predominantly White, compared to 7 percent for a dissident. For an alternative indicator of racial views, we examine the relationship between adherence to religious exceptionalism and racial resentment. The *racial resentment* measure ($\alpha = .91$) is an assessment of the degree to

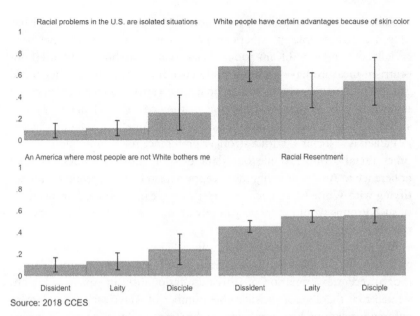

FIGURE 3.8 Predicted probabilities and values of attitudes toward racial issues
and racial groups given adherence to American religious exceptionalism
*Note: Predicted values were generated using coefficient estimates from logit and
OLS regression models that control for biblical literalism, religious tradition,
religious behaviors, personal demographics, and political ideology. Capped lines
mark the estimated 95 percent confidence intervals.*

which respondents believe Blacks have violated national norms. Racial
resentment has been linked to opposition for a variety of racially progressive policies and candidates. Those who score high on the measure
believe Blacks' demands for government aid and help are unfair, which
leads them to oppose policies such as affirmative action and welfare
(Kinder and Sanders 1996). Those who score low on the measure believe
Blacks have suffered serious setbacks due to historic discrimination and
still require government assistance, leading them to be more supportive
of policies aimed at assisting Blacks. Our analysis finds that the dissidents score significantly lower than the laity and disciples. The laity
score 9 points higher, while the disciples score 10 points higher, than
dissidents.

Another way of uncovering support for a racial hierarchy is by examining preferences for one racial group over another. To examine this
preference, we use a measure of ethnocentrism adapted from research by
Cindy Kam and Donald Kinder. Kam and Kinder find that ethnocentrism

explains a variety of policy preferences as well as vote choice and has played a strong role in American politics whenever issues have been racialized (Kinder and Kam 2009). Those who score high on their ethnocentrism measure have a strong preference for Whites over other racial groups, while those who score low on it have a strong preference for racial minorities over Whites. Our analysis of the 2010 Knowledge Networks survey finds that each increment of support for American religious exceptionalism is associated with a stronger preference for Whites compared to other racial groups. While our data do not allow the inference that adherence to American religious exceptionalism is the equivalent of identifying with White supremacist groups, we have little doubt that members of such groups would score very highly on our American religious exceptionalism scale.

We move next to attitudes about the religious roots of the nation and attitudes toward religious groups. Andrew Whitehead and Samuel Perry's (2020) recent examination of Christian nationalism in America demonstrated that there are a considerable number of Americans who want to enforce a religious hierarchy where Christians are at the top. Katherine Stewart's (2019) examination of Christian nationalist organizations details how they have been able to advance policies at the local, state, and national level to try to advance Christianity in this religious hierarchy. Our results demonstrate strong evidence that increased adherence to American religious exceptionalism is also linked to support for this specific religious hierarchy. The first piece of evidence demonstrating disciples' support for a religious hierarchy is their beliefs about which religion serves as the basis for the nation. When asked if the United States was founded as a Christian nation, we find 61 percent of Americans agreeing. Figure 3.9 shows the results from the analysis of this question and finds that a dissident has a relatively high level of support for this statement with a 66 percent chance of agreeing. For a laity and a disciple, the odds are 76 percent and 97 percent, respectively.

This bias in favor of Christians is further demonstrated when the respondents indicated their agreement with the statement "non-Christians create immoral policies." In this case, a dissident has an 11 percent chance of agreeing with this statement, while a laity has a 37 percent chance. For a disciple, the odds are 60 percent. This stepwise increase further indicates the connection between American religious exceptionalism and an American religious hierarchy. This in turn leads to a source of grievance for the influence Christians have in contemporary America. Both a laity and a disciple are almost twice as likely to believe Christians

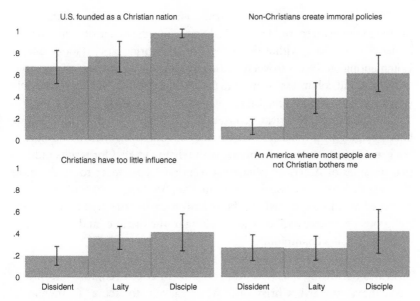

FIGURE 3.9 Predicted probabilities of attitudes toward religious issues and religious groups given adherence to American religious exceptionalism
Note: Predicted values were generated using coefficient estimates from logit and OLS regression models that control for biblical literalism, religious tradition, religious behaviors, personal demographics, and political ideology. Capped lines mark the estimated 95 percent confidence intervals.

have too little influence compared to a disciple. This grievance is further demonstrated in the anxiety of being in a non-Christian dominant nation. When asked about whether they were bothered by the possibility of America no longer being majority Christian, we find that a dissident and a laity both have a one in four chance of agreeing; however, a disciple has a 41 percent chance of agreeing.

The preceding analysis taps critical concerns about religion in the United States. As we noted in Chapter 1, several politicians have explicitly argued that the Constitution and other early documents established the nation as a Christian nation. Several others have lamented about the growing number of non-Christians being elected to office. Katherine Harris, in her failed 2006 US Senate campaign, went so far as arguing that electing non-Christians to office was "legislating sin."[4] Others have bemoaned the election of Muslims to the House of Representatives as well as to local offices. In 2006, reacting to Keith Ellison becoming the first Muslim to serve in the House of Representatives, Rep. Virgil Goode

(R-VA) fulminated that "we are leaving ourselves vulnerable to infiltration by those who want to mold the United States into the image of their religion, rather than working within the Judeo-Christian principles" (Goode 2007). Commenting on the controversy caused by Goode's comments, conservative radio host and columnist Dennis Prager stressed that the "Bible was the only relevant religious text in the United States" and having Muslims in Congress "would undermine American civilization."[5] Furthermore, there is increasing handwringing over the increasing number of Americans who are not identifying as Christian or not identifying with religion at all. Our results indicate that disciples of American religious exceptionalism appear to be the most concerned about these issues. When the then presidential candidate Trump promised an adoring crowd at Liberty University in 2016 that he was going to "protect Christianity," he was speaking to the disciples and letting them know they had a champion.[6]

The analysis of attitudes toward specific religious groups further demonstrates the strong bias that adherents of American religious exceptionalism have toward Christians. When asked to score Evangelicals, Catholics, and Muslims on a feeling thermometer, with 0 representing very cold feelings toward that group and 100 representing very warm feelings, we find overall Americans have the warmest feelings toward Catholics, followed by evangelicals, and Muslims. Our analysis demonstrates that the expected relationships as adherence to religious exceptionalism is associated with higher scores for Catholics and evangelicals, but lower scores for Muslims. The disciples feel 4 points warmer toward Catholics and 6 points warmer toward evangelicals, while feeling 11 points cooler toward Muslims. The cool reaction to Muslims is expected, as American Muslims represent a group that has been much maligned for much of American history with anti-Muslim bigotry only intensifying over the past two decades (Shortle and Gaddie 2015; Dana, et al. 2019; Lajevardi 2020). However, the warmer feelings toward Catholics represents that they have become an accepted group and have moved from the outsider status to being part of prototypical America.

Additional evidence regarding religious attitudes demonstrates distinct patterns by which people assign negative traits to religious groups. The respondents were asked the extent to which the adjectives "violent" and "lazy" described Christians and Muslims. From these responses we subtracted the Muslim score from Christian score to create a measure representing religious ethnocentrism. Those who score high on the measure are more likely to attribute these negative traits to Muslims than Christians and those who score low are more likely to associate them with Christians than Muslims. We find a progressive increase in Christian ethnocentrism as a laity scores significantly higher than a dissident and a disciple scores significantly higher than a laity.

Beyond holding animus toward Muslims, we are also concerned with how these religion-based animosity manifest in the policy arena. After the events of September 11, American Muslims faced greater scrutiny and attempts to control their behavior. They became the victims of an increasing number of hate crimes from private individuals, and there were calls for government action to control the group. Law enforcement increased surveillance of mosques and several states and localities sought to curb the freedoms enjoyed by Muslim residents. In 2010, a national controversy arose over the building of a Muslim community center two blocks away from the World Trade Center site. Conservative bloggers pejoratively referred to it as the "Ground Zero mosque" and brought in national politicians to help them rally national opposition (Boorstein 2010). In the face of the strong opposition, the developer halted the plan and eventually turned it into luxury condominiums (Kaysen 2017). Analyses of public opinion polling found 52 percent of Americans opposed the building of the cultural center. Figure 3.10 demonstrates overall opposition to the Muslim cultural center as even a dissident has a 54 percent chance of disapproving its construction. However, we see that even with this fairly high baseline of opposition, a laity and a disciple express significantly higher probabilities of opposing the mosque's construction. A laity has a 66 percent chance of opposing it, while a disciple has a 74 percent chance.

In addition to public pressure to prevent the construction of mosques, states and localities have attempted to curtail what conservative activists threaten is the "Islamification" of America. In 2010, the citizens of Oklahoma voted to add an amendment to their state constitution which banned the use of Sharia law in legal cases. The amendment was struck down by a federal judge. Meanwhile, other states and localities continue to attempt to enact policies to prevent the building of mosques. We examined support for allowing localities to control the building of mosques using two state polls in Oklahoma and Kentucky, respectively. Both polls find a third of the respondents agree with giving such powers to localities. Our analysis of the relationship between religious exceptionalism and support for local control over mosque construction finds that the support for these policies is driven by the disciples of religious exceptionalism. In the Oklahoma poll, we find a 19-point gap between the dissidents and disciples. In the Kentucky poll, the gap is 13 points.

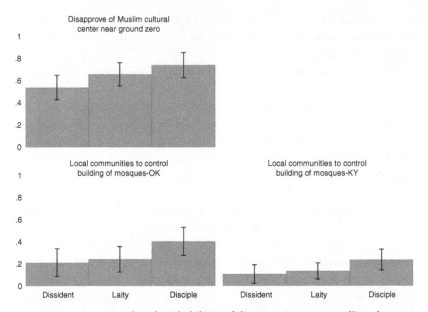

FIGURE 3.10 Predicted probabilities of disapproving or controlling the construction of Muslim cultural centers and mosques given adherence to American religious exceptionalism

Note: Predicted values were generated using coefficient estimates from logit regression models that control for biblical literalism, religious tradition, religious behaviors, personal demographics, and political ideology. Capped lines mark the estimated 95 percent confidence intervals.

The final dimension of our analyses for this chapter examines an aspect of American citizenship that has been underexamined in recent years, gender. The rise of the #MeToo movement and the unsuccessful campaign for president run by Hillary Clinton in 2016 have sparked increasing discussion about the role of gender in shaping American citizenship. Throughout America's history, the full citizenship status of American women has been questioned. Examples of the more problematic features of Americanness from a gendered lens include the fact that women were not guaranteed the right to vote until 1920; the continued failure to enact an Equal Rights Amendment; persistence of a pay gap between men and women; and increased publicity to the epidemic of sexual assault and harassment that has persecuted women across American society. As argued earlier, the prototypical American has historically been White, Christian, and male. The results thus far have established that the disciples of American religious exceptionalism favor a nation where Whites and

Christians – in fact, White Christians – are in charge. To ask the obvious question, do they also favor a world where men are in charge? Given that adherence to religious exceptionalism is associated with traditionalism and strict hierarchies, we expect to find the disciples are more supportive of a gender hierarchy. To test this, we examine attitudes regarding the validity of women's claims of mistreatment along with a scale that measures the perception White men are threatened in current society. Figure 3.11 demonstrates there is a considerable gap between the dissidents and disciples as the disciples are more likely to discount the validity of women's complaints.

A disciple is significantly more likely to agree that women complain when losing in a fair competition that both a dissident and a laity. Regarding sexual assault claims, both a laity and a disciple are significantly more likely to discredit accusations than a dissident. Finally, we examine the perceived threat to White men using in current society using a scale ($\alpha = .90$) of attitudes related to beliefs about improper treatment of men, an increasing feminine society, and perceptions that Whites are

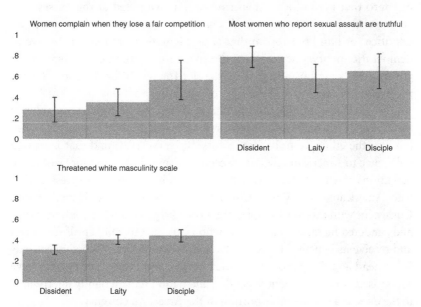

FIGURE 3.11 Predicted probabilities and values of attitudes related to the legitimacy of women's complaints and the belief White masculinity is under attack given adherence to American religious exceptionalism
Note: Predicted values were generated using coefficient estimates from logit and OLS regression models that control for biblical literalism, religious tradition, religious behaviors, personal demographics, and political ideology. Capped lines mark the estimated 95 percent confidence intervals.

paying an undue price for diversity. The mean score on the measure is 0.46 and a closer examination of its relationship with religious exceptionalism finds that a laity and a disciple are more likely to view White men as being under greater threat than a dissident. Consistent with Du Mez's (2020) argument about the nature of American religious nationalism, we see that American religious exceptionalism is associated with support for racial, religious, and gender hierarchies.

3.3 CONCLUSION

Americans are very proud to be American. In this chapter, we show that this is in no small part due to the particular understanding of their country as exceptional and divinely ordained to play a special leading role in the world. Those who ascribe to the American religious exceptionalism worldview are especially likely to say that they are proud to be American, though this is also true for Americans who do not necessarily buy into that mythology. Americans are, as we noted at the outset, just very proud of their nation. But disciples are also more likely to adopt an uncritical or blind patriotism that is problematic from the perspective of democratic theory since it limits the space for legitimate criticism of the government's actions and makes it easier for would-be despots to wrap themselves in religion and the flag to justify their actions.

The other signal finding in this chapter is that while Americans embrace the idea of a civic nation, distinct from the ethnic nations of Europe, they also fall into the ethnic trap. In fact, across our surveys we find that increased adherence to American religious exceptionalism is linked to more restrictive definitions of what it means to be American with respondents expressing that true Americans are White, Christian, and born in the United States. Consistent with this, the disciples are more likely to enforce racial, religious, and gendered hierarchies that limit who is justified to call herself American and receive its benefits. These results bolster arguments of scholars, such as Whitehead and Perry (2020), Du Mez (2020), and Butler (2021), who have showcased how race, religion, gender, and nation remain tightly intertwined in the eyes of a considerable portion of the American citizenry.

Such beliefs contribute to a hostility to newcomers, a fact we hasten to stress that precedes the heightened levels of xenophobia and racism in the Trump anti-immigrant platform. President Trump might have doubled down on the worst instincts of his fellow Americans, but he did not invent or imagine the fear and paranoia with which White, Christian America views immigration. Understanding why this is, is the purpose of Chapter 4.

4

What Do We Owe Strangers?

You shall also love the stranger, for you were strangers in the land of Egypt.
Deuteronomy 10:19

American immigration policy responds to ideological concerns and economic stress, and has little to do with factual immigration trends and patterns (Massey 1999). Due to the nature of American territorial expansion and the genocide of native peoples, Americans have assumed they can control who could become a citizen and who could inhabit the nation. This is in contrast to their European counterparts whose territorial expansion required the incorporation of large populations residing in the lands newly acquired (Zolberg 2006). As a result, from its inception, immigration has presented America's cities and towns with a cultural challenge over how to define their attachment to their nation and region. One grievance to the King in the Declaration of Independence was that the colonists were unable to attract desirable inhabitants and keep out the undesirables (Zolberg 2006). The new nation sought to increase its labor force quickly and cheaply, but from the beginning there was a shared understanding of what types of people were suitable to consider as fellow citizens and who did not make that cut.

State governments were responsible for establishing immigration policy in the early years of the nation. They pursued a distinctly Protestant agenda. In the 1800s, smaller towns and cities made notable recruitment efforts to court the (perceived) culturally assimilable members of majority-Protestant nations. The most obvious example is the state-led recruitment campaign of Swedish and German workers in the late nineteenth century, which led one-sixth of the population of Sweden to migrate to the American Midwest for railroad work (Judd and Swanstrom 2012, p. 23). Elite mistrust of urban immigrant voting blocs – who were predominantly Catholic – led several states to limit the number of representatives who could serve cities in the state legislature (Judd and Swanstrom 2012, p. 42). In the post-Civil War era, states such as California, New York, and Louisiana sought to control the flow of "undesirable immigrants" who sailed through their ports. California's procedures entailed inspecting immigrants' moral character; for this privilege, immigrant passengers were charged a price of 75 cents.

After a series of court cases gave rise to pressure from both domestic and international interests, the Supreme Court placed immigration control under the purview of the federal government in 1875 (Zolberg 2006). The federal government redoubled earlier state efforts to curate an image of the ideal American citizen – religious elements featured heavily in this process. A majority of the first federal restrictions on immigration were based on "moral" or religious grounds. For example, in addition to barring immigrants identified as poor, diseased, politically dangerous, and Chinese laborers, immigrants who had been charged with crimes of moral turpitude, sex work, and polygamy were disqualified from entering the country. It is significant that most of these laws reflected a religious narrative about who should be allowed to immigrate. The anti-Chinese stipulation was partially responding to White labor groups' political maneuvering in California, but moreover stemmed from popular stereotypes of the time, which viewed Chinese immigrants as the cultural antithesis of the American prototype (Chang 2003; Kil 2012). Chinese immigrants were not only of a different race, but did not subscribe to Western religious teachings, and like other immigrant groups they spoke little to no English. Stereotypes about Asian immorality were a large part of this narrative, which pointed to incidents of sex trafficking to cause alarm and persuade differently minded groups to support regulations limiting Asian immigration (Bald 2013; Kibria, Bowman and O'Leary 2014).

Cultural narratives of the ideal citizen were paramount to the nation's rich history of religiously inspired immigration policies (Tichenor 2002). However, non-Christian religious groups have been especially vulnerable targets of restrictive policies such as entry quotas and cruel expulsion procedures. For example, the bracingly honestly named Chinese Exclusion Act of 1882 prohibited all Chinese immigration to America – this law was not reversed until sixty years later in 1943 (Kil 2012). Its restrictiveness is mirrored by the Trump-era executive order that sought to ban immigration from seven majority-Muslim countries. Another example is the Immigration Act of 1917, which barred immigration from "the Asiatic Zone," targeting the admission of Hindu and East Indians. No one has been spared such disdain, not even refugees fleeing violence. In 2015, under President Obama, regional efforts to resettle Syrian refugees began in several states, but these were halted in 2017 due to Trump's Muslim ban. During World War II, the federal government denied Jewish refugees' admission and even heightened visa requirements for Jews hoping to flee the Shoah to America (Tichenor 2002). Today Trump and other right-wing politicians invoke this age-old playbook to oppose the resettlement of Afghan refugees fleeing their country after the Taliban defeated the United States in the twenty-year war that began after September 11, 2001.

Historically, the link between religion and immigration policy has been defined by national narratives placing religious values and identities at the forefront of who can be admitted. However, religious identity alone has not protected immigrants from strict immigration control measures. This is because immigrant newcomers' religious identities are only part of a broader national narrative positing that moral and religious values – defined by White Christian Protestantism – make some groups assimilable to America's culture, whereas others are deemed fundamentally incompatible with what it means to be American.

4.1 ATTITUDES TOWARD IMMIGRANTS

In this chapter, we address American immigration opinion. America's various panics about immigration are rooted in the dim view of immigrants held by its majority population. Some scholars attribute negative attitudes toward immigrants to economic competition, while others point to the perceived cultural threat posed by immigrant newcomers. September 11, 2001, allowed anti-immigration activists to securitize the immigration debate. President Trump and his anti-immigration tsar Stephen Miller relied on tapping into each of these dimensions, as his campaign and presidency pushed stringent immigration restrictions to mobilize his base of White Christian voters. Trump launched his campaign by focusing on the security dimension by claiming that rapists and murderers – who he shamelessly equated to Mexicans at large – were freely entering the country in droves. As president, he continued to argue the nation was admitting the wrong type of immigrants by lamenting the entrance of people from "shithole countries" (Barbash 2019). Furthermore, by controlling immigration, he promised, he would reinvigorate the American economy, and save factory jobs that were either moving abroad or going to immigrants. Trump's and Americans' increasing uneasiness about immigration is not an isolated concern. Right-wing nationalism is gaining steam across Europe with neo-Nazi movements on the rise and majority populations indulging in fearmongering over the alleged economic, cultural, and security threat posed by immigrants (Givens 2005; Malhotra, Margalit and Mo 2013; Givens, Navarre and Mohanty 2020). A major factor in the success of the Leave campaign in the United Kingdom was the ability of anti-immigrant forces such as the United Kingdom Independence Party (UKIP) to stoke xenophobia and bigotry against outsiders (Gest 2016). In India, a toxic mix of religious nationalism and xenophobia has led to a Citizenship Amendment Act and a call for a National Register of Citizens (Barbora 2019; Nagarwal 2021).

Are anti-immigrant attitudes driven by economic self-interest or cultural superiority? The economic self-interest explanation suggests that labor market competition shapes unwelcoming attitudes toward immigrants, as the result of individual economic vulnerability. Additionally, immigrants are portrayed as leeches on the social safety net who overwhelm public services (Marrow 2011). Such beliefs were the impetus behind California's 1994 Proposition 187, which banned undocumented immigrants from accessing nonemergency public healthcare and public education. Many scholars focused on the economic ramifications of immigration initially suggested a large role of economic influences on American immigration attitudes (Frey 1995; Camarota 1997; Huber and Espenshade 1997; Borjas 1999). The result was that economic or material factors were thought to be major forces in determining hostile immigration attitudes (Olzak 1992). For instance, Neil Malhotra, Yotam Margalit, and Hyunjung Mo find that those living in high-technology countries express higher levels of opposition to H-1B visas, because the recipients of such visas, which are intended to allow American companies to hire high-skilled foreign workers, pose a direct labor market threat to their interests (2013).

Cultural theories argue that understanding immigration opinion requires an understanding of group identity, which in turn must be informed by theories of social identity and self-categorization (Tajfel 1981; Fiske 2011). Cultural models' theorizing has further been complemented by in-depth historical accounts of the crucial role of group politics in federal and state immigration policy and procedural norm formation

(Tichenor 2002; Ngai 2014). Among the most cited social identity-based accounts of immigration opposition, one set posits racial identity effects, while another posits national identity effects. Studies on racial identity effects demonstrate that anti-Mexican and anti-Latinx attitudes explain immigration opposition (Lee, Ottati and Hussain 2001; Lee and Ottati 2002; Alba, Rumbaut and Marotz 2005; Brader, Valentino and Suhay 2008; Abrajano and Hajnal 2015), while others have concluded a more generalized array of group-based prejudices and xenophobia are at play (Pérez 2008; Kinder and Kam 2009; Brader, et al. 2010). This literature is bound by the premise that Americans who oppose immigration hold a specific racial image that guides their decision-making. Often these cultural threat perceptions have been tied to economic threats in the political rhetoric, such as right-wing pundit Lou Dobbs's data-free histrionics that undocumented immigration is devastating the American middle class (2006). In doing so, a tight web of cultural and economic justifications for opposing immigrants has galvanized the public to sense immigrants as a threat (Calavita 2014). These cultural concerns were at the heart of Samuel Huntington's angst about the influx of immigrants whom he perceived as not assimilating and not being committed to the nation (2004). Even though research refutes his thesis (de la Garza, Falcon and Garcia 1996; Citrin, et al. 2007), Huntington's concerns about a growing unassimilated and uncommitted group of immigrants leading to the nation's ruin resonate with a large number of Americans (Citrin, Reingold and Green 1990; Citrin, et al. 1997; Sniderman, Hagendoorn and Prior 2004; McDaniel, Nooruddin and Shortle 2011).

Given that the adherents of American religious exceptionalism hold a strong attachment to the idea of a nation and possess a distinct understanding of the nation's culture, we expect them to fear the various threats that outsiders pose. The results in Figure 4.1 demonstrate that disciples of American religious exceptionalism express greater concerns about the economic and cultural threats posed by immigrants.

Beginning with concerns about how immigrants threaten economic self-interests, such as taking "wanted" jobs and using up public services, we find a laity scores higher than a dissident and a disciple scores significantly higher than both of them. When we probe perceptions of cultural threat, such as the notion immigrants refuse to adapt to and pose a threat to traditional values, we find a similar pattern as a laity scores higher than a dissident and a disciple scores higher than both. To be fair, our data make clear that Huntington's xenophobia is shared by most Americans, be they dissidents, laity, and disciples, and, further, a comparison of the two models

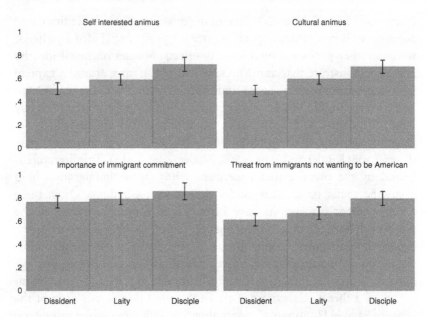

FIGURE 4.1 Predicted values and probabilities of attitudes toward immigrants
*Note: Predicted probabilities and values were generated using coefficient estimates
from logit and OLS regression models that control for biblical literalism, religious
tradition, religious importance, worship attendance, personal demographics, and
political ideology. Capped lines mark the estimated 95 percent confidence
intervals.*

demonstrates that both self-interest and cultural threat provoke equal
concern. In our data, Americans place heavy stress on immigrant commitment, which we measure via an index (α = .88) capturing the importance
respondents place on immigrants' commitment to the nation and their
desire to be American. Across our American religious exceptionalism
scale, our survey respondents place great stress on the need for immigrants
to be loyal; however, disciples are especially insistent on such loyalty tests.

In a different test, we flip the script and ask respondents how worrying
they find hypothetical immigrants who do not profess a loyalty to the
nation or do not express a desire to become American. We combine
responses into what we call a *nonloyal-immigrant threat* scale (α = .83).
Unsurprisingly, disciples are most concerned about such immigrants, and
dissidents are least threatened by them.

Our last analysis of attitudes toward immigrants examines perceptions
of status. In particular, we are interested in the extent to which groups

from specific global regions are perceived as being here legally versus illegally. Much of the anxiety over immigration has been about undocumented immigration and the fear people who should not be in the United States are illegally making their way into the nation and destroying it from within (Berg 2009; Ngai 2014). This was a major concern of candidate Trump, and President Trump used all available tactics to target undocumented immigrants while fueling right-wing paranoia through tweets and speeches warning about the threat they pose to the nation.

In our surveys, a plurality of Americans (36.5 percent) associate Europeans with legal immigration, while just a quarter of associated people from Latin America with the same. The analysis of the relationship between adherence to the tenets of American religious exceptionalism and the perceived legal status of these groups demonstrates that Europeans are strongly associated with legal immigration by dissidents, laity, and disciples (see Figure 4.2). This does not surprise us, given that Europeans, specifically northern and western Europeans, have historically been viewed as the ideal immigrants (Brader, Valentino and Suhay 2008; Abrajano and Hajnal 2015). Interestingly, we find that the disciples are significantly more likely to associate people from Latin America with legal immigration than are dissidents; however, the disciples are significantly less likely to associate those from Asia with legal immigration compared to the dissidents. We lack the data to test a plausible mechanism for this divergence, but our working hypothesis would be that disciples are more likely to worry that Asian immigrants are not Christian and that they represent cultures that threaten American norms, which would be consistent with America's long and continued history of anti-Asian bigotry (Chang 2003; Kil 2012; Ngai 2014). And, just as depressingly, we should emphasize that fully two-thirds of those surveyed associate people from Latin America with illegal immigration. In fact, the probability any respondent in our survey thinks this way is so high that there are no statistically significant differences based on adherence to American religious exceptionalism.

4.2 FLOW OF IMMIGRATION

We turn in this section from perceptions of immigrants to analyzing preferences for different immigration policies. Overall, our data show that disciples are more likely to want to limit the amount of immigration, provide fewer services to immigrants, and offer harsher punishments. There is little support for increasing the rate of immigration across the

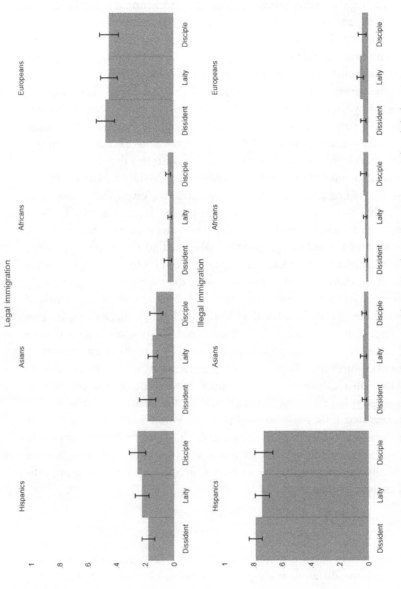

FIGURE 4.2 Predicted probabilities of perceived immigration status by global region

Note: Predicted probabilities were generated using coefficient estimates from logit regression models that control for biblical literalism, religious tradition, religious importance, worship attendance, personal demographics, and political ideology. Capped lines mark the estimated 95 percent confidence intervals.

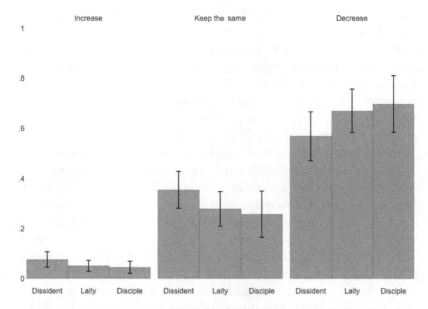

FIGURE 4.3 Predicted probabilities of attitudes toward the rate of immigration
Note: Predicted probabilities were generated using coefficient estimates from logit regression models that control for biblical literalism, religious tradition, religious importance, worship attendance, personal demographics, and political ideology. Capped lines mark the estimated 95 percent confidence intervals.

board (see Figure 4.3). In a very real sense, while liberal activists might wish to paint President Trump and his advisors Steve Bannon and Stephen Miller as extremists, the sad truth is the draconian anti-immigration policies pursued across US presidential administrations, and the relentless demonizing of undocumented immigrants, has exhausted any support for increased immigration. America, often a reluctant host, is now actively closing its doors.[1]

In our survey, dissidents appear to be the most open to immigration as they are significantly more likely to state that immigration should increase or be kept the same compared to a laity or disciple. However, we still find strong support for decreasing immigration even among the dissidents. A dissident has a 57 percent chance of stating the nation needs to decrease its rate of immigration, while the odds for a laity and a disciple are 67 percent and 70 percent, respectively.

We do find evidence for the hypothesis anti-immigration activists have succeeded by focusing on undocumented immigration in their talking points. When asked specifically about reducing both legal and illegal immigration, we find the disciples are highly supportive of reducing both forms of immigration. The dissidents express little support for reducing legal immigration, while expressing a high level of support for decreasing illegal immigration. Of course, given our earlier reported finding that Americans associate Latin American-origin residents in general with undocumented immigration, this distinction means little in practice. In effect, criticizing illegal immigration has become a socially acceptable way to express one's support for lower immigration overall.

America's desire to reduce immigration is reflected in its attitudes about what types of services immigrants should be able to access. As Hiroshi Motomura explains, Americans' view that legal resident non-citizens are less deserving is part of another widely held myth of "citizenship by contract" where legal immigrants are expected to "read the fine print" and happily adhere to limits on their rights, even if that entails seemingly illiberal actions, such as deportation for minor legal offenses (2006, 2014). According to this myth, immigrants should accept fewer legal protections in order to prove their worthiness, loyalty, and abiding nature to their host country.[2] In other words, while they are perceived as more deserving than unauthorized immigrants, many Americans view legal immigrants as less deserving than current citizens.

The overall preference for citizens notwithstanding, documented immigrants do enjoy a markedly preferred status relative to undocumented immigrants. Americans are more supportive of providing services, such as public medical services (68.4 percent) and workmen's compensation (74.7 percent) for documented immigrants, compared to the undocumented (11.9 percent and 13.6 percent, respectively). Further, they are more forgiving of transgressions by documented immigrants. We find that fewer than a quarter of Americans express support for detaining and deporting documented immigrants convicted of a crime, while more than three-fourths of Americans support this action for the undocumented. The analyses summarized in Figure 4.4 demonstrates little differentiation between the groupings as a dissident, laity, and a disciple seem to agree regarding reduced access to services and protections for the undocumented. However, when it comes to documented immigrants, we find that a dissident is more open to giving them services and protections, while a laity and a disciple are less supportive. The odds of a dissident supporting medical access to a legal immigration are 73 percent, while being 66 percent and 64 percent for a laity and a disciple, respectively. We see the same pattern regarding workmen's compensation; a dissident has

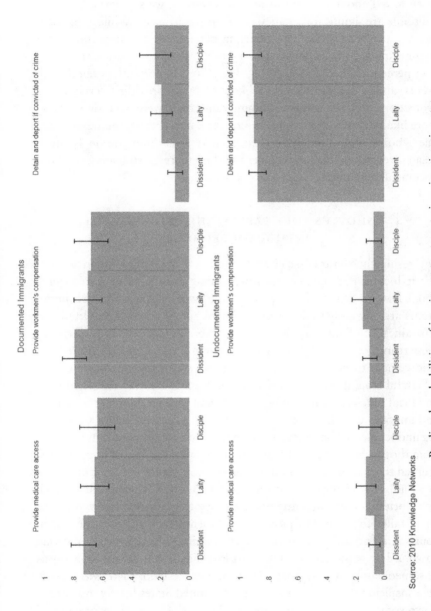

FIGURE 4.4 Predicted probabilities of immigrant treatment given immigration status

Source: 2010 Knowledge Networks

Note: Predicted probabilities were generated using coefficient estimates from logit regression models that control for biblical literalism, religious tradition, religious importance, worship attendance, personal demographics, and political ideology. Capped lines mark the estimated 95 percent confidence intervals.

a 79 percent chance of preferring this protection, while a laity and a disciple have a 70 percent and 68 percent chance, respectively. Finally, when asked about detainment and deportation, we see that a laity and a disciple are significantly harsher in their punishment. While a dissident has a 9 percent chance of supporting detainment and deportation for committing a crime, a laity has a 19 percent chance and a disciple has a 23 percent chance of supporting this action. Importantly, even though a laity and a disciple were less likely to favor providing services and protections to a documented immigrant, they were still significantly more likely to offer these opportunities to a documented immigrant than one who is undocumented. Their anxiety over immigration is much greater regarding the undocumented, but there is still anxiety about documented immigrants.

4.3 SHOW US YOUR PAPERS: THE UNDOCUMENTED IMMIGRANT PROBLEM

Our results thus far reveal a clear distinction between how Americans feel about documented and undocumented immigrants. The fear and concerns about how to deal with the perceived growth in undocumented immigrants are great, especially in the southern border states (Lee, Ottati and Hussain 2001; Dunaway, Branton and Abrajano 2010). In response to these rising concerns, Arizona passed State Bill 1070, which required law enforcement to determine the immigration status of individuals during a "lawful stop, detention, or arrest." The 2010 law also restricted state and local officials from limiting enforcement of federal immigration laws and imposed punishments on those protecting, employing, or transporting undocumented immigrants. The bill was met with significant backlash from those who recognized it as state-mandated racial profiling. Protests erupted throughout the nation and several companies and civic organizations announced boycotts of the state of Arizona. Undeterred by such opprobrium, other states attempted to copy this law (Wallace 2014), but either failed to get the law passed or had them struck down by the federal courts. In 2012, the Supreme Court unanimously supported allowing Arizona law enforcement officers to investigate the immigration status of someone who was stopped, detained, or arrested if there was reasonable suspicion the person was not in the United States legally, but struck down some of the other provisions of SB 1070. Our analysis of national attitudes toward this law found that, in 2010, close to three-fourths of Americans agreed with this policy.

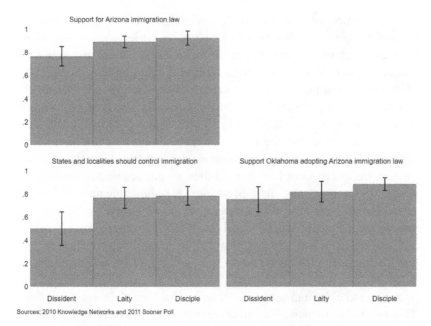

Sources: 2010 Knowledge Networks and 2011 Sooner Poll

FIGURE 4.5 Predicted probabilities of support for Arizona immigration law and giving states greater power in creating immigration laws
Note: Predicted probabilities were generated using coefficient estimates from logit regression models that control for biblical literalism, religious tradition, religious importance, worship attendance, personal demographics, and political ideology. Capped lines mark the estimated 95 percent confidence intervals.

Figure 4.5 shows high support for the law among all three groupings, but also that a laity and a disciple score significantly higher than a dissident. To see how this plays out at the state level, we use the 2011 Oklahoma Sooner Poll, where we find two-thirds of respondents believe states should be given more power to create immigration laws. Further, more than three-fourths of respondents believe the state should adopt an immigration law similar to Arizona's. Even with this high level of support among Oklahoma residents, we still find significant differences. For instance, the modal Oklahoma dissident is on the fence about giving states autonomy to create their own immigration enforcement laws. A dissident has a 50 percent chance of supporting giving states this power, whereas the odds for a laity and a disciple are 77 percent and 78 percent, respectively. However, there is strong support for Oklahoma adopting a similar law to Arizona's SB 1070 among all three categories, with disciples leading the charge.

The question of how to handle undocumented immigrants extends beyond policies requiring proof of citizenship or legal residence. There have been intense debates about undocumented immigrants and their children. Given that part of the situation is caused by the consequences of American immigration and foreign policy, such as eliminating the Bracero Program, which allowed for migratory labor, or contributing to intensifying the violent conflicts in Central America (Massey and Pren 2012), some argue that the undocumented should be allowed either to become citizens or to gain permanent residency status. Complicating this further, the question of how the children of undocumented immigrants should be treated has also presented a policy dilemma. Congress attempted to address this concern in 1986 when it passed the Immigration Reform and Control Act, which provided farm workers and longtime residents with legal status. In 2001, Senators Dick Durbin and Orrin Hatch introduced the Development, Relief, and Education for Alien Minors Act (DREAM Act) as a way to provide protections to undocumented immigrants who entered the United States as minors. This bill failed to pass, but other versions of it have been introduced since then. President George W. Bush attempted to address this issue with the Secure Border, Economic Opportunity and Immigration Reform Act of 2007. The bill included measures to increase border security, a guest worker program, and a process by which undocumented immigrants could gain legal status and eventually citizenship. The act proposed undocumented immigrants pay a penalty, learn English, pass a background check, pay taxes and have several years of employment in order to gain legal residency status. If they were able to meet these criteria, they would be eligible to apply for citizenship, but they would be put at the "back of the line" (Krutchik 2007). The bill that was introduced in the Senate received support from several Democrats, but eventually died as senators from both sides of the aisle assailed it. Seeing the inability to get immigration reform through Congress, President Obama issued an executive order establishing a policy of Deferred Action for Childhood Arrivals (DACA), which provided a renewable two-year reprieve from deportation and allowed recipients to obtain work authorization. Using proposals from the DREAM Act, DACA was intended to provide a solution to the dilemmas associated with undocumented immigrants who had lived in America for most of their lives. As soon as the policy was announced, it was met with harsh criticism and accused of providing amnesty for law breakers. Furthermore, several politicians and pundits cited DACA as the reason for a sharp increase in the number of unaccompanied minors attempting to cross the US border. Research quickly made clear that there is no evidence for such an association (Amuedo-Dorantes and Puttitanun 2016), but the political damage had been done. Upon entering the White House, President Trump promised to rescind DACA and did so in September of 2017. On June 18, 2020, a 5–4 majority of the US Supreme Court decided that Trump's reasoning was arbitrary and capricious and allowed DACA to remain in place. But until Congress finds enough political courage to legislate this issue, hundreds of thousands of young people will remain vulnerable to deportation to countries they never knew.

Figure 4.6 uses data from the 2014 Kentucky Poll to demonstrate how a person in each of our categories feels about resolving the undocumented immigrant problem. As expected, a disciple is least supportive of providing a pathway for citizenship for undocumented immigrants. However, between the three options this is the most likely to be chosen by a disciple. A disciple has a 42 percent chance of supporting the right of

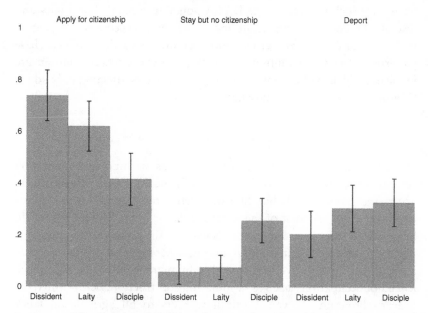

FIGURE 4.6 Predicted probabilities of support for citizenship for undocumented immigrants and their children
Note: Predicted probabilities were generated using coefficient estimates from logit regression models that control for biblical literalism, religious tradition, religious importance, worship attendance, personal demographics, and political ideology. Capped lines mark the estimated 95 percent confidence intervals.

undocumented immigrants to apply for citizenship, while having a 25 percent chance of allowing them to stay as permanent residents, and a 33 percent chance of choosing deportation. This pattern of choosing a path to citizenship over the other options is the same for a dissident and a laity. Furthermore, they are more likely to choose deportation over permanent residence. At least in these Kentucky data, the main policy options of interest are providing a pathway to citizenship or outright deportation, which reflects the polarized debate on this issue. Of course, Kentucky is not America, and so caution should be applied generalizing from these data beyond the Bluegrass state.

Hardline views are also evident when we assess support for providing a pathway to citizenship or permanent residency status for those who entered the United States as children, but these views evolve over time. We find no significant difference between the dissidents and disciples in the 2011 Sooner Poll or the 2012 Religious Worldviews Survey, but data from the 2018 Cooperative Congressional Election Study (CCES) demonstrates a increasing support for DACA over the decade. By 2018, a dissident is virtually a lock to support the DACA policy ($p = 0.93$). For a laity and disciple the odds are 87 percent and 86 percent, respectively, indicating that even disciples have grown more favorable to this policy. These patterns reflect the evolution of policy preferences where children are involved, which evoke greater leniency than policies affecting only adults (Merolla, Ramakrishnan and Haynes 2013).

4.4 IMMIGRANTS AND THE WORKFORCE

One of the underlying concerns of the various attempts at immigration reform is the importance of immigrants in the American workforce. In 2017, the Bureau of Labor Statistics estimated foreign-born workers constituted 16.9 percent of the American labor force. The nation would be unable to meet its economic needs without the presence of immigrants who fill a variety of occupations requiring either a certain skill level or that are undesirable to native-born workers. Immigrants have taken on physical labor occupations, such as farming and construction. Before 1965, the Bracero Program allowed Mexican workers to fill agricultural labor shortages on a temporary basis. However, the program was eliminated as reports of abuses, such as extremely low wages, unacceptable working conditions, and corruption in allocating work opportunities, became public (Massey, Durand and Malone 2002). The elimination of the program did not stop farmers from recruiting Mexican workers of course. As

Douglas Massey and Karen Pren note, it "shifted from a de jure guest-worker program" to a "de facto program" as farmers hired undocumented workers (2012). The Bracero program's weaknesses and eventual elimination are seen as a key factor in the rise of the number of undocumented immigrants (Massey, Durand and Malone 2002; Massey and Pren 2012). At the other end of the skill continuum, there are also concerns about labor shortages associated with high-skilled positions, such as technology-intensive occupations. The H-1B visa was established for employers to recruit workers with high skills in specialized occupations (Malhotra, Margalit and Mo 2013). In 2017, more than two-thirds of H-1B visa petitions approved were for computer-related occupations, indicating the high demand in this area (USCIS 2018). Additionally, the public views low-skilled workers as more of a threat than high-skilled workers (Brader, Valentino and Suhay 2008; Hainmueller and Hiscox 2010), which may explain why the Trump administration sought to make the education criteria required for immigration more restrictive (Hauslohner 2019).

Our analysis of employment policy attitudes begins with the criteria respondents would propose for awarding an immigrant a temporary work visa. A plurality (44 percent) of respondents would award a visa to someone with a special skill, while 43 percent of respondents favor offering visas to offset labor shortages. Four percent would approve a visa for someone with an extraordinary ability, and about 10 percent of the respondents support providing no employment-based visas at all. We find no evidence that these attitudes are correlated with adherence to American religious exceptionalism except regarding how best to address labor shortages. A disciple (36 percent) is significantly less likely to support a visa for this situation than a dissident (44 percent).[3] In addition to asking about awarding visas, we used data from our 2010 Knowledge Networks Survey to examine support for the guest worker program. Here we find that about a third of Americans favor a formal guest worker program. A dissident is more supportive of this program, but the overall levels of support are fairly low. A dissident has a 33 percent chance of supporting, while a laity has a 20 percent and a disciple a 26 percent chance. Finally, when asked about whose responsibility it is to ensure that only documented workers are hired, we find that the respondents put the onus on the employer. Using the data from the 2011 Sooner Poll, we find overwhelming support for a policy requiring employers to verify the immigration status of would-be workers with 81 percent of respondents in favor. Even with this overall high level of support we find a disciple has a greater probability of favoring this policy compared to a dissident or a laity. These results indicate that when it comes to employment, a dissident, laity, and a disciple are not fiercely divided, but that a disciple has more intense views about immigration issues related to employment.

4.5 RELIGIOUS PREFERENCES IN IMMIGRATION

One of the more controversial issues associated with immigration is religion. Even though the United States trumpets the separation of church and state and does not formally recognize a specific religion as the religion of the nation, the historical record makes clear that elites and the public regard the United States as a Protestant Christian nation. This implicit belief explains the numerous panics during its history the nation has suffered over fears that Catholics, Jews, and Muslims would invade the nation and undermine its Protestant purity (Brodkin 1998; Schrag 2010). Persistent efforts to control the building of mosques, along with state legislatures introducing legislation to protect themselves from Sharia law, demonstrate the current concerns over a perceived Muslim invasion. This is why President Obama generated such outrage when he described the United States as "one of the largest Muslim countries in the world" (Obama 2009a), and why conservative opponents thought labeling him a "secret Muslim" was a smear. Perhaps the cruelest instance of this paranoia has been the effort to refuse the resettlement of refugees fleeing the Syrian civil war because they are Muslim. President Trump stoked such bigotry by banning or limiting travel from certain Muslim-majority nations. Referred to as the "Muslim ban" by opponents and President Trump alike, it was one of many controversial – and successful – anti-immigration policies from his administration (Collingwood, Lajevardi and Oskooii 2018; Kanno-Youngs 2020).

A strong adherent of American religious exceptionalism is much more suspicious of allowing non-Christians into the nation and likely to wish to establish blockades to their entry (see Figure 4.7). In 2008, when presented with the idea of reducing non-Christian immigration, there was relatively low support. However, a disciple and a laity were significantly more likely to support this immigration plan than a dissident. In 2018, when confronted by an actual ban on immigration by citizens of certain Muslim-majority nations and resettlement of Syrian refugees, we see that even a dissident is wary of allowing Muslims into the nation. A dissident has a 40 percent chance of supporting President Trump's Muslim ban and

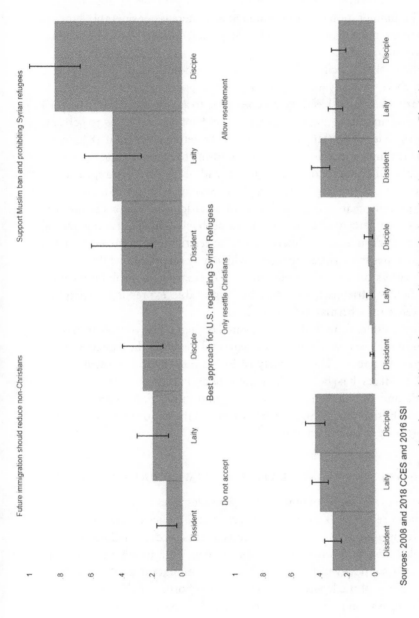

FIGURE 4.7 Predicted probabilities of support limiting the immigration of non-Christians

Note: *Predicted probabilities were generated using coefficient estimates from logit regression models that control for biblical literalism, religious tradition, religious importance, worship attendance, personal demographics, and political ideology. Capped lines mark the estimated 95 percent confidence intervals.*

Sources: 2008 and 2018 CCES and 2016 SSI

rejecting the agreement to resettle Syrian refugees. For a laity, the odds of supporting such policies increases to 45 percent, but for a disciple it is 84 percent. When confronted with the reality of being able to limit Muslim immigration into the United States, there is considerable support from those in the dissident and laity categories, and there is overwhelming support among disciples.

When asked specifically about how to respond to the Syrian refugee crisis, there is clear hesitancy among the respondents, but a dissident is least anxious about these arrivals compared to a laity or disciple. The odds of a dissident stating that the refugees should not be accepted is 30 percent, while the odds of agreeing with the original resettlement plan is 38 percent. For a laity and a disciple, the odds of choosing to renege on the agreement are higher than the odds of continuing with it. A laity has a 39 percent chance of supporting not accepting Syrian refugees compared to a 28 percent chance of agreeing with resettlement. For a disciple the odds are 43 percent and 26 percent, respectively. One interesting finding is that all groups are unlikely to prefer restricting resettlement in the United States to Christian refugees, which may reveal that while respondents express an implicit preference for decreasing or prohibiting non-Christian resettlement, they feel uncomfortable expressing an explicit preference for Christian refugees.

These results fit with the findings in Chapter 3 that demonstrated the biases of the disciples toward Christians and the belief the United States is a Christian nation. Their anxiety of losing their nation to seculars and non-Christians has been well documented (Parker and Barreto 2013; Shortle and Gaddie 2015; Jones 2016), and in reaction to these threats they establish limited views of who is a part of the nation and who gets the opportunity to join the nation.

4.6 TRUMP ADMINISTRATION AND IMMIGRATION POLICY

Our final examination of immigration attitudes assesses how adherence to American religious exceptionalism is related to policy decisions made by the Trump administration. The previous discussion demonstrated that the disciples were supportive of his "Muslim ban," but to what extent were they also supportive of some of his other immigrant policies, such as building a wall the length of the US–Mexico border or the controversial family separation policies which led to children being held in cages?

Figure 4.8 demonstrates the disciples are committed to the border wall. Our analysis of the 2018 CCES data finds that a disciple is almost three

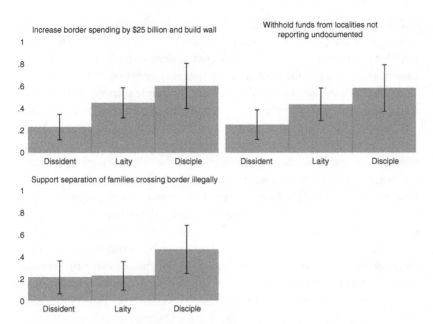

FIGURE 4.8 Predicted probabilities of support for President Trump's
immigration policies
*Note: Predicted probabilities were generated using coefficient estimates from logit
regression models that control for biblical literalism, religious tradition, religious
importance, worship attendance, personal demographics, and political ideology.
Capped lines mark the estimated 95 percent confidence intervals.*

times more likely to support the building of the border wall than
a dissident. Along with the border wall, President Trump's campaign
promised to implement a more active deportation policy. The Obama
administration, which deported more people than any prior administration, claimed its enforcement priority targeted those who posed a national
security threat, had serious criminal convictions, or were recent border
crossers. For the Trump administration, standing on the shoulders of the
Obama legacy, all undocumented persons were of equal concern, regardless of criminal history or length of residency (Ryo 2019). This policy led
to a series of high-profile raids by Immigration and Customs Enforcement
(ICE) and public backlash. In opposition to the Trump administration's
policy stance and fears of how the ICE raids may create greater harm for
immigration communities, a few local governments refused to cooperate
with ICE. In response, the Justice Department attempted to withhold
federal funds from these "sanctuary cities"; however, this threat was

overturned by a federal judge (Yee 2017). The judicial branch's ruling goes against the popular opinion of the disciples, and no doubt fuels their populist concerns of an out-of-touch elite undermining America. As in the case of the border wall, we find a disciple is supportive of punishing the "sanctuary cities" by withholding funds. A disciple is more than twice as likely to support this response to noncooperation compared to a dissident. The final and probably the most controversial immigration policy of the Trump administration has been the family separations at the border. In an attempt to increase the enforcement of the administration's "zero-tolerance" policy on undocumented immigration, the Department of Homeland Security (DHS) entertained the idea of family separations as early as March 2017, just two months after Trump was inaugurated in front of a small crowd of die-hard fans in thrall to his voicing of their White nationalist grievances. In the face of public outcry over the idea, DHS pretended to reverse course, but, out of the public eye, implemented the plan starting in October of 2017. When discovered, the family separation policy faced immediate and harsh backlash from pro-immigration and civil rights activists (Dickerson 2018). During the controversy over family separations, the then Attorney General Jeff Sessions defended the controversial policy by referring to Romans 13, which calls on Christians to follow the laws of the land. Despite his efforts at religious rationalization, the administration faced intense public pressure and eventually ended the practice in June 2018. A PRRI Poll found that 53 percent of Republicans expressed approval with family separation policies (Palmer and Igoe 2019). Our analysis of support for family separation confirms that increased adherence to American religious exceptionalism increases the probability that one supports this policy.

4.7 CONCLUSION

An enduring divide in immigration attitudes exists between disciples and dissidents. Disciples feel particularly threatened by immigrants in economic, cultural, and national-symbolic terms, whereas dissidents are less likely to share these concerns. In terms of public perceptions of documented immigrants' and undocumented immigrants' origins, the differences are less glaring, making clear the damage of enduring media narratives about immigrants and criminality (Farris and Silber Mohamed 2018). The disciple–dissident divide carries into their immigration-flow attitudes, with disciples supporting the reduction of all forms of immigration, including legal immigration. Coupled with our analysis of how respondents associate immigration with particular origin regions, we surmise this is because disciples are more likely to perceive legal immigrants as Latinx, which makes disciples less likely to grant moral authority to these perceived cultural outsiders. The disciples' strong restrictionist spirit is further evidenced in the disciples' extreme opposition to undocumented immigration, wariness of non-Christian immigrants, and ardent support for Trump's most aggressively anti-immigrant orders.

A striking finding across our analyses of immigration attitudes is the growing crystallization of attitude divergence between dissidents and disciples on every issue. It is not surprising Trump's involvement accelerated this divide. His calls for a border wall and promise to punish sanctuary cities allowed disciples a release valve to express freely their support for his vocal and extreme forms of immigration restrictionism. In supporting their favored politician's extremism, disciples of American religious exceptionalism draw on a pre-existing vision of deservingness to exclude perceived culturally undesirable groups. And, as Trump has been able to depend on the disciples' support, his views have grown increasingly extreme, as he is emboldened to go further than ever thought viable before – and still receive endless praise in return. While the policy of family separations at the border stoked liberal outrage in 2017, its politicization resulted in increasing support from Trump's base. Clearly, toddlers and children in cages is a fair price to pay to make America White, Christian, and great again.

5

Evangelizing American Religious Exceptionalism

And I will make of you a great nation, and I will bless you and make your name great, so that you will be a blessing. I will bless those who bless you, and him who dishonors you I will curse, and in you all the families of the earth shall be blessed.

Genesis 12:2–3

He says, "You are My war-club, My weapon of war; And with you I shatter nations, And with you I destroy kingdoms. "With you I shatter the horse and his rider, And with you I shatter the chariot and its rider.

Jeremiah 51: 20–21

I will magnify Myself, sanctify Myself, and make Myself known in the sight of many nations; and they will know that I am the LORD.

Ezekiel 38:23

Mine eyes have seen the glory of the coming of the Lord;
   He is trampling out the vintage where the grapes of wrath are stored;
   He hath loosed the fateful lightning of His terrible swift sword;
   His truth is marching on.

Julia Ward Howe, Battle Hymn of the Republic

The past two decades have thrusted Americans' attention to the outside world. The end of the Cold War and the collapse of the Soviet bloc confirmed, for many Americans, a self-image as defenders of freedom, democracy, and all things good in the world. The events of September 11, 2001, and subsequent military campaigns in Iraq and Afghanistan, however, forced many Americans to focus upon global issues and crises. The emergence of the Islamic State as a new source of global terror, an ugly civil war in Syria in which the United States faced another proxy war against a resurgent Russia, an increased probability of conflict with a nuclear North Korea, a counterproductive Iran policy, and military defeat in Afghanistan have brought American national security strategy under greater scrutiny. Beyond concerns about physical threats, increasing global economic competition and growth in Asian markets, specifically China, has allowed pro-isolationists to stoke economic angst in Americans only dimly aware of the fact that the United States has benefited immeasurably from free trade. Instead, daily reports about the outsourcing of American jobs along with concerns about the global value of the dollar have caused Americans to move from finding their economic place in their nation to finding it in the world as they grapple with the reality of competing in a global marketplace. Finally, as the self-appointed flag bearer of freedom and liberty for the world, the United States must decide how to respond to humanitarian crises as it seeks influence through relief efforts to countries afflicted by conflicts, environmental disasters, and disease.

Concerns about threats to the well-being of the nation conflict with a desire to play the role of a global hegemon, which American religious exceptionalism assumes is a God-given privilege. This chapter illuminates how Americans view their role globally and how these attitudes are influenced by American religious exceptionalism. By focusing on the history of American Grand Strategy and the role of religion in shaping it, we demonstrate how adherence to American religious exceptionalism influences the decision-making of political elites since the early days of the nation. We then describe the structure of American foreign policy attitudes and our expectations for the role of American religious exceptionalism in shaping mass public opinion about how American power should be deployed globally. Our survey data allow us to analyze the linkage between American religious exceptionalism, core values in foreign policy attitudes, and attitudes toward specific policies. We find that adherents to religious exceptionalism distinguish themselves in a unique normative view of America's role in the world.

5.1 RELIGIOUS EXCEPTIONALISM AND AMERICAN GRAND STRATEGY

Americans require a righteous cause to explain and justify their nation's actions abroad. Moralized narratives of the United States' foreign policy success have led critics to lambast leaders for their magical claims that "God has a special providence" for the United

States (Mead 2001). Other critics struggle to find coherence in American foreign policy strategy, arguing Americans lack the concentration span to focus on the range of issues demanding a hegemon's attention. However, scholars of American foreign policy reject the notion that American foreign policy is juvenile or incoherent, arguing that critics focus on the wrong aspects of foreign policy (Milner and Tingley 2015; Kertzer and Zeitzoff 2017). For European nations, foreign policy was a constant game of climbing the European politico-military hierarchy (Mead 2001; Preston 2012). By playing this game, nations became locked into long-term conflicts and alliances and created highly centralized governments that restricted the rights and liberties of their citizens (Rhodes 2018). The United States approached foreign policy differently, as a new nation whose understanding of its founding and purpose was distinct. The Founders feared that engaging in foreign policy such as their European forebears would harm the young nation and prevent it from becoming the global leader God intended. Seeking to protect the emerging temple, the national leaders chose to engage the world through trade as opposed to politics. As George Washington stated in his farewell address:

The great rule of conduct for us in regard to foreign nations is, in extending our commercial relations, to have with them as little political connection as possible. So far as we have already formed engagements, let them be fulfilled with perfect good faith. Here let us stop.[1]

The luxury of an ocean separating them from Europe allowed Americans to stay out of the politico-military struggle dictating European foreign relations for centuries (Preston 2012). With this freedom, Americans chose to "be in the world, but not of it." They engaged the world through trade and resisted succumbing to the activities that defiled others. By staying out of the schemes of European nations, the United States was able to cultivate its exceptionalism (Mead 2001; Rhodes 2018). In his July 4 address of 1821, John Quincy Adams explains why this was the best path to take:

[America] well knows that by once enlisting under other banners than her own, were they even the banners of foreign independence, she would involve herself, beyond the power of extrication, in all the wars of interest and intrigue, of individual avarice, envy, and ambition, which assume the colors and usurp the standard of freedom. The fundamental maxim of her policy would insensibly change from liberty to force. The frontlet on her brows would no longer beam with the ineffable splendor of freedom and independence; but in its stead would soon be substituted an imperial diadem, flashing in false and tarnished luster the murky radiance of dominion and power. She might become the dictatress of the world; she would be no longer the ruler of her own spirit.[2]

From the perspective of the Founding Fathers of the United States, the political and military scheming of European nations encouraged militarism and debt, and reduced liberty, all of which contributed to their impurity. If the United States were to engage in such behavior, it would no longer be exceptional. Avoiding entanglements and protecting America from European nations' political and military intrigues would instead allow the United States to emphasize liberty and republicanism, two aspects critical to their case for the nation's exceptionalism.

Reflecting on this choice to play a different role on the world stage, some argue that the United States was isolationist for much of its history. This could not be further from the truth. As Walter Russell Mead and Michael Green demonstrate, foreign policy was a critical part of the nation's development (Mead 2001; Green 2017). The prestige of the Secretary of State was only second to that of the president. Furthermore, twelve of the first fifteen presidents of the United States had some role in foreign relations, with six serving as Secretary of State. As George Washington emphasized in his farewell address, American foreign policy needed to focus on trade. To provide and maintain the liberty they promised their citizens, America's leaders needed to provide a strong economy. To accomplish this, opening and maintaining markets for American goods, specifically its agricultural goods, was crucial.

Even though trade was the primary focus of early American foreign policy, the United States did have to enter the fray with European nations. The colonies were no strangers to war (Byrd 2013). Colonists engaged in numerous wars with Native Americans, the French, and Spanish long before engaging their war for independence from the British. Each of these military campaigns was animated by a sense of religious zeal as clergy cited biblical passages and developed sermons to motivate amateur soldiers to kill for their country. The Bible became a book of war stories giving generals words of motivation and soldiers words of comfort. Invoking texts such as Exodus 15:3 "The Lord is a Man of War" and Jeremiah 48:10 "Cursed is he who does the work of the Lord with slackness, and cursed is he who keeps back his sword from bloodshed," clergy engrained an image of a God who would unflinchingly inflict divine wrath on any opposition to his Will. This image of God justified America's use of its military might to protect trade and maintain dominance in the Western hemisphere (Byrd 2013; Green 2017).

By 1815, the US Navy established a permanent squadron in the Mediterranean to combat the Barbary pirates and by 1822 squadrons had been established in the Caribbean and Pacific. By 1843 the US Navy had an established presence on every major continent and virtually every ocean, and American soldiers had seen combat in all these theaters (Mead 2001). The Monroe Doctrine, which perceived any attempt by European nations to expand in the Western Hemisphere as a threat to America's peace and safety, was an effort to protect the holy land the United States had created from foreign threats. If Spain and France were able to increase their influence in South America and Mexico, it would place nations beholden to them at the American border. One of the incentives for annexing Texas into the Union was a paranoia Texas might develop strong relations with the British leading to it becoming a proxy for British interests. Similarly, the Mexican–American war sought in part to keep British and French interests out of the western half of the nation (Rhodes 2018). These attempts to expand the nation were not solely about security; the fervent belief in the yoke of Manifest Destiny also justified westward expansion. Once dominion had been established securely from sea to shining sea, the United States began to reach beyond the continent. God had chosen it, and in His Honor, Americans had built a magnificent temple befitting their city upon a hill; now it was an article of their faith to evangelize to the world.

The strategy of building and protecting the national temple was dominant until the end of the nineteenth century, when national ambition expanded to colonialism abroad. Americans no longer felt simply being a shining "city upon a hill" was enough to change the world. To fulfill its divine mission, the nation had to engage the world by sharing its knowledge. President William McKinley's administration marked the transition from building the temple to embarking on a crusade. Under McKinley, with strong support from Congress, the nation began what some historians refer to as "Progressive Imperialism" (McDougall 1997, 2019). The Progressives believed their technological, cultural, and political advancements represented the height of civilization and the rest of the world, specifically the "non"-civilized world, would benefit from American intervention (Moore 2017). Much like Jesus's message in the Sermon on the Mount, these Americans argued that the nation should not "hide its light under a bushel." Such activities were sanctioned, even championed, by religious and secular leaders who were convinced that

America's great advances practically made it a sin not to spread the "Good News" to the world (Strong 1893; McCartney 2011; McDougall 2019). The United States framed its new interventionist foreign policy as fulfilling the mission of the "Good Samaritan" (McDougall 2019). Rev. W. S. Rainsford, Rector of the St. George's Church in Manhattan where the city's most powerful and influential residents worshipped, invoked the parable of the Good Samaritan in a pamphlet calling for American intervention in Cuba and imploring the nation to carry out its divine duty:

War is an evil and brings great evils in its train. But again I repeat there is one thing far worse than war, for it is the fruitful womb from which all wars are born: it is the spirit which selfishly, supinely, sits at home in comfort and national plenty, when the divinely given rights of freedom and justice are denied to our next-door neighbour; it is the growing, sluggish indifference to torture and wrong. This in the eyes of God is far worse than war; for it inevitably leads to wholesale death, death of the soul, and the blasting and decay of all that is worthy in civilization. (1902, p. 185)

His fellow Americans heeded this call to save foreign souls, even by force if the recipients of America's largesse were not enlightened enough to be grateful. A late arrival to the Great Game, the United States proved a quick study and soon claimed control of territories in Asia, the Caribbean, and Latin America, launching the nation into an era of imperialism that had been exclusively the arena of European powers (McDougall 1997; Moore 2017). Given that a previous generation had devoutly sworn off European-style political and military expansionism, this change of heart was noteworthy, but those who justified the new approach saw a through line to the nature of America and its Founders. One of the most vocal supporters of this expansion, Albert Beveridge, on the cusp of a political career as two-term Senator from Indiana and chair of the Senate Committee on Territories, saw imperialism as the nation's divine duty:

Have we no mission to perform, no duty to discharge, to our fellow man? Has God endowed us with gifts beyond our deserts and marked us as the people of His peculiar favor, merely to rot in our own selfishness, as men and nations must, who take cowardice for their companion and self for their deity-as China has, as India has, as Egypt has?

Shall we be as the man who had one talent and hid it, or as he who had ten talents and used them until they grew to riches? And shall we reap the reward that waits on our discharge of our high duty; shall we occupy new markets for what our farmers raise, our factories make, our merchants sell – aye, and please God, new markets for what our ships shall carry? (1898)

Spreading the American gospel was thus a humanitarian endeavor – that it also served American self-interests was simply further confirmation of the nation's divine favor. Americans had been plotting to annex Cuba for decades and saw a chance for expansion through ousting the Spanish. Furthermore, these actions were justified by an extreme level of paternalism. Wielding the intellectual cudgel of Social Darwinism, interventionists argued Anglo-Saxon culture and values would save the world (McCartney 2011; McDougall 2019). Given their self-image as rescuers rather than conquerors, these American crusaders did not think to offer guarantees of independence to the recipients of their "humanitarianism" (Moore 2017; McDougall 2019). President McKinley omitted the recognition of Cuba as an independent nation in his call for war with Spain, and Congress explicitly eschewed language requiring the nation to recognize Cuban independence (McCartney 2011).

So fervent was the missionary zeal that the American gospel was often spread at the point of a gun. Reports of abuses of power in the Philippines led many to argue that the nation was a despot, much as the Spanish had been before America's arrival, or, once upon time, the Egyptians were to the Israelites. In his second inaugural address, at the dawn of what was to be the American Century, President McKinley dismissed this notion with a full-throated exposition of the virtuousness of the American cause:

The American people, intrenched in freedom at home, take their love for it with them wherever they go, and they reject as mistaken and unworthy the doctrine that we lose our own liberties by securing the enduring foundations of liberty to others. Our institutions will not deteriorate by extension, and our sense of justice will not abate under tropic suns in distant seas.[3]

What about the Filipino rebels who fought American occupation? McKinley argued they were an unrepresentative group that rejected the greatness of American liberty:

We are not waging war against the inhabitants of the Philippine Islands. A portion of them are making war against the United States. By far the greater part of the inhabitants recognize American sovereignty and welcome it as a guaranty of order and of security for life, property, liberty, freedom of conscience, and the pursuit of happiness. (McKinley 1901)

Senator Beveridge was more candid in his justification of using American power to "liberate" Cubans and Filipinos:

The Opposition tells us that we ought not to govern a people without their consent. I answer, the rule of liberty that all just government derives its authority from the consent of the governed, applies only to those who are capable of self-government.

We govern the Indians without their consent, we govern our territories without their consent, we govern our children without their consent. How do they know that our government would be without their consent? Would not the people of the Philippines prefer the just, humane, civilizing government of this Republic to the savage, bloody rule of pillage and extortion from which we have rescued them? (1898)

Filled with the spirit of Progressive Imperialism, President Theodore Roosevelt built the "Great White Fleet" which circumnavigated the globe to demonstrate the power of the United States. As the most vocal champion of Progressive Imperialism, Roosevelt worked to extend America's power in the Caribbean and Latin America. He helped orchestrate Panama's independence from Colombia for the construction of the Panama Canal and sheltered Caribbean nations in severe debt to European nations (McDougall 1997; Moore 2017).

Inspired by the same intellectual lineage, President Woodrow Wilson contended America would bring peace to the world and endeavored to accomplish this through mediation and international law. Wilson believed the great nations of the world, specifically the United States and Great Britain, could work together to bring about global peace and prosperity. Unlike Roosevelt, who presented the military in a bellicose fashion, Wilson cast their job as being the world's police force (McDougall 2019). Consider his 1914 commencement address to the United States Naval Academy:

It ought to be one of your thoughts all the time that you are sample Americans – not merely sample Navy men, not merely sample soldiers, but sample Americans – and that you have the point of view of America with regard to her Navy and her Army; that she is using them as the instruments of civilization, not as the instruments of aggression. The idea of America is to serve humanity, and every time you let the Stars and Stripes free to the wind you ought to realize that that is in itself a message that you are on an errand which other navies have sometimes tunes forgotten; not an errand of conquest, but an errand of service.[4]

This contributed to Wilson's unwillingness to enter World War I. He was driven by his belief either the Allies would win the war or he could negotiate a peace (McDougall 2019). President Wilson positioned the naval forces to provide "armed neutrality" to enforce international law; however, this was an insufficient deterrent to Germany's imperial ambitions. When it became apparent the Allies were on the brink of defeat and facing growing threats to American interests, Wilson called for the nation to enter the war. In his April 1917 address to Congress requesting a declaration of war against Germany, he invoked a language the

Founders and Puritan forebears would have recognized. The United States, protectors of peace, justice, and international law, must act now:

> Neutrality is no longer feasible or desirable where the peace of the world is involved and the freedom of its peoples, and the menace to that peace and freedom lies in the existence of autocratic governments backed by organized force which is controlled wholly by their will, not by the will of their people. We have seen the last of neutrality in such circumstances.
>
> We are at the beginning of an age in which it will be insisted that the same standards of conduct and of responsibility for wrong done shall be observed among nations and their governments that are observed among the individual citizens of civilized states.[5]

Victory over the German forces, Wilson hoped, would allow him to fulfill his vision of co-operation between nations through international law, and shaped his approach to the Treaty of Versailles and the establishment of the League of Nations. Ironically, while Wilson's views found support among the European nations, he could not convince his fellow Americans of their virtue. Americans questioned what such an approach might mean for their independence and feared long-term commitments. Because of this the League of Nations was not ratified by the US Senate and Wilson's hopes for the United States to lead a global community were dashed (McDougall 1997).

The national crusade stalled for several decades as the Axis Powers began to move through Europe and Asia. Even though President Franklin Delano Roosevelt attempted to rekindle the crusading spirit through speeches to Congress and his fireside chats, he was unable to rouse the public to action (McDougall 2019). Throughout his campaign to get the nation to make a stronger commitment to halt the progression of the Axis Powers, Roosevelt emphasized religious freedom as a cornerstone of democracy and liberty (Preston 2012). Roosevelt argued that America could not remain an island as totalitarian governments took over the rest of the world. In his 1940 State of the Union Address, he stated: "We must look ahead and see the kind of lives our children would have to lead if a large part of the rest of the world were compelled to worship a god imposed by a military ruler, or were forbidden to worship God at all" (Roosevelt 1940). Roosevelt gained support among theologians, such as Reinhold Niebuhr, who moved from pacifism to calling for government action. Couching their argument in the doctrine of Christian realism, which viewed "foreign policy as a series of realistic choices between relative good and lesser evils" (Preston 2012, p. 306), Niebuhr and other Christian realists contended no nation, not even the United States, was innocent. However, some nations were more sinful than others and it was the responsibility of nations that were closer to God, like the United States, to act to prevent these more sinful nations from causing greater harm (Preston 2012). Through Roosevelt's calls for action and the emergence of Christian realism to provide a theological justification for action, Americans grew more supportive of military intervention against Hitler. On December 8, 1941, in response to the attack on its naval installation in Pearl Harbor, Hawai'i, America declared war on Japan. Declaration of war against Germany followed three days later on December 11. As the nation formally entered World War II, President Roosevelt channeled Wilson's spirit and entreated all nations to confront the evil and lawlessness of the Axis Powers. He established national days of prayer and used his fireside chats to lead the nation in prayer (Preston 2012). In his 1942 "The Century of the Common Man" speech, Vice President Henry Wallace made an emphatic statement about the religious duty of Americans to fight the evil of the Nazis. Wallace argued that not confronting Hitler would allow "Satan [to be] turned loose on the world" and that "the violence preached by the Nazis is the devil's own religion of darkness." He acknowledged Americans' aversion to war, but insisted they must be willing to make an exception in the case of Hitler. Wallace contended Americans will "fight with a tireless enthusiasm until war, and the possibility of war, have been removed from this planet." In his concluding remarks, Wallace made it clear that this was a Manichean battle between the forces of God and the forces of Satan:

No compromise with Satan is possible. We shall not rest until the victims under the Nazi and Japanese yoke are freed. We shall fight for a complete peace as well as a complete victory.

The people's revolution is on the march, and the devil and all his angels cannot prevail against it. They cannot prevail, for on the side of the people is the Lord. (1942)[6]

As in the Revolutionary War, America's military leaders invoked religious rhetoric to empower their soldiers. In his D-Day message, General Dwight D. Eisenhower informed his soldiers that they were "about to embark on the Great Crusade" and asked for "the blessing of Almighty God upon this great and noble undertaking" (Eisenhower 1944). This sense of divine blessing encouraged soldiers to sing military songs, such as "Praise the Lord and Pass the Ammunition" and "God is my Co-pilot," that overtly mixed religiosity with militarism (Preston 2012). President Harry S. Truman's proclamation of victory in Europe called for a National

Day of Prayer and began thus: "The Allied armies, through sacrifice and devotion and with God's help, have wrung from Germany a final and unconditional surrender" (Truman 1945b).

The victory over Japan did not receive the same unanimous jubilation. Because this victory required the use of two nuclear bombs, moral concerns abounded among both clergy and those within the Truman administration (Preston 2012). President Truman attempted to ease these concerns by stating that "American foreign policy is based firmly on fundamental principles of righteousness and justice." He characterized America's atomic program as part of a "sacred trust" with the rest of the world and looked forward to a day when such weapons no longer existed. He concluded his speech by stating: "We shall pursue that course with all the wisdom, patience, and determination that the God of Peace can bestow upon a people who are trying to follow in His path" (Truman 1945a).

World War II changed America's approach to global leadership. Though it had rejected the League of Nations two decades earlier, the United States now joined the newly formed United Nations and implemented the Marshall Plan to help rebuild war-ravaged Europe. In the process of vanquishing one enemy, another emerged. The Soviet Union had been viewed with suspicion before the war but were accepted as allies during it. Much of the discussion of the godless communist halted during the war effort to sustain an uneasy alliance. With Hitler vanquished, and a victorious America ready to ascend to its rightful place as defenders of freedom and democracy, a new enemy emerged. Portraying the spread of Communism as a global threat, the United States appointed itself the primary force to stop its expansion. To combat this new antagonist, the Truman Doctrine called for new military alliances in Western Europe that could keep Soviet expansionism at bay. The cautions of the Founders against foreign entanglements were but faint echoes from a more naïve bygone era (McDougall 1997; Mead 2001).

In less than half a century, the United States went from being outside of European politico-military machine to becoming its engine. Religious rhetoric fueled it. From the outset of the Cold War, President Truman framed it in religious terms. In a 1946 address to the Conference of the Federal Council of Churches, he celebrated the victories of World War II, but warned of new dangers:

Now that we have preserved our freedom of conscience and religion, our right to live by a decent moral and spiritual code of our own choosing, let us make full use of that freedom. Let us make use of it to save a world which is beset by so many threats of new conflicts, new terror, and new destruction.

In that same speech, Truman asked the nation's houses of worship to band together to set the world right and protect it from these new dangers.

This is a supreme opportunity for the Church to continue to fulfill its mission on earth. The Protestant Church, the Catholic Church, and the Jewish Synagogue–bound together in the American unity of brotherhood–must provide the shock forces to accomplish this moral and spiritual awakening. No other agency can do it. Unless it is done, we are headed for the disaster we would deserve. (1946)[7]

In a 1951 address Truman delineated the god-fearing morality of America and the godless deviance of communism:

For the danger that threatens us in the world today is utterly and totally opposed to all these things. The international Communist movement is based on a fierce and terrible fanaticism. It denies the existence of God and, wherever it can, it stamps out the worship of God.

Our religious faith gives us the answer to the false beliefs of communism. Our faith shows us the way to create a society where man can find his greatest happiness under God. Surely, we can follow that faith with the same devotion and determination the Communists give to their godless creed. (1951)[8]

In these heady early days of the Cold War, the nation developed what Jonathan Herzog refers to as "the spiritual industrial complex," a contrived attempt to increase religiosity among Americans as a method of battling communism (Herzog 2011). The government, private businesses, entertainment, and religious organizations worked together to bring religion to the forefront of the American conversation (Gunn 2009; Herzog 2011). National Security Council policy papers, such as NSC 68 and NSC 162/2, reveal the depth of the Truman and Eisenhower administration's obsession with the growth of communism, which they viewed as a great evil. NSC 68 paints the United States as the emblem of justice and liberty, whereas the USSR was system of "complete subversion."[9] The report characterizes the Soviet Union as "animated by a new fanatic faith, antithetical to our own," a threat not only to the United States, but also to civilization as a whole. Communism, NSC 68 warned, advocated a faith where "The system becomes God, and submission to the will of God becomes submission to the will of the system." No institution was immune, with the communist threat lurking in the corners of labor union halls, school cafeterias, media houses, and even churches. Combating the spread of communism required the United States to maintain a strong military force, practice a higher level of discipline, and sacrifice freedoms. Issued three years later, in 1953, NSC 162/2 doubled down on the existential threat of communism, and argued that the United States must embrace an expanded global role and mobilize "the spiritual and martial resources necessary to meet the Soviet threat."[10] Through the Truman and Eisenhower administrations and guided by foreign policy advisors such as George Kennan and John Foster Dulles, the United States mounted a holy crusade against communism (Inboden 2008; Gunn 2009; Herzog 2011). This crusade aimed not merely to stop the spread of communism, but also sought to reshape the world in America's image in the process (Preston 2012).

To achieve these lofty ends, America's leaders had to mobilize the public. As they had from the days of the nation's founding, leaders relied on religion to align Americans with their agenda to combat communism. A religious revival followed, reaffirming the United States as a covenant nation righteously standing vigil against godless communism. When introducing the bill that would place the motto "In God We Trust" on American currency, Representative Charles E. Bennett (D-Florida) pointed to communism as the basis for this needed change:

I sincerely hope that the Senate will give its prompt approval to this proposal. In these days when imperialistic and materialistic communism seeks to attack and destroy freedom, we should continuously look for ways to strengthen the foundations of our freedom. At the base of our freedom is our faith in God and the desire of Americans to live by His will and by His guidance. As long as this country trusts in God, it will prevail. To serve as a constant reminder of this truth, it is highly desirable that our currency and coins should bear these inspiring words, "In God We Trust." (U.S. Congress 1955)

America's anti-Communist religious revival was not led simply by paranoid politicians; clergy embraced their central role in advancing the crusade against communism. Evangelical clergy, who were highly patriotic and already saw themselves as the redeemers of the world, were most supportive of the crusade. In working with the government, they moved into the American mainstream while carrying out their heavenly duties (Gunn 2009; Herzog 2011; Preston 2012). Faced with the specter of Godless communism, once-pacifist Evangelical leaders changed their tune. To them, disarmament and demobilization were no longer options because the divine imperative of defeating the Soviet Union required the United States to have the world's greatest military. Preachers such as evangelist Billy Graham became prominent voices in American public life as they lambasted communism's evils. Here is Graham at his 1946 Los Angeles Tent Revival: "Communism is not only an economic interpretation of life, communism is a religion that is inspired and directed and motivated by the Devil himself that has declared war against almighty God" (Graham 1949). Like Graham, Harold John Ockenga, a founder of the National Evangelical Association, argued that, because communism denied God, communists could not be trusted and attempts to negotiate were foolish. He warned his flock that communists wished to sow dissent in the American public and suggested they funded and influenced the civil rights movement. Ockenga also accused liberal Christian leaders who wanted to find a way to work with communist leaders as either being naïve or supportive of the communist cause. Most importantly, Ockenga urged Christians to support the nation's military and the building of a strong military force capable of deterring communism's growth (Ockenga 1961).

As it raged on, the Cold War continued to be framed as a religious crusade of good versus evil, with politicians finding support from evangelical leaders. However, this support would wane as the nation dealt with the repercussions of the Vietnam War and Americans tired of the constant tension between the United States and the Soviet Union. Even Billy Graham softened his rhetoric toward communists (Preston 2012). Nevertheless, the essential difference between the two superpowers was still fundamentally about good versus evil, an idea captured memorably by Reagan's moniker of "Evil Empire." In his 1983 remarks to the Annual Convention of the National of Association of Evangelicals, Reagan recounted his admiration of a man who stated he loved his daughters so much he would rather see them die believing in God "than have them grow up under communism and one day die no longer believing in God" (Reagan 1983). And since defending God required the biggest and best bombs, the president admonished secular and religious leaders who called for nuclear disarmament:

So, I urge you to speak out against those who would place the United States in a position of military and moral inferiority. ... So, in your discussions of the nuclear freeze proposals, I urge you to beware the temptation of pride – the temptation of blithely declaring yourselves above it all and labeling both sides equally at fault, to ignore the facts of history and the aggressive impulses of an evil empire, to simply call the arms race a giant misunderstanding and thereby remove yourself from the struggle between right and wrong and good and evil. (Reagan 1983)

When, at long last, the Berlin Wall was dismantled and the Soviet Union disintegrated, America celebrated the defeat of its mightiest opponent.

Vanquishing the mortal threat of communism reaffirmed its divine exceptionalism but victory left America facing an existential dilemma. Five
decades of war-footing, starting with defending the American way of life
against Nazi Germany and Imperial Japan, followed almost immediately
by wars against communism in Korea, Vietnam, and countless other
proxy states around the world, had defined America's purpose in the
world. The military-industrial complex, against which Eisenhower had
once cautioned, had triumphed and mushroomed, giving America the
most powerful military the world had ever known. But with communism
vanquished, to what purpose would such fearsome firepower be turned?
Some in Washington still wanted a crusader state; others bemoaned the
neglect years of crusades abroad had rendered at home. Under Presidents
George H. W. Bush and Bill Clinton, foreign policy was still framed along
moral terms; however, these early post-Cold War presidents embraced
a more realist approach to foreign policy, casting America in the role of
a global police force. Their national foreign policy strategies focused on
reigning in rogue nations along with promoting democracy, free trade,
and religious liberty. The Bush administration's invasion of Panama and
the first Iraq War were framed as moral causes. But, unlike in earlier years,
where communism was engaged across the globe, now there were many
other rogue nations that went unchecked because they did not pose
immediate threats to America's trading or energy interests. This left religious conservatives and liberals feeling betrayed (Preston 2012). Yet the
rich vein of American religious exceptionalism was ever available to be
mined by presidential speechwriters. President Clinton, in his remarks at
the National Cathedral Memorial Service for those killed in bombings of
US embassies in Kenya and Tanzania in 1998, evoked the missionary spirit
in characterizing the Americans who perished in the bombing:

In the book of Isaiah it is written that the Lord called out, "Whom shall I send, and
who will go for us?" And Isaiah, the prophet, answered, "Here am I, Lord; send
me." These Americans, generous, adventurous, brave souls, said, "Send me. Send
me in service. Send me to build a better tomorrow." And on their journey they
perished, together with proud sons and daughters of Kenya and Tanzania. (1998)

Calling for divine aid for America's battle against its new enemies, Clinton
continues:

All of us must stand together with our friends from Kenya and Tanzania and other
peace-loving nations – yes, in grief, but also in common commitment to carry on
the cause of peace and freedom, to find those responsible and bring them to justice,
not to rest as long as terrorists plot to take more innocent lives, and in the end, to

convince people the world over that there is a better way of living than killing others for what you cannot have today. For our larger struggle, for hope over hatred and unity over division, is a just one. And with God's help, it will prevail. (1998)

Three years later, the nation renewed its crusading zeal as the attacks on September 11, 2001, shook the nation to its core. President George W. Bush said those who had perpetrated those attacks hated democracy and liberty. Furthermore, since there can be no neutral side in a battle between good and evil, President Bush warned that any nation showing sympathy to those who would harm America would be considered an enemy. In his remarks at the National Day of Prayer and Remembrance Service, Bush implored divine consolation, while also warning that America would not be denied its vengeance:

War has been waged against us by stealth and deceit and murder. This Nation is peaceful, but fierce when stirred to anger. This conflict was begun on the timing and terms of others. It will end in a way and at an hour of our choosing. (2001)

As the nation launched its military actions in Afghanistan, where it aimed to defeat the Taliban regime that it blamed for the September 2011 attacks, and Iraq, where it was searching for nonexistent weapons of mass destruction, America found its purpose again. Once again, America was on a crusade to spread the gospel of democracy and freedom. Indeed, the language used in the fight against terrorism echoed the language used to combat communism. In a February 2002 speech Attorney General John Ashcroft argued that America's actions were about freedom:

Our fight against terrorism, then, is a defense of our freedom in the most profound sense: It is the defense of our right to make moral choices – to seek fellowship with God that is chosen, not commanded. This freedom is respected and nurtured in our society of laws. It is respected in our right to choose how or if we worship God. It is nurtured in our fundamental belief of equality before the law. By attacking us, terrorists attack not just the system of government that supports this freedom, but freedom itself.

The conflict that confronts us is not Christian versus Muslim, or Muslim versus Jew. Even as we seek justice in Afghanistan for those who attacked us on September 11, we extend our hands in aid and comfort to a war-torn people. As we pursue justice, we respect life. As we seek to reprimand the guilty, we also seek to give assistance to the innocent.

This is not a conflict based in religion. It is a conflict between those who believe that God grants us choice and those who seek to impose their choices on us. It is a conflict between inspiration and imposition; the way of peace and the way of destruction and chaos. It is a conflict between good and evil. And as President Bush has reminded us, we know that God is not neutral between the two. (2002)

Ashcroft's insistence that the wars in Afghanistan and Iraq were not anti-Islam campaigns were undercut by other members of the Bush administration who openly portrayed the purpose of these military campaigns as the protection of Christianity from the evils of Islam (Miles 2004). The Defense Department's deputy undersecretary for intelligence, Lieutenant General William G. Boykin, made presentations to religious groups – often in uniform – describing these wars as protecting Christianity. In other presentations he argued that God placed President Bush in the White House for the purpose of combatting the evil besieging the nation. In one address he stated that the nation was attacked "because we're a Christian nation . . . and the enemy is a guy named Satan" (Arkin 2003). In another, he elaborated thusly, "Ladies and gentlemen, this is your enemy. It is not Osama bin Laden, it is the principalities of darkness. It is a spiritual enemy that will only be defeated if we come against them in the name of Jesus and pray for this nation and for our leaders" (Lei 2003).

President Barack Obama entered the White House on a message of hope and change, promising to disentangle the nation from its crusades and to focus on making the nation better and changing the world by example as opposed to force. As a presidential candidate he made the following argument in a *Foreign Affairs* article:

America cannot meet the threats of this century alone, and the world cannot meet them without America. We can neither retreat from the world nor try to bully it into submission. We must lead the world, by deed and by example. (2007, p. 7)

President Obama's approach seems to indicate a preference for a less unilateral approach to international conflict, but his reasoning and justification for the use of American power would have been very familiar to the Christian Realists who provided the theological cover for FDR's entry into World War II. Obama unabashedly invoked moral and religious language in his discussion of foreign policy. While ostensibly seeking to construct a different model of American leadership, he was no less explicit in his belief in American exceptionalism than any of his predecessors. In his Nobel Peace Prize lecture, acknowledging the irony of the Commander-in-Chief of the US military winning such an award while the nation was in the midst of two wars, Obama invoked the concept of a "just war" to defend past and future American military action:

Over time, as codes of law sought to control violence within groups, so did philosophers and clerics and statesmen seek to regulate the destructive power of war. The concept of a "just war" emerged, suggesting that war is justified only when certain conditions were met: if it is waged as a last resort or in self-defense; if the force used is proportional; and if, whenever possible, civilians are spared from violence. (2009b)

After genuflecting fleetingly in the direction of the ideology of nonviolence of Mahatma Gandhi and Martin Luther King, Obama returned to the Christian realism of Niebuhr:

But as a head of state sworn to protect and defend my nation, I cannot be guided by [Gandhi's and King's] examples alone. I face the world as it is, and cannot stand idle in the face of threats to the American people. For make no mistake: Evil does exist in the world. A non-violent movement could not have halted Hitler's armies. Negotiations cannot convince al Qaeda's leaders to lay down their arms. To say that force may sometimes be necessary is not a call to cynicism – it is a recognition of history; the imperfections of man and the limits of reason. (2009b)

Obama's repeated invocations of American exceptionalism laid the foundation for the Trumpian version of the same. As president, Donald Trump openly invoked American superiority and called on the nation to redeem itself. Like Obama, Trump wanted to end the crusades and rebuild the temple that is America, to Make America Great Again as it were. Preaching a populism reminiscent of Jesus kicking over the tables and expelling the merchants in order to cleanse the temple, President Trump argued that previous presidents had failed the nation by building bad foreign trade deals, entering international pacts, and prosecuting unsuccessful military campaigns. Emphasizing America First, he unapologetically placed self-interest at the center of his presidency. In his own interest was the support of White evangelical voters, which led Trump to use religious rhetoric repeatedly in campaign speeches and to mobilize the National Guard to tear gas peaceful protestors so that he could have a photo-opportunity in front of historic St. John's Church in Lafayette Square, holding a Bible upside down. During his campaign he professed the need to protect Christianity and vilified Muslims. He attempted to reduce immigration from majority Muslim nations. In a sop to the Israeli right and to hardline pro-Israeli American lobbyists, President Trump recognized Jerusalem as Israel's capital, which set off alarms throughout the Middle East (Toosi 2018).

From John Winthrop to Donald Trump, American religious exceptionalism is the animating force behind American identity and its foreign policy. The unshakeable faith that America is a chosen people, a city on a hill that must be defended against those who would corrupt and destroy it while feeling the weight of the responsibility to evangelize abroad, is a constant. In the next section, we show that these ideas exist not just as elite rhetoric but form a consistent and reliable explanation for how the mass public understands America's foreign policy choices.

5.2 AMERICAN PUBLIC OPINION TOWARD FOREIGN POLICY

The role of public opinion in foreign policy has been much maligned by research showing it lacks stability, structure, and influence on policy-making (Holsti 2004). Alexis de Tocqueville commented, "I have no hesitation in saying that in the control of society's foreign affairs democratic governments do appear decidedly inferior to others" (1945, p. 245). Foreign policy realists, such as Hans Morgenthau, viewed public opinion as a nuisance – a vestige of the emotional and irrational masses (1948). Walter Lippmann agreed: "Public opinion has been destructively wrong at critical junctures" (1955, p. 20). According to realists, the uninformed public stifled the decisions of the well-informed and was "a dangerous master of decision when the stakes are life and death" (p. 20). Gabriel Almond further criticized the American public as inattentive to foreign policy, which he feared led to mass indifference and the utter absence of any discernible attitude structures in the American psyche (1950). The "Almond-Lippmann consensus" was supported by other research finding that Americans were ill-informed about domestic issues and even more uninformed about foreign issues (Bailey 1948; Kriesberg 1949; Cottrell and Eberhart 1969). Quite damningly, Phillip Converse demonstrated the instability of American attitudes on domestic issues – a negative attribute that only worsened on foreign policy issues (Campbell, et al. 1960; Converse 1964). Many scholars concluded that the unknowledgeable masses rendered public opinion irrelevant to foreign policy decisions (Campbell, et al. 1960; Kelman 1965). Studies of Congress and the presidency supported these conclusions, finding little connection between public opinion and legislative and executive decision-making (Miller and Stokes 1963; Caspary 1970; La Feber 1977). Bernard Cohen found some officials to be especially indignant at the idea that public opinion influences national foreign policy, demonstrating further the disconnect between the American people and foreign policy outcomes (1972). Other scholars asserted that when public opinion and government policy are aligned, it is because political elites had provided clear cues for the partisan publics to follow (Zaller 1992; Berinsky 2009). The overwhelming thrust of this scholarship is that elites need not pander to public opinion – they are the ones manipulating it.

Some scholars reject this conclusion. One piece of evidence to contradict this assumption is that political leaders are very concerned with opinion polls (Jacobs and Shapiro 1995), and it is worth noting that, as early as 1968, Doris Graber claimed that public opinion was influential even in the early years of the Republic, including for seminal foreign policy achievements such as the Louisiana Purchase and the Monroe Doctrine (1968). Ole Holsti highlights a number of firsthand accounts by bureaucrats and pollsters who confirmed that public opinion is a factor in foreign policy decisions (2004), though perhaps one should expect politicians in a democratic setting to claim this. Benjamin Page and Robert Shapiro note that changes in public opinion often preceded changes in foreign policy, suggestive of a causal relationship where the public influences elite decision-making, not vice versa (1982). John Aldrich and his colleagues argued that foreign policy views, expressed in electoral outcomes, are critical for the public to influence governmental decisions (2006). Other political scientists, such as Larry Bartels (1991) and Christopher Wlezien (1996), report a correlation between public opinion and defense spending. Studies also found that elite cues do not have the effects that were previously assumed (Gelpi 2010; Levendusky and Horowitz 2012), and that social peers might be as important in shaping foreign policy opinions as are elites (Kertzer and Zeitzoff 2017). While evidence remains that elites manipulate and ignore public opinion, and that the average American is woefully ignorant of international politics, this body of research provides suggestive evidence that the American public's opinion does influence the room elites have to maneuver abroad.

Scholars have also sought to refute the assumption that American foreign policy attitudes are unstable (Caspary 1970; Holsti 2004). Page and Shapiro argue that the changes in attitudes we see over time are not due to randomness, but are a response to real-world events (Page and Shapiro 1982, 1992; Shapiro and Page 1988). John Mueller's analysis of public opinion during the Korean and Vietnam wars finds that public opposition to both wars rose in response to battle deaths (1973). This sensitivity of public opinion to casualties has been demonstrated in a series of papers by Scott Gartner and Gary Segura (Gartner, Segura and Wilkening 1997; Gartner and Segura 1998, 2000; Gartner, Segura and Barratt 2004). Others find that public opinion sometimes attempts to force leadership's hand in one direction or the other, in predictable and rational ways. For example, they may push for more action from doves, while calling for more restraint from hawks (Mayer 1992; Nincic 1992). In this way, aggregate public opinion appears highly reasonable and restrained – even stable, in contradiction to the pessimistic conclusions of early foreign policy realists.

Along with these rebuttals to attitude instability and policy disconnectedness arguments, scholars have demonstrated a high level of structure in American foreign policy attitudes. Even though Americans possess low levels of foreign affairs knowledge, they can rely on overarching principles and values to decide whether to support or oppose a policy. Ole Holsti contends that low levels of information may increase the use of some types of attitudinal structure in order to lower the cognitive costs of decision-making (2004). Eugene Wittkopf along with Holsti and James Rosenau established two attitudinal dimensions structuring foreign policy attitudes: co-operative internationalism and militant internationalism (Wittkopf 1986, 1990; Holsti and Rosenau 1993). Scholars have confirmed these two dimensions and argue that a third dimension, isolationism, should be considered. Whereas Wittkopf and Holsti and Rosenau treated isolationism as the rejection of both co-operative and militant internationalism, others hypothesize that it represents its own distinct dimension (Chittick, Billingsley and Travis 1995; Rathbun 2007). Each of these dimensions has been credited with providing a structure to foreign policy attitudes, even if citizens lack detailed knowledge of particular world events. Co-operative internationalism, also referred to as multilateralism (Chittick, Billingsley and Travis 1995) and community (Rathbun 2007), represents a support for others abroad and for the principle of working toward common goals (Holsti and Rosenau 1990; Wittkopf 1990). Those at the high end of the dimension are supportive of institutions such as the United Nations and collaborating with other nations to solve global problems. Militant internationalism, also referred to as militarism (Hurwitz and Peffley 1987), emphasizes deterrence and the need to look and act strong to the world. Any sign of weakness on the part of the nation is viewed as an invitation for aggression from other nations (Rathbun, et al. 2016). Finally, isolationism represents the desire to turn inward and avoid foreign entanglements (Chittick, Billingsley and Travis 1995; Rathbun 2007). Many have argued that isolationism has dominated American foreign policy; however, as these examples show, this is not the case. Bear Braumoeller has led a revision of the commonplace narrative that the United States became highly isolationist after World War I (2010). In his analysis, the failure to ratify the League of Nations was a product of a well-mobilized minority rather than representing a collective *zeitgeist*.

Figure 5.1 demonstrates the trend in American attitudes along these three dimensions from 1992 to 2018.

We measure militarism using a Gallup Poll question about whether it was important for the United States to lead the world militarily. The data demonstrate that most Americans consistently believe having the world's top military is important. Co-operative internationalism is measured using an assessment of the United Nations. Gallup asked respondents, "[d]o you think the United Nations is doing a good job or poor job in trying to solve the problems it has had to face?" Americans are unlikely to state that the United Nations is doing a good job. This appears to be primarily in reaction to the United Nations' reluctance to support the United States' erroneous decision to invade Iraq after the September 11, 2001, attacks. Our measure of isolationism is agreement with the statement, "[t]he United States should mind its own business internationally and let other countries get along the best they can on their own," which was compiled using responses to Gallup and Pew surveys. This trend shows a moderate level of support with most Americans subscribing to this more isolationist viewpoint in 2013. To offer an international

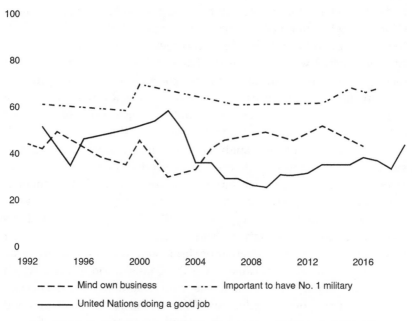

FIGURE 5.1 American support for isolationism, militarism, co-operation (1992–2017)

comparison, Timothy Gravelle, Jason Reifler, and Thomas Scotto applied measures of each of these dimensions to surveys in the United States, United Kingdom, France, and Germany (Gravelle, Reifler and Scotto 2017). They found Americans were significantly less isolationist than the other nations, and much more militaristic. On the co-operative internationalism dimension, Americans were on par with citizens of the United Kingdom and France, but are significantly less supportive than Germans. What explains this structure of Americans' foreign policy attitudes? And why are some Americans more likely than others to embrace particular foreign policy positions?

5.3 MORALITY, RELIGION, AND FOREIGN POLICY ATTITUDES

Since independence, morality has been a central aspect of American foreign policy. Part of the idea of American exceptionalism is the belief that Americans just have better values than other nations. Unlike other nations whose actions are driven by pure self-interest, when the United States engages in global affairs, Americans believe it reflects strong moral character (Morgenthau 1948; Wilson 1998; Guth 2012). Studies continually demonstrate the importance of moral predispositions in providing the foundation for American foreign policy attitudes (Hurwitz and Peffley 1987; Kertzer, et al. 2014; Rathbun, et al. 2016). Jon Hurwitz and Mark Peffley find "core values," such as ethnocentrism and morality of warfare, form the basis of how Americans structure their foreign policy attitudes (1987). Focusing on attitudes toward a social hierarchy or national community, Brian Rathbun finds these values are associated with support for military superiority, international aid, and protecting human rights (2007). For Joshua Kertzer and colleagues, who ground their study in Moral Foundations Theory, individualizing foundations (harm/care and fairness/reciprocity) are associated with co-operative internationalism, while binding foundations (authority/respect, in-group/loyalty, and purity/sanctity) are associated with militarism (2014). Meanwhile, Brian Rathbun and his colleagues, using Schwartz's measure of ten value domains, find that militarism, co-operative internationalism, and isolationism are each associated with distinct values (2016). Conservation values, which emphasize stability and compliance with traditions, are associated with greater support for militarism. Universalism, an appreciation and concern for the welfare of all, is related to greater support for co-operative internationalism. Isolationism is associated with higher levels of conservation and lower levels of benevolence. Through a series of experiments, Sarah Kreps and Sarah Maxey demonstrate that American support for military humanitarian interventions is based in the belief that the nation has a moral responsibility as opposed to concerns about cost or strategic consequences (2018).

Existing scholarship establishes the importance of values in shaping how Americans think about foreign policy. An important source of value systems is religion. Religion serves as an integral part of value development and application because it teaches individuals about who they are and how to operate in the world (Roof 1976; Leege 1993; Warner and Walker 2010). Clifford Geertz draws the most direct connection between religion and values when he states: "In sacred rituals and myths, values are portrayed not as subjective human preferences but as the imposed conditions for life implicit in a world with a particular structure" (1973, p. 131). Scholars who have examined the connection between religion and the values structuring foreign policy find a consistent linkage. Samuel Huntington famously argued that with the fall of the Soviet Union, the battles would no longer be over ideology but religion, which he saw as the basis for what he called civilizations (1996). Several studies find that Huntington's "clash of civilizations" thesis resonates with the public. As Zeev Maoz and Errol A. Henderson (2020) demonstrate, leaders benefit from the use of religious rhetoric when they are able to portray the opposition as being religiously dissimilar. Through America's history, this religious dissimilarity rhetoric was used to provide a religious basis for war with Native Americans, the French Catholics, Nazis, and Communists. In response to the September 11, 2001, attacks, several studies found that American Christians dismissed theological similarities between themselves and Muslims and that such conscious decoupling contributed to their greater support for military action in Iraq (Cimino 2005; Smidt 2005; Uddin 2019). Joshua Wu and Austin Knuppe find that when Americans learn that the victims of violent oppression are Christians, they are more likely to support military intervention compared to when the victims are Muslim (2016). Robert Johns and Graeme Davies compare American and British support for military strikes against a hypothetical nation developing nuclear weapons and find that there is greater support for launching these strikes against Muslim nations as opposed to Christian nations. Furthermore, they find religion plays no role in British support for these actions, but higher American support for anti-Muslim strikes is driven by Christian subjects in their experiment (2012).

More fine-grained analysis of various religious traditions reveals differences in the visions for how America should engage the world. Alfred Hero's analysis of the relationship between religious affiliation and foreign policy attitudes over a three-decade period found that each religious tradition had a distinct position. Hero found that Catholics and Black Protestants were more isolationist than their White Protestant counterparts, but their policy preferences changed over time. Catholics became less supportive of militarism, while becoming more supportive of co-operative internationalism (1973). Other research has shown similar differences across different religious traditions (Daniels 2005; Guth 2010b; Taydas, Kentmen and Olson 2012), clergy (Hadden 1967; Quinley 1974; Tipton 2007), and political elites (Rosenson, Oldmixon and Wald 2009; Collins, et al. 2011). Amnon Cavari argues that these differences in foreign policy views have been exacerbated by increased party polarization among the traditions (2012). Scholars have also found differences across commitment levels. Comparative studies have found a positive link between frequency of religious practices and militarism at the individual and national level (Alexander 2017; Petrikova 2018). However, an examination of American attitudes finds that religious service attendance is linked to decreased support for militarism and more extreme actions, such as torture (Green 2007; Malka and Soto 2011; Kilburn and Fogarty 2015). Paul Djupe and Brian Calfano find that those who regularly attend worship services are more likely to be exposed to inclusive messages that may decrease their support for unilateralism. However, when exposed to messages emphasizing exclusivity, they are more likely to reject co-operative internationalism and support self-interested actions (2013a).

One of the most robust set of findings has been the connection between religious beliefs and foreign policy. Specifically, scholars argue that those who hold strict religious views, such as the inerrancy of their religious texts, are more likely to endorse militarism and express suspicion of co-operative internationalism (Williams, Bliss and McCallum 2006; McCleary and Williams 2009; Guth 2013). Others argue that the core values of Christian traditionalism contribute to support for militarism by encouraging hierarchical authoritarianism, dogmatism, and nationalism (Barker, Hurwitz and Nelson 2008). Much of the differences between White evangelical Protestants and other Christians can be traced to differences in beliefs (Jelen 1994; Guth, et al. 1996; Mayer 2004; Guth 2010b). Paul Froese and Cristopher Bader find that those who hold an authoritarian view of God are more likely to frame world events as a battle between good and evil, making military service a sacred duty (2010). Those who view God as benevolent see war as man failing God, while views of an authoritative God lead to more hawkish attitudes among Democrats (Thomson Jr and Froese 2016). This relationship is so strong that the level of support for militarism among Democrats who believe in an authoritative God is indistinguishable from Republicans who hold the same image. Most recently, Joseph Baker and Andrew Whitehead demonstrated that images of a masculine God is associated with greater support for military action (Baker and Whitehead 2020). This masculine image of God is reminiscent of the Christianity preached during the Revolutionary War, era of Liberal Imperialism, and the Cold War. Rebecca Glazier demonstrates that providential beliefs, the idea that there is a divine plan, make citizens more accepting of foreign policy initiatives framed in religious terms (2013). Finally, Americans who adopt a "sacralization ideology," a belief that religious and secular institutions should collaborate more closely, were more supportive of US policy in Iraq (Froese and Mencken 2009). We read these studies as confirming that religion, in its many varied forms, is a crucial element in shaping the structure of foreign policy attitudes.

5.4 AMERICAN RELIGIOUS NATIONALISM AND FOREIGN POLICY ATTITUDES

We expect American religious exceptionalism to be a robust contributor to foreign policy attitudes. Specifically, we view American religious exceptionalism as a structuring component in American public opinion. In line with research showing ethnocentrism is a core value that informs general postures, we think of exceptionalism as informing the three dimensions of foreign policy attitudes (Hurwitz and Peffley 1987; Kinder and Kam 2009). Because of their belief in the divinely ordained superiority of the nation, we expect those who score high on our exceptionalism measure to score low on measures of co-operative internationalism. We expect the opposite relationship regarding militarism. The belief of national superiority should be associated with a want to build a strong military as well as a higher likelihood of viewing military action as the preferred response to conflicts. Finally, American religious exceptionalism emphasizes the nation has a divine mission to complete. Because of this, we expect those who adhere to religious exceptionalism to be supportive of engaging the world. However, we believe the sense of superiority will encourage global engagement when it explicitly benefits the nation. Because of their placement on these three dimensions, we contend adherents of American religious exceptionalism will embrace the crusading spirit of foreign policy. Much like the efforts of the early twentieth century and the Bush era, we expect the disciples of religious exceptionalism to engage the world forcefully, but on their terms and always in line with a narrow reading of America and its interests.

5.5 ATTITUDES TOWARD THE MILITARY

We begin by examining the relationship between adherence to American religious exceptionalism and military service. Using data from 2018, we check first if respondents served in the military or if an immediate family member served. Disciples are most likely to report a personal or familial connection to the military (55.3 percent) though dissidents are not far behind at 49.1 percent and the laity is at 46 percent. These differences are not significant statistically, indicating there are no substantive differences in military service among these groups.

Moving to attitudes about the military and the use of military action, Figure 5.2 demonstrates the linkage between adherence to American religious exceptionalism and militarism. These results support the idea of God being a "man of war." In general, there is considerable support for the military among the various groupings. But, as expected, disciples hold the military in higher regard and are much more supportive of using it to solve problems. Beginning with the *militarism* measure ($\alpha = .64$; see Gravelle, Reifler and Scotto 2017), we find a laity scores significantly higher than a dissident and a disciple scores significantly higher than both. This pattern is consistent across all the various measures of militarism. Americans are generally supportive of having a strong military and accord some level of sanctity with the military; however, the disciples of American religious exceptionalism are more vociferous in their endorsement of military dominance and extolling the virtues of the military.

Moving to admiration of the military, we find evidence of the sacredness of duty. This result is based on our analysis of a *military conservatism* index ($\alpha = .71$), which measures support for male conscription, the importance of citizens sacrificing their lives for the nation, and honoring those who are willing to sacrifice (Philpot 2017). There is considerable support among each of the groupings, but a disciple is significantly more supportive of this ideology than a dissident or a laity. Along with these attitudes toward the military and the need for military power, we

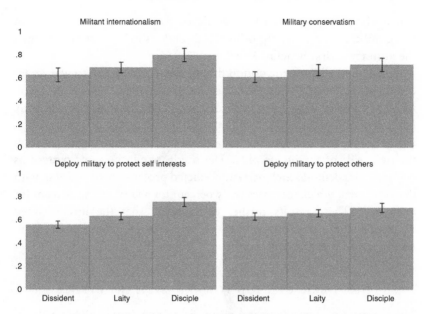

FIGURE 5.2 Predicted values and probabilities of support for militant internationalism, military conservativism, and reasons for military action
Note: Predicted probabilities and values were generated using coefficient estimates from logit and OLS regression models that control for biblical literalism, religious tradition, religious importance, worship attendance, personal demographics, and political ideology. Shaded areas mark the estimated 95 percent confidence intervals.

are also concerned with when citizens think the military should be deployed. Specifically, we are interested in support for the deployment of the military in situations directly benefitting the nation and situations where military intervention may be more in aid of others. To get at these different motivations for the use of force, we created two indices that address deploying the military for national self-interest and deploying it for the interest of others. The *self-interest* measure ($\alpha = .59$) addresses support for sending the military to protect the oil supply, to destroy terrorist camps, and to spread democracy. The *selfless* measure ($\alpha = .55$) captures support for defending allies, intervening in genocides and civil wars, and upholding international law. We find that a disciple of American religious exceptionalism scores higher on both measures but the gap between disciples and dissidents is larger for the self-interest measure than for the selfless measure. These findings indicate that even though a disciple is more supportive of military action in general, who benefits from the action matters. While a dissident is more supportive of using military force to help others, a disciple is most supportive when the military action benefits America.

To examine directly the notion that God supports going to war under certain conditions, we analyze agreement with the statement, "God requires the faithful to wage wars for good." The statement taps directly into the notion of the nation's military actions being part of a divine plan. Furthermore, it emphasizes the innocence of the nation by arguing it is on the right side of the divine plan. The results show the same pattern as before: a dissident has an 8 percent predicted probability of agreeing with this statement, which increases to 15 percent for a laity and 32 percent for a disciple. These results further demonstrate that the link between American religious exceptionalism and support for militarism is via an image of a God of war and wrath.

5.6 PUBLIC OPINION TOWARD MILITARY EVENTS

The analysis thus far investigates respondents' reactions to abstract global issues and how the nation should use the military; however, our interest is in how adherence to religious exceptionalism is related to attitudes about specific military operations that have shaped the nation's political landscape. Figure 5.3 provides the results from examining the linkage between religious exceptionalism and attitudes about the role of the military in Iraq, Afghanistan, and Iran.

Even though Americans express admiration for the military, they became increasingly frustrated with some of the nation's recent military operations. In March 2005, Gallup found that 23 percent of Americans believed sending the troops to Iraq was a mistake, whereas by August 2010, 55 percent of Americans believed this. In November 2001, two months after the September 11 attacks, Gallup found that only 9 percent of Americans believed sending troops to Afghanistan was a mistake, whereas by November 2010, 39 percent believed it was a mistake. Overall, respondents were highly supportive of withdrawing troops from Iraq as 81 percent of them agreed with this action. However, our multivariate analyses find that a dissident is more supportive of this policy than a laity and a disciple. The support for removing troops from Afghanistan was close to three-fourths even in 2010. The less controversial nature of the invasion of Afghanistan may explain why there are no significant differences between the groups. We suspect disciples were much more enthusiastic about invading Iraq in the first instance, and

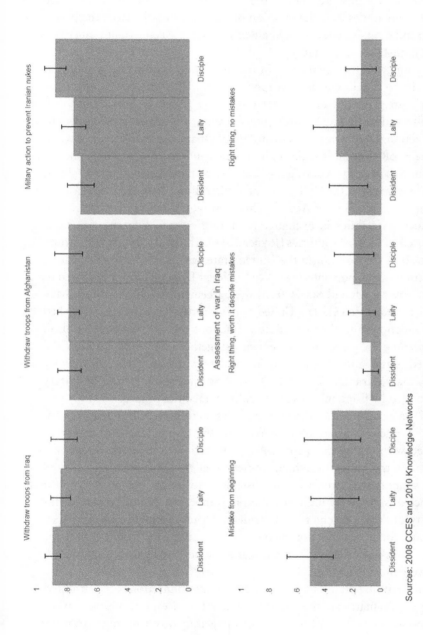

FIGURE 5.3 Predicted probabilities of support for US military actions

Note: Predicted probabilities and values were generated using coefficient estimates from logit and OLS regression models that control for biblical literalism, religious tradition, religious importance, worship attendance, personal demographics, and political ideology. Shaded areas mark the estimated 95 percent confidence intervals.

Sources: 2008 CCES and 2010 Knowledge Networks

supporting withdrawal is tantamount to admitting that the decision to do so had been a mistake. Indeed our analysis shows that dissidents were most likely to describe the invasion of Iraq as a mistake from the beginning, and disciples were most likely to say that it was the right thing to do even if mistakes were made.

Another international crisis in recent years concerns Iran's increased capacity to develop nuclear weapons. Within US policy circles, there has been a great deal of debate over the proper response. Some, like 2008 presidential candidate Senator John McCain, called for immediate military action. In contrast, President Barack Obama, who defeated McCain in the 2008 election, sought a diplomatic route to control Iran's nuclear armament. In 2015, working the United Kingdom, Russia, France, China, and Germany, the Obama administration brokered the Joint Comprehensive Plan of Action. This plan would require Iran to reduce its nuclear facilities in exchange for lifting certain economic sanctions imposed by various countries (Joyner 2016). The deal was met with strong opposition on the right in the United States as many saw it as placating a hostile state. Upon entering office President Donald Trump promised to withdraw the United States from the agreement, which he did in May 2018 (Landler 2018). The United States shortly thereafter reestablished past sanctions and then issued new sanctions on Iran, which led to Iran threatening to leave the agreement altogether. Tensions between the United States and Iran peaked in January 2020 after the US military assassinated Iranian General Qassem Soleimani, and Iran's military responded by firing missiles at US military facilities in Iraq.

When asked in 2010 about military action to prevent Iran from advancing its nuclear program, 73 percent of the respondents to our survey agreed with taking this action. An examination of support for military action on the Iran issue and adherence to religious exceptionalism found that support was driven by the disciples. A disciple has an 88 percent chance of supporting military action in Iran, compared to 76 percent for a laity and 71 percent for a dissident. Given disciples' near-universal support for military action against Iran in 2010, we would expect the champions of President Trump's aggressive posture against Iranian leaders were most likely disciples.

The bottom half of Figure 5.3 addresses the connection between adherence and evaluation of the 2003 invasion of Iraq. Respondents were asked to choose from five options: (1) Invading Iraq was a mistake from the beginning; (2) it was a mistake, but worth the costs; (3) it was the right thing, but mistakes were too costly; (4) it was the right thing despite mistakes; and (5) it was the right thing and there were no mistakes. The plurality choice among the respondents was that it was a mistake from the beginning with 44 percent choosing this option, followed by 23 percent stating it was the right thing and worth it despite the mistakes. The respondents were least likely to indicate that it was the right thing with no mistakes as only 5 percent chose this option. We display the three most interesting results regarding how adherence to American religious exceptionalism is related to the evaluation of the Iraq invasion. The strongest finding from these analyses is that a dissident has a significantly higher probability of believing the invasion was a mistake from the beginning compared to a laity or a disciple. A disciple, on the other hand, is more likely to think the invasion was the right thing to do despite the mistakes. Finally, the probability a respondent thinks the invasion was right and there were no mistakes is low across the board.

The United States invaded Iraq under false pretenses about the presence of weapons of mass destruction in March 2003. The ensuing war lasted almost a decade with almost 5,000 American casualties and hundreds of thousands of Iraqi deaths, mostly civilians. In our survey, conducted in 2010, a year before the war formally ended, dissidents, laity, and disciples agree mistakes were made, but disciples were more likely to try to defend the invasion, albeit only lukewarmly. These findings reveal the upper bounds of support for costly interventions are defined by adherence to religious exceptionalism. Publics in general are unlikely to support costly and protracted wars, especially in the modern era where measurable victories no longer exist, as the ignominious end to the Afghanistan conflict underscores. In the political environment following the Iraq War, when an entire nation was exasperated by an unattainable victory alongside numerous deaths in the name of fictional weapons of mass destruction and an unsubstantiated link to Iraq's involvement in the September 11 attacks, it takes a true believer to justify military intervention.

5.6.1 Views on International Co-operation

Our analysis of co-operative internationalism, reported in Figure 5.4, demonstrates that while disciples are not more opposed to the abstract notion of co-operation, they are more opposed to specific instances of co-operation. Starting with the *co-operative internationalism* scale ($\alpha = .71$), we find only small differences between the three groups, though disciples appear most open to co-operative internationalism here. However, our

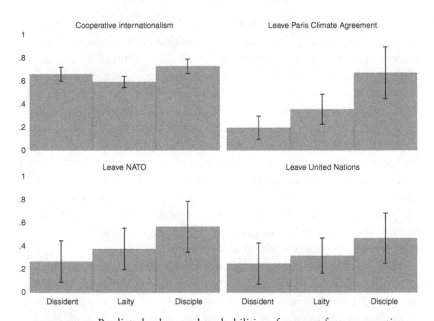

FIGURE 5.4 Predicted values and probabilities of support for co-operative internationalism, US withdrawal from international organization, and unilateral action given adherence to American religious exceptionalism
Note: Predicted probabilities and values were generated using coefficient estimates from logit and OLS regression models that control for biblical literalism, religious tradition, religious importance, worship attendance, personal demographics, and political ideology. Shaded areas mark the estimated 95 percent confidence intervals.

examination of specific acts of co-operation reveals a contradictory pattern.

When asked about memberships in formal multilateral partnerships, such as the North Atlantic Treaty Organization (NATO) and the United Nations (UN), disciples are most open to withdrawing from them. President Trump, who has openly courted the hardcore adherents of American religious exceptionalism, openly criticized the nation's international partnerships, even going so far as threatening to leave the United Nations, NATO, and the Open Skies Treaty. Furthermore, during the height of the coronavirus pandemic in 2020, he announced America's withdrawal from the World Health Organization, which he accused of being beholden to hostile nations and not being forthright with information about the virus. This move was promptly reversed when President Biden came into office.[11] Our analyses find that President Trump would receive a high level of support from the disciples for leaving NATO and other international institutions. The disciples are significantly more likely to support this move than the dissidents and the laity. A disciple has 57 percent probability of supporting such a move, which is more than twice that of a dissident. This pattern is the same for leaving the United Nations. The laity and dissidents are significantly less likely to support this move than the disciples. Furthermore, the probability of a disciple supporting this policy is almost twice that of a dissident.

The 2016 Paris Climate Agreement serves as a specific case of the nation coming into conflict with the United Nations over environmental policy. The agreement, which calls on nations to commit to policies that reduce greenhouse gas emissions to combat climate change, has been portrayed by climate-change skeptics as a threat to the domestic energy sector. President Trump announced in June 2017 his intention to withdraw the United States from this landmark agreement (Shear 2017). This was another policy move that President Biden quickly reversed once in office. Consistent with our earlier results, the disciples are the ones leading support for Trump's policy. A disciple is three times more likely to support leaving an international agreement than is a dissident and almost twice as high as a laity. Even though we initially found disciples to be supportive of the abstract notion of co-operative internationalism, over and over, our examination of actual foreign policy options demonstrates the disciples are more supportive of unilateral action and quite wary of any multilateral collaboration. Their support for co-operative internationalism may stem from the attitude that they are willing to work with other nations, but only if the United States dictates all decisions.[12]

Another example of American resistance to co-operative internationalism is endorsement of President Trump's decision to recognize Jerusalem as the capital of Israel. The city of Jerusalem has been a primary contention in the Israeli–Palestinian conflict. The city is of sacred importance to Jews, Christians, and Muslims. When President Trump made the announcement, he was rebuked by the international community, which regarded the decision as dangerous and a threat to peace in the Middle East. Domestically, the president was understood to be catering to demands of pro-Israel groups and evangelical Protestants (Landler 2017). Evangelicals see the recognition of Jerusalem as Israel's capital as critical to completing a biblical prophecy linked to millennialism (Lewis 2010). A majority of respondents (57 percent) to the 2018 CCES supported this move, the bulk of whom we classify as belonging to the laity and disciple groupings based on their affinity to American religious exceptionalism. Interestingly this was one of the few Trump foreign policy stances that President Biden did not reverse immediately upon being sworn in. Given the high levels of partisan polarization along religious lines, the extent to which this endeared him to the laity and disciples is most likely minimal at best.

An additional measure of support for co-operative internationalism is the willingness to enter trade partnerships. For the early US republic, maintaining trade partnerships allowed the burgeoning nation to sustain itself and become a global power. Because of this, trade policy has been relevant to elites along with the masses. Those who ascribe to liberal international relations theory argue that strong trade partnerships can reduce hostilities, because the nations become entwined and harm to one may cause harm to the other (Mansfield and Pollins 2001; Russett and Oneal 2001). The reduction of conflict may have national benefits, but the citizens of the nations may be more resistant to trade depending on their personal circumstances. At the individual level self-interest and predispositions influence support for trade liberalization. Those who see themselves as the losers in these agreements are more resistant to elite rhetoric in favor of these agreements (Kleinberg and Fordham 2010; Rudra, Nooruddin, and Bonifai 2021). Additionally, attitudes regarding trust in others and assumptions of national supremacy are also linked to opposing trade liberalization (Daniels and von der Ruhr 2005; Hainmueller and Hiscox 2006; Kaltenthaler and Miller 2014). Furthermore, the economic uncertainty brought about by globalization has encouraged a rise in religious nationalism (Kinnvall 2004). Since the early nineties, Americans have become increasingly supportive of foreign trade with 70 percent of Americans believing it was an opportunity for growth in 2018 (Jones 2018b); however, there has been consistent opposition to it among religious conservatives (von der Ruhr and Daniels 2003; Daniels and von der Ruhr 2005; Guth 2010a). During his presidential campaign, Donald Trump tapped into this distrust by consistently targeting free trade agreements as one of the evils limiting the nation's greatness.

Our analysis of the linkage between adherence to American religious exceptionalism and trade policy demonstrates that Trump's opposition to trade liberalization had fans among the disciples of American religious exceptionalism. Figure 5.5 demonstrates disciples consistently express a disdain for free trade and support increasing tariffs on imported goods. When asked to choose between promoting free trade and implementing more trade restrictions, we find that the disciples lean toward restrictions more than the dissidents and laity. Even with this higher level

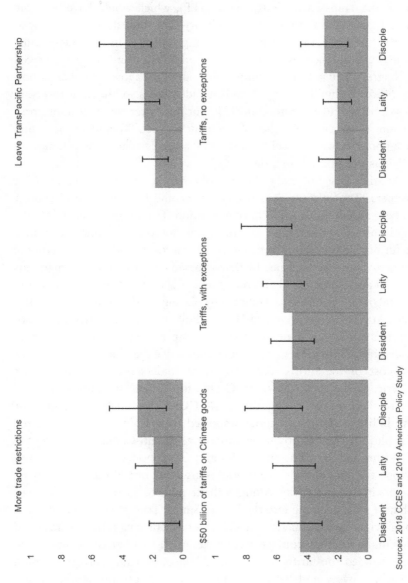

FIGURE 5.5 Probabilities of support for trade policy given adherence to American religious exceptionalism

Note: Predicted probabilities and values were generated using coefficient estimates from logit and OLS regression models that control for biblical literalism, religious tradition, religious importance, worship attendance, personal demographics, and political ideology. Shaded areas mark the estimated 95 percent confidence intervals.

Sources: 2018 CCES and 2019 American Policy Study

of support, there is still a less than one in three chance that a disciple will choose restrictions over free trade, which underscores that free trade in the abstract still enjoys widespread popular support. We next move to feelings about the Trans-Pacific Partnership (TPP), which would have been the largest regional trade agreement in history. The trade deal was developed as a method to counter China's growing influence in the Indo-Pacific. While championed by the Obama administration, it never faced a Congressional vote and Trump pulled out of the agreement once assuming office (Granville 2017). President Biden has also hinted at reversing this decision and reentering the TPP, but only after concerns about protections for workers and the environment are met. We find a progression in support for withdrawal from the TPP as one's adherence to American religious exceptionalism grows.

Another aspect of trade is the use of tariffs in negotiating with trading partners. Tariffs serve as a source of income for nations and protect domestic products from foreign competition. Trump has employed tariffs, specifically aimed at China, in a futile attempt to revive American manufacturing. However, this tactic has come at a cost as several sections of the economy have been harmed by the increased costs of importing materials (Flaaen and Pierce 2019). Trump ignited a US trade war with China and several other nations who retaliated by placing tariffs on American goods. The August 2019 Harvard-Harris Poll found that two-thirds of Americans think it is necessary for Trump to confront China over its trade policy; however, 74 percent acknowledge that Americans will bear the cost of the tariffs and 63 percent understand that tariffs hurt Americans the most (Harvard Center for American Political Studies/ Harris Poll 2019). Using the 2018 CCES, we analyze support for $50 billion in tariffs on goods imported from China and find that the disciples are significantly more supportive of anti-China tariffs than the dissidents and laity. But support for anti-China policy is widespread even among the laity and dissidents, and is arguably one of the only unifying factors in America today. Along with attempts to decrease the volume of Chinese goods coming into the United States, Trump has also attempted to reinvigorate the American steel industry by placing tariffs on steel and aluminum products from select countries in March of 2018. In June 2018, he expanded the tariffs to Canada, Mexico, and the European Union (Lynch, Dawsey and Paletta 2018). Eventually, certain nations would become exempt and return to the status quo, but, in the interim, many noted the negative economic impact on the United States from these tariffs (Long 2019). Our analysis of the public's attitudes toward the steel and aluminum tariffs finds that Americans are more supportive of the tariffs when exceptions are made for Canada, Mexico, and the European Union. This remains the case when examining how adherence to American religious exceptionalism relates to these attitudes. Consistent with our earlier findings, the disciples are more likely to express support for these tariffs than the dissidents. Finally, when asked about implementing the tariffs with no exceptions, we find much lower support and no significant differentiation between the categories. These tariffs were another policy that President Biden had been looking to reverse; however, changes in the global economy due to the on-going COVID-19 pandemic, a sputtering domestic economy, and a challenging legislative landscape leaves the Biden administration limited room to maneuver as it seeks to balance the desire to foster foreign partnerships with the imperative of securing domestic jobs (Lynch 2021).

5.6.2 Isolationism Beliefs

The last dimension of foreign policy attitudes we examine is isolationism. The United States has often been criticized for its isolationist inclination. This tendency was even stronger during the Trump presidency, a central tenet of which was "America First," which was manifested by a series of actions of reneging on international commitments and posturing with China and the European Union. However, one of the tenets of American religious exceptionalism is that the United States has an imperative to save the world from its evils. This has contributed to the nation taking on the role of a crusader state and attempting drastically to change the world into its own image. However, some have argued that engaging the world will tarnish the image of the nation.

Disciples are more supportive of isolationism in the abstract, but believe that the nation has a responsibility to the world (see Figure 5.6). They score significantly higher than the dissidents and laity on the *isolationism* measure ($\alpha = .77$), indicating support for the nation keeping to itself and staying out of the problems of other nations. However, when asked about the nation's responsibilities to the world, we see a rejection of isolationism and support for the belief that the United States has numerous obligations to the world, specifically regarding the spread of democracy, capitalism, and freedom. In the 2012 Religious Worldviews Survey, respondents placed themselves between two statements about the global role of the nation. One of the statements posited that the nation had a responsibility to the world, while the other argued that the nation

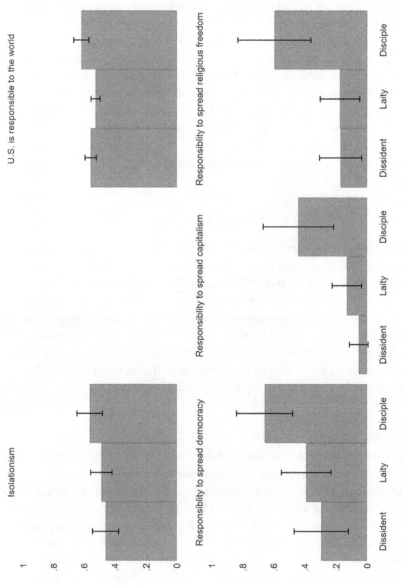

FIGURE 5.6 Predicted values and probabilities of support for isolationism and belief that the United States has a responsibility to spread certain values to the world given adherence to American religious exceptionalism

Note: Predicted probabilities and values were generated using coefficient estimates from logit and OLS regression models that control for biblical literalism, religious tradition, religious importance, worship attendance, personal demographics, and political ideology. Shaded areas mark the estimated 95 percent confidence intervals.

would be better off if it stayed home. Lower values indicate that respondents prefer the United States staying at home, while higher values indicate they feel closer to feeling the United States has a responsibility to the world. The predicted values indicate a dissident and a laity do not lean toward either option, while a disciple leans toward a global responsibility for the nation.

When we ask if the nation has the responsibility to spread specific values to the world, we do witness large differences. The respondents were asked if they agreed the United States had a responsibility to spread democracy, capitalism, and freedom of religion to the world. These three themes have been central planks in the nation's crusade to save the world. The results demonstrate that the disciples of religious exceptionalism have a significantly greater chance of agreeing that the nation has a responsibility to spread each of these values than the dissidents and laity. The gap between the dissidents and disciples regarding these obligations ranges between 37 and 43 percentage points. The high level of support among the disciples for these crusading values suggests their support for isolationism is conditional. If the need to engage the world is to promote American values, isolationism is not an option. Because of this, leaders constantly invoke these values as justifications for engaging the world, whether it be through military action, diplomacy, or trade.

5.7 CONCLUSION

Our empirical findings reinforce our argument of the power of religious exceptionalism in the United States, especially in its ability to shape American foreign policy attitudes. We find strong statistical evidence that religious exceptionalism is associated with attitudes across three dimensions: militarism, co-operative internationalism, and overall preferences toward engagement with the international community. Disciples of religious exceptionalism voice significantly more support for the military than dissidents – in the abstract sense of pure admiration for the institution as well as in the specific sense of supporting US military operations and military-led invasions. Next, disciples express less support for using the military to aid other countries and tend only to support co-operative internationalism when the benefits to the United States are immediate and obvious. Finally, disciples clearly prefer that the United States engage the world rather than isolate itself from global affairs, reflecting their commitment to evangelizing the American way-of-life to the rest of the world.

It is hard to overstate the importance of religious exceptionalism to its disciples' view of American foreign engagement. While the ideology powerfully shapes attitudes and behaviors across domestic and foreign policy realms alike, disciples can ultimately look upon American foreign policy to accomplish the nation's divine mission: to spread national values to the rest of the world. Because of this, its disciples strongly link their views of America's divinity to nearly blind support for the nation's military endeavors, especially when these operations place America first. This chapter reveals the popularity of political actions in the name of national narcissism. However, it also works to dispel the notion all America First supporters favor isolationism. If anything, disciples welcome engagement with the global community, but only as long as there are resources to be gained for God's nation.

6

Governing the Temple

Let every person be subject to the governing authorities. For there is no authority except from God, and those that exist have been instituted by God. . . . For rulers are not a terror to good conduct, but to bad. Would you have no fear of the one who is in authority? Then do what is good, and you will receive his approval, for he is God's servant for your good. But if you do wrong, be afraid, for he does not bear the sword in vain. For he is the servant of God, an avenger who carries out God's wrath on the wrongdoer.

Romans 13: 1, 3-4

The Constitution of the United States, for instance, is a marvelous document for self-government by Christian people. But the minute you turn the document into the hands of non-Christian and atheistic people they can use it to destroy the very foundation of our society.

Pat Robertson, The 700 Club, Dec 30, 1981

Disciples of American religious exceptionalism view the nation as a sacred place worthy of worship. For them, the nation is a temple where they can engage in worship and celebrate the divine greatness of the nation. By displaying the flag, honoring the military, and fiercely upholding their preferred national traditions, disciples demonstrate their fealty to the nation and gratitude for its divine blessings. On the other hand, there are the dissidents who reject the idea of the nation being sacred or having a divine place in the world. They are less concerned with outward displays of commitment and express greater openness to the world. The preceding chapters illuminated how disciples and dissidents define the "true" members of the American congregation along with who can gain access to the temple. Furthermore, we established where disciples stand on how the American nation-as-temple and its congregants should engage the world. This chapter explains how the dissidents and disciples believe the temple should be governed. Specifically, we examine beliefs about how the temple should be led and how to interpret the relationship between the congregation, the American public, and its clerics – America's political leaders. Furthermore, we examine which gospel disciples and dissidents believe should be preached, expressed through ideological preferences, along with their preferences for a national religious sect (political party), and for a high priest of the nation (presidential vote choice). Finally, we examine the work of the disciples; their commitment to worship has been demonstrated, but what is their commitment to the promotion and maintenance of the temple? To do this, we utilize our rich survey data to explicate how Americans believe the nation should structure its decision-making, the ideologies they believe should guide the nation, as well as their partisan commitments, vote choice, and leader evaluation. By understanding how its adherents want the temple governed, we can better understand where to situate religious exceptionalism in the larger discussion of American politics.

6.1 TYPES OF GOVERNANCE

The divergence between dissidents and the disciples about how best to govern the nation is illuminated by comparing support for various modes of governance. Max Weber's seminal definition of the state as a political organization that "claims the monopoly of the legitimate use of physical force" (1946, p. 76) would suggest that we need to understand how the public views decisions to use force in order to comprehend the public's beliefs about how the nation should be governed. The United States has long prized itself as the beacon of democracy and, as Chapter 5 demonstrated, disciples of American religious exceptionalism strongly believe it is the nation's duty to spread the good news of democracy to the world, at gunpoint if need be. Direct democracy is the classical vision we have of democracy; however, scholars such as E. E. Schattschneider have noted it asks too much of citizens and is not a realistic form of governance (1975). Elite maneuvering and intellectual support for an elite-based democratic system resulted in modern mass democracies choosing varieties of republican forms of governance. This system frees citizens from the mundane day-to-day decisions about government, while providing them the routine power to choose who will make these decisions. Additionally, the nation delegated different decision-making powers to separate institutions to prevent one set of decision-makers from dictating the nation's path. The Founders created a set of checks and balances they hoped would make it difficult for the whims of one institution to go unchecked by another. This system stands in stark contrast to other forms of government, such as autocracies and oligarchies. In autocracies, such as dictatorships and monarchies, the power of the government is concentrated in the hands of a single person or party, and the executive's decisions are not limited by the laws or the public. In an oligarchy, decisions are made by a ruling few. Those who enjoy status as members of the power elite are chosen for certain attributes, such as family heritage, religion, or military authority (Winters 2011). For instance, in a theocracy the ruling elite are chosen from the ranks of religious institutions, while in a stratocracy they are chosen from the military.

The content of American religious exceptionalism ideology pulls its adherents in conflicting directions. Even though disciples champion the spread of liberal democratic ("American") values, we expect them also to express antidemocratic attitudes. Their uncritical patriotism and higher levels of social dominance orientation indicate they may support democracy in theory, but not necessarily in practice, especially when to do so might endanger American interests or challenge the inherent legitimacy of American leadership.

To examine how adherence to American religious exceptionalism influences support for various forms of government, our surveys asked respondents to indicate whether they believed certain forms of government are good or bad. The results, presented in Figure 6.1, demonstrate that they are equally supportive of direct and representative democracy. Furthermore, they are all significantly more supportive of representative democracy than direct democracy. However, when we move to nondemocratic forms of government, we find significant differences, as increased adherence is associated with greater support for autocratic and oligarchic forms of government.

In our 2019 survey, we find, quite troublingly, that disciples and the laity – high and moderate adherents of American religious exceptionalism, respectively – are willing to countenance supporting a strong leader who can make decisions without interference from Congress or the Courts. These respondents are also more supportive of technocracies (let experts lead) and stratocracies (let the military lead). Technocracies are oligarchic forms of government where those with high levels of education and skill make decisions. A disciple has a 72 percent probability of supporting this notion followed by a laity at 52 percent and a dissident at 31 percent. This

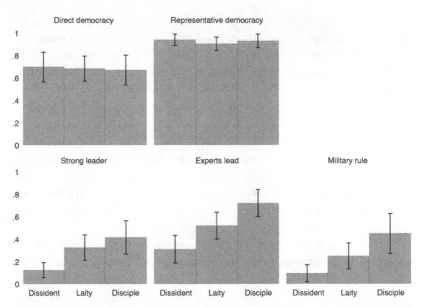

FIGURE 6.1 Predicted probabilities of support for various forms of government given adherence to American religious exceptionalism
Note: Predicted probabilities were generated using coefficient estimates from logit regression models that control for biblical literalism, religious tradition, religious importance, worship attendance, personal demographics, and political ideology. Capped lines mark the estimated 95 percent confidence intervals.

relationship may be a bit surprising given that disciples have been known to be skeptical of academic and professional elites. However, it is important to note that the statement discusses taking the decision power away from politicians, which would indicate a greater distrust for politicians than of experts. Indeed, further analysis of populist attitudes will illuminate the distrust the disciples have of politicians. Finally, we find that increased adherence to American religious exceptionalism is associated with significantly higher probability of believing military rule is good. A dissident is markedly opposed to this as she has a 9 percent chance of supporting this form of government; however, a laity is more open to it with a 24 percent probability. Fitting with the previous results, we see that a dissident is most open to this with 44 percent probability. Even though these results indicate a nondemocratic bias among the disciples, it is important to recall that disciples' support for representative democracy is significantly higher than their support for these nondemocratic forms of government. Still, the disciples' openness to alternative undemocratic forms of government is indeed unique to them as a group and fits with research that has found this group to be opposed to democratic ideals, especially when they lose power (Parker and Barreto 2013; Stewart 2019).

6.2 THE RELATIONSHIP BETWEEN THE PRIESTS AND THE CONGREGATION

We have established an important foundation for this chapter: disciples have authoritarian and nondemocratic tendencies, but they are still most likely to support democratic rule. Part of the support for democratic forms of government comes from American religious exceptionalism's emphasis on the myth of the innocence of the nation and its "true" members. This myth paints a portrait of an idyllic relationship between government and citizens where the leaders and the masses are pure and mutually engaged in advancing the greatness of the nation. This emphasis on purity contributes to populist attitudes, which argues that the problems of the nation are not due to policy complexities, but due to impurities in the leadership. Populist rhetoric is routinely associated with nationalism as both seek to cleanse the nation. Benjamin De Cleen notes the similarities between the two, specifically separating the world into distinct groups and emphasizing sovereignty (2017). But while nationalism's focus is the nation, populism's focus is the people. Furthermore, scholars contend populism is a "thin" ideology, meaning that it is limited in the political questions it can address compared to thick ideologies that offer a broad and coherent set of responses to political questions (Stanley 2008; Bonikowski 2016; Wettstein, et al. 2016). In the twentieth century, southern politicians such as Huey Long and George Wallace combined their populism with the ideology of White supremacy to cement their power in Louisiana and Alabama, respectively (Lee 2006). In the 2016 election, populism made a comeback as candidates from both parties preached their own versions. Senator Bernie Sanders (D-Vermont), who lost out to Secretary Hillary Clinton for the Democratic presidential nomination, paired socialism with populism, arguing passionately for the need to scour government of corporate influence and provide the masses with what they truly earned. The Republican Party nominated Donald Trump, who promised to "drain the swamp" of Washington, DC, and to take the fight to corrupt politicians who he accused of betraying America. His effective pairing of populism with nationalism appealed to White grievants about their place in modern America and allowed him to secure the Republican Party's nomination and eventually the presidency (Gusterson 2017; Bonikowski 2019).

At its core, populism advances three distinct ideas about the homogeneity of the people, the corruption of elites, and the importance of unrestrained popular sovereignty (Wettstein, et al. 2016). Populists believe the people are virtuous and have a common cause and are more than willing to contribute to the good of the nation. Elites, by contrast, are corrupt and seek to subvert the gains of the people for their own selfish interests, endangering the nation. Finally, populists believe power should be taken from the elites and restored to the people to put the nation on the right track. It is the presence of these three attitudinal dimensions that animate populist attitudes and direct the populist ideology. Accordingly, we utilize a three-dimensional measure of populism to examine the relationship between American religious exceptionalism and populism. Disciples of religious exceptionalism are always alert for any attempts to corrupt the people. This is what fuels their highly restrictive definition of who is truly American along with their suspicion of immigrants. The emphasis on purity is extended to leadership as leaders who do not fit their definition of what it means to be an American are viewed as dangers. A prime example is Article Two of the US Constitution limiting eligibility for the Office of the Presidency to "natural-born citizens." A more contemporary example is the outrage and discomfort many Americans expressed over the increasing number of Muslims being elected to local, state, and national offices.[1] Furthermore, populists seek to maintain or increase the sovereignty of the nation, through avoiding long-standing international agreements as well as maintaining a superior military. Conspiracy theories that the sovereign power of the people is being undermined by shadowy international cabals of bankers and UN diplomats fuel righteous populist calls to defend the nation against foreigners.

All of this leads us to expect that the disciples of American religious exceptionalism are more likely to identify with these three dimensions of populism. To test this claim we employ a three-dimensional index to gauge support for populism.[2] Each dimension is measured using a scale of four attitudinal items. The *belief in a virtuous people* scale ($\alpha = .74$) is comprised of beliefs about the homogeneity of the people, their shared values, their ability to pull together, and how they define good character. The *anti-elite* scale ($\alpha = .59$) consists of beliefs that members of Congress lose touch with ordinary people, that differences between the elites and the people are larger than the differences between the people, that ordinary people have no influence, and that politicians talk instead of act. The *sovereignty of the people* scale (α = .77) is comprised of attitudes regarding giving the people the final say, asking the people about important issues, giving the people decision-making power instead of politicians, and the need for members of Congress to follow the will of the people. Across these survey items, which tend to receive quite a lot of support across respondents, disciples score highest, demonstrating their affinity to populism.[3]

Americans in general all hold "the people" in high regard, but disciples score significantly higher on this dimension. However, given the results from the analysis in the earlier chapters, the image of who exactly are "the people" likely differs across respondents. The same pattern emerges when examining anti-elitism. All our respondents score high on this dimension, demonstrating the general suspicion Americans have toward elites, but this suspicion is significantly stronger among the disciples than it is among the laity and dissidents. The largest gap concerns the sovereignty of the people, which receives the greatest emphasis and support from disciples relative to other respondents. This further demonstrates the commitment to populism among the disciples. Given the popularity of "taking our country back" rhetoric among the disciples of religious exceptionalism, we should not be surprised they seek greater influence over the nation's decisions. These findings suggest the disciples are populists; but populism is a short-term ideology used to help groups gain power (Bonikowski 2016). It is effective only if the group believes its voice is not heard or if they feel threatened. This is partly why President Trump's re-election campaign slogan switched from "Make America Great Again" to "Keep America Great."[4] Furthermore, it was his populist rhetoric that encouraged the belief among his supporters that the 2020 election was stolen from him – and by extension, therefore, from them – and the violence that ensued, culminating in the attack on the US Capitol on January 6, 2021.

6.3 THE GOSPEL OF AMERICAN RELIGIOUS EXCEPTIONALISM

Understanding populism illuminates how disciples and dissidents view their relationship to the government and its leadership; however, populism's ability to explain policy preferences is limited. In this section, we examine how American religious exceptionalism affects attachment to political ideologies. Chapter 2 demonstrated that disciples are more likely to identify as conservatives when asked to identify themselves on a unidimensional scale. This is helpful, but incomplete. As Tasha Philpot demonstrates, a person may be conservative in one area but liberal in another (2017). Thus, it is important to note how adherence to American religious exceptionalism correlates with certain ideological dimensions. This chapter examines attachment to four distinct political ideologies: social welfare, religious conservativism, laissez-faire, and racial conservativism. Each of these measures is comprised of three items related to how government should behave. The *social welfare* scale ($\alpha = .78$) is comprised of items regarding the government's duty to protect the less fortunate even in the face of debt. The *religious conservatism* ($\alpha = .83$) items assess support for the government's active promotion of religious instruction, increasing religious influence, and governing based on biblical principles. The *laissez-faire* scale ($\alpha = .74$) consists of items related to the belief government regulation, involvement, and management is detrimental to society. Finally, the *racial conservatism* scale ($\alpha = .69$) represents the belief that government should not be involved in solving racial inequalities and that groups calling for government support are overly dependent. These dimensions represent only a few of the ideological dimensions that exist, but we believe they provide a well-rounded picture of what the disciples want from their government.

We expect adherence to American religious exceptionalism to be associated with attitudes placing greater blame on the individual than on the nation. Because the nation is perceived as pure and innocent, any problems individuals may experience are their own fault. Furthermore, we expect the disciples to perceive those who are not successful or require government help to be deviants. Much like James Morone's (2003) discussion of the Puritan tradition in American politics and policy, we believe the disciples will see little reason for government involvement in people's lives, unless it is to reinforce proper behavior. As such, we expect the disciples to be less supportive of government action in the areas of social welfare and racial equality and more supportive of a laissez-faire approach to policy. The exception will be in support for government assistance in advancing religious teaching, because disciples believe religious education fosters good citizenship. Our data confirm these expectations. For example, increased adherence to American religious exceptionalism is associated with increased support for government advancing religious instruction and protecting religious traditions. President Trump's attempts to make prayer a part of the school day sits well with the disciples as they believe this is part of the government's role.[5] Interestingly, there are no significant differences regarding the role of the government in the economy. The predicted values for a person in each of these categories are relatively high, comporting with the popular notion that Americans generally support free markets over government involvement in economic affairs. Finally, our analysis of racial conservatism confirms that an increase in adherence is associated with opposing the government having a role in solving racial equality issues. In this case, the dissidents score significantly lower than both the laity and disciples. This result corresponds well with the findings in Chapter 3, which revealed the positive relationship between adherence and White animus toward racial minorities.

6.4 SECTS AND HIGH PRIESTS

Having established a clear disciple–dissident gap in preferences in government types, understandings about relationships between the people and government, and visions of the ideal function of government, we turn now to partisanship. Partisan identities are critical to representative politics because they provide frameworks by which citizens and leaders can make sense of and express their expectations for government and policy issue stances (Campbell, et al. 1960; Aldrich 1995; Philpot 2017). Even though the Founding Fathers frowned on the idea of political parties, which they worried would divide the nation, parties ultimately served a critical purpose in helping decision-makers to work together and elect candidates to office (Aldrich 1995). Throughout American history, for issues ranging from centralizing the government to slavery, regulating the railroads to the gold standard, all the way to today's culture wars, political parties have taken sides and deliberated fiercely (Chambers 1972; Aldrich 1995; Campbell 2006). The public has in turn taken cues from these impassioned debates, and the result has been the American public's enduring attachment to partisanship (Campbell, et al. 1960). Given the centrality of parties in American political life, it is important to understand how adherence to American religious exceptionalism correlates with party identification.

Over the past half-century, we have observed a re-sorting of the parties along religious grounds. Whereas in the early part of the twentieth century religious groups were spread out among the parties, today we see a clear delineation between religious and partisan groups. The relationship between the most ardent supporters of American religious exceptionalism, White evangelical Protestants, and the Republican Party has crystallized (Green 1996; Layman 2001; McDaniel and Ellison 2008; Compton 2020). Many of the prominent disciples of American religious exceptionalism, such as Billy and Franklin Graham, have developed a strong and public partnership with Republican leaders. In 1988, Pat Robertson sought the nomination for president in the Republican primary with a campaign that tightly entwined his vision of the government with conservative Christian values (Johnson, Tamney and Burton 1989; Compton 2020). Furthermore, Republican candidates have actively sought the support of the disciples by employing increasingly religious rhetoric and actively engaging in culture wars (Layman 2001; Domke and Coe 2008; Keddie 2020). President Ronald Reagan is noted for bringing religious elites into the fold by actively using language connecting the nation with a higher power. Other Republican presidents followed suit, most notably President George W. Bush, whose efforts to connect divine power to the nation have been detailed earlier in this book. Most recently, President Trump used overt language to recruit the nation's disciples during his presidential campaign (Rozell and Whitney 2018; Whitehead, Perry and Baker 2018; Keddie 2020). Figure 6.2 demonstrates religiously orthodox White Protestants' increased affinity for the GOP since 1980. In 1980, only 41 percent of White Protestants identified or leaned Republican – by 2016, 76 percent did. Similar patterns exist in the evolution of vote choice among White Protestants: Ronald Reagan garnered 42 percent of their votes in 1980, whereas Donald Trump secured 78 percent of their votes in 2016.

Finally, much of the discussion of partisanship today focuses not just on how individuals identify, but how they feel about the opposition party. Affinity for one's own party along with an intense dislike of the opposing party has become a critical aspect of American politics and elections (Abramowitz and Webster 2016; Abramowitz and McCoy 2019). Figure 6.2 also demonstrates how the difference in feeling thermometer scores for the Democratic and Republican Parties has grown with a bias toward the GOP among White conservative Protestants. In 1980, religiously orthodox White Protestants held neutral attitudes toward the parties, meaning they scored each party the same. By 2016, they scored Republicans 18 points higher than Democrats. A closer examination of this trend finds that this increased gap is not due to a warmer feeling toward the Republican Party, but cooler feelings toward the Democratic Party. Whereas the average thermometer score for Republicans was unchanged, the score for Democrats plummeted from 58 in 1980 to 26 in 2016. Using religiously orthodox White Protestants as a proxy, these results indicate the GOP has been able to capture the attention of the disciples, while the Democrats have lost them.

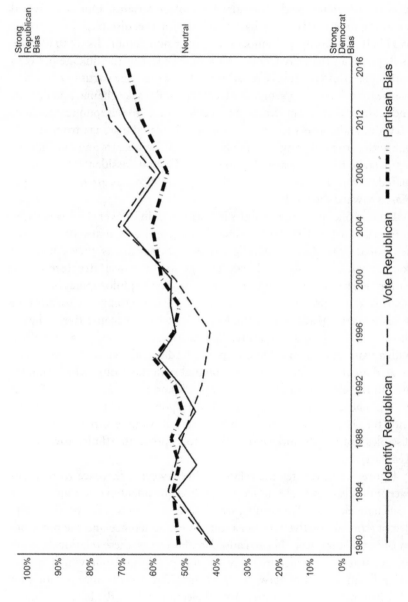

FIGURE 6.2 White conservative Protestant partisan identification, presidential vote choice, and partisan bias between 1980 and 2016

As a more direct test of the relationship between adherence to American religious exceptionalism and partisanship, we use our survey data to predict partisan identification as a function of the respondent's level of adherence and a standard set of covariates. Our data reveal a major gulf in partisanship based on our measure: disciples are 35 points less likely to identify as Democratic and 45 points more likely to identify as Republican than dissidents.[6] As a further test of the linkage between partisanship and religious exceptionalism, we examine partisan bias using the mean thermometer scores for Democrats, Barack Obama, and liberals and subtracting them from the mean scores for Republicans, John McCain, and conservatives. The measure is scaled to range from zero to one with zero indicating a strong bias toward Democrats and one indicating a strong bias toward Republicans. We find dissidents are slightly biased toward Democrats, while the laity and disciples are more strongly biased toward the GOP.[7]

Finally, one of the major shifts in partisan politics over the few decades is the rise of the Tea Party, which has championed many of the ideas associated with American religious exceptionalism as they sought to counter what they see as drastic change in the power structure of the nation (Parker and Barreto 2013). Drawing on the philosophies of groups such as the John Birch Society, the Tea Party attempted to advance a reactionary agenda within the Republican Party because they believed the nation was losing its culture. The election of a Black president along with advancements for other groups not traditionally viewed as American created greater anxiety for those affiliated with the group, which culminated in the election of Donald Trump (Parker 2018; Towler and Parker 2018). The 2014 Kentucky Poll asked respondents if they sympathized with the Tea Party. Here we find clear substantive differences as the disciples are significantly more likely to express an affinity toward the Tea Party.[8]

Figure 6.3 illustrates the relationship between adherence to religious exceptionalism and vote choice across three presidential elections and one US Senate election. The results, which include a control for partisanship, demonstrate a positive relationship between adherence and the probability of voting for a Republican candidate. However, these relationships are not consistently significant. There are only two instances in which there is a significant difference between the groups. The first instance is voting for Mitt Romney in the 2012 presidential election, where the laity are significantly more likely to vote for him than the disciples; however, the difference between the dissidents and the disciples is not significant. The second

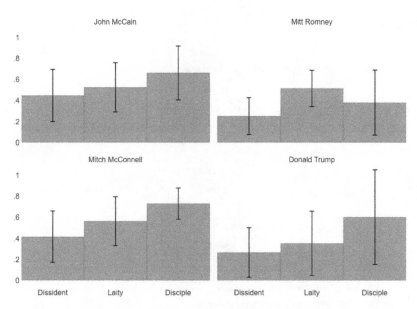

FIGURE 6.3 Predicted probabilities of vote choice given adherence to American religious exceptionalism

Note: Predicted probabilities and values were generated using coefficient estimates from logit regression models that control for biblical literalism, religious tradition, religious importance, worship attendance, personal demographics, political ideology, and partisanship. Capped lines mark the estimated 95 percent confidence intervals.

is the 2014 Kentucky Senate race between Senate Minority Leader Mitch McConnell and Democratic challenger Allison Grimes. The race was viewed as an opportunity for Democrats to pick up a Senate seat as McConnell was becoming increasingly unpopular with Kentucky voters and had faced a primary challenger who aligned himself with the Tea Party (Weisman 2014). Because of these factors, the race was nationally important and resulted in more than $85 million spent by the campaigns and outside groups. McConnell eventually won with 56 percent of the vote (Berinsky, Huber and Lenz 2012; Cillizza 2013). We find that Senator McConnell can owe some of his victory to the disciples as they were significantly more likely to vote for him. Controlling for partisanship, a dissident has 41 percent probability of voting for McConnell, while a disciple has a 73 percent chance. In contrast, the minor differences in Figure 6.4 between the categories in the analysis of presidential vote choice can be attributed to accounting for ideology and partisanship. As

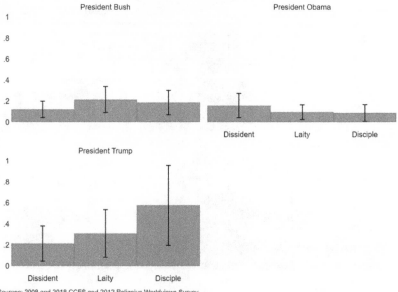

FIGURE 6.4 Predicted probabilities of presidential approval given adherence to American religious exceptionalism
Note: Predicted probabilities were generated using coefficient estimates from logit regression models that control for biblical literalism, religious tradition, religious importance, worship attendance, personal demographics, political ideology, and partisanship. Capped lines mark the estimated 95 percent confidence intervals.

has been long established, both are the strongest predictors of presidential vote choice (Campbell, et al. 1960; Philpot 2017).

Another indicator of partisan leanings is presidential approval. Figure 6.4 displays how adherence to American religious exceptionalism is related to approval for President George W. Bush and President Obama. By the end of his presidency, Bush was criticized for the failing economy and failures of the invasion of Iraq and, to a lesser extent, of Afghanistan. His post-September 11, 2001, approval rating high of 90 percent had eroded substantially by November 2008 to just 28 percent. As Figure 6.4 illustrates, the end of Bush's presidency was marked with paltry support among the dissidents who were very unlikely to approve of how he was handling the job. While the concerns about Bush were shared widely, the laity and disciples remained more supportive of his presidency until the very end.

Our examination of President Obama's job approval finds the expected negative relationship as both the laity and disciples express lower levels of approval for him than do dissidents.[9] In contrast to President Obama, who was disliked intensely by the disciples of American religious exceptionalism, President Trump was a godsend. There is a 37-percentage point difference between a dissident and a disciple regarding approval of President Trump. A dissident has a 21 percent chance of expressing approval, while the odds for a disciple are 58 percent. During and after his time in the White House, Trump has openly courted this group. He brought its most public disciples into his administration. He invested in forging a strong bond with this group, which in return has provided him with unwavering support.

6.5 THE CHURCH OF TRUMP?

From the beginning of his campaign in 2016, President Trump openly courted American religious nationalists, especially Christian nationalists. His promise to protect Christianity at Liberty University along with his antagonism of Muslims has made him the darling of those who believe the nation is betraying its religious basis. His efforts have been rewarded by the relatively unflinching support for Trump among Christian conservatives, such as White evangelical Protestants. The 2020 PRRI American Values Survey finds that 42 percent of White evangelical Protestants state that there is almost nothing President Trump could do to lose their support. Furthermore, 55 percent of White evangelicals believe Donald Trump has been called by God to lead during this critical time in the United States. This commitment to Trump bordering on religious fanaticism was on display during the assault on the US Capitol on January 6, 2021, as numerous insurrectionists displayed religious symbols, such as the Christian flag, the ichthys symbol, and handwritten signs declaring their righteousness in supporting President Trump.[10] Most notably, one insurrectionist carried an elongated flag which read "Jesus is my savior" and "Trump is my President." Another had an American flag altered to read "Make America Godly Again" on its white stripes.

In their 2020 American Values Survey, the Public Religion Research Institute (PRRI) asked respondents a variety of questions related to which candidate they associated certain attributes: strong religious beliefs, uses religion as a political weapon, is chosen by God, and models religious values. The respondents were allowed to choose Donald Trump, Joe Biden, neither, or both. These items were combined to create a measure of the perceived piety of President Trump ($\alpha = .72$). Our analysis of how this perception correlates with the belief that God has granted America a special role finds that a respondent who completely

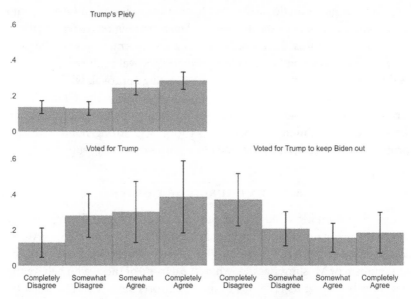

FIGURE 6.5 Predicted values and probabilities of believing President Trump's piety, voting for President Trump, and reason for vote given agreement with the belief that God has granted America a special role in human history

Note: Predicted probabilities were generated using coefficient estimates from logit regression models that control for biblical literalism, religious tradition, religious importance, worship attendance, personal demographics, political ideology, and partisanship. Capped lines mark the estimated 95 percent confidence intervals.
Source: Author analysis of the 2020 PRRI American Values Survey.

agrees with this idea of the nation is twice as likely to believe Trump is pious than one who disagrees with it. In addition to being more likely to view President Trump as having a high level of religious ideals, those who completely agree were also more likely to say they intended to vote for Trump in the 2020 election. Furthermore, among those who said they would vote for President Trump, those who believe in the divinity of the nation were *less* likely to explain their vote intention as motivated by wanting to keep Joe Biden out of power. This indicates that those who believe the nation has a divine role to play in human history cast their vote for Trump because they believed he should be in office instead of just seeking to keep his opponent out of office. These data from the PRRI's 2020 American Values Survey support the idea that President Trump was able to tap into the vision of a divinely inspired and directed nation to attract voters (see Figure 6.5).

The results in Figure 6.6 demonstrate the allure President Trump held among the disciples of American religious exceptionalism. Disciples are supportive of Trump's consistently brash leadership style, and are much more likely to agree with the sentiment that since things are so bad, the nation needs a leader who will break the rules. Disciples' support for Trump is further evident in their dismissal of accusations against him. When asked about the more general accusation that the Trump administration colluded with the Russian government to secure victory in 2016, the relationship with religious exceptionalism is in the expected direction even though we control for partisanship which dominates the underlying regression model. The most serious set of accusations leveled at President Trump at the time was that he illegally withheld funds from Ukraine to pressure its leadership to investigate his political rivals, specifically Joe Biden. These accusations led the House of Representatives to impeach the president. Analyses found Americans were split on the impeachment as

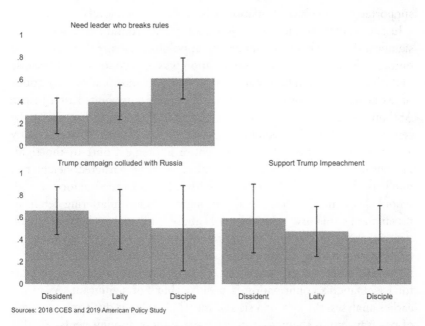

Sources: 2018 CCES and 2019 American Policy Study

FIGURE 6.6 Predicted probabilities of approving of President Trump's leadership style and believing Trump campaign and Trump administration committed illegal activity

Note: Predicted probabilities were generated using coefficient estimates from logit regression models that control for biblical literalism, religious tradition, religious importance, worship attendance, personal demographics, political ideology, and partisanship. Capped lines mark the estimated 95 percent confidence intervals.

approval for the impeachment ranged from 46 percent to 51 percent (Newport 2020). We find a similar polarization in our data though again this model is swamped by partisanship. Even though the disciples of American religious exceptionalism were less likely to believe in wrong-doing on the part of the Trump campaign or Trump administration, it is clear that partisanship is a much stronger factor in shaping these attitudes (though, of course, religious exceptionalism today is a strong predictor of partisan identity).

In a separate analysis of specific Trump policy decisions and appoint-ments, we find strong support among the disciples. During his first two years, President Trump nominated two Supreme Court Justices, Neil Gorsuch and Brett Kavanaugh. Both men faced controversial confirmation hearings. The confirmation of Justice Gorsuch followed Senator Mitch McConnell (R-Kentucky), the Republican majority leader in the Senate, refusing to hold confirmation hearings for Merrick Garland during the last year of President Obama's presidency. Only 45 percent of Americans supported Gorsuch's confirmation, which is the lowest level of support for a Justice confirmed since 1991 (Jones 2017). We found that disciples are significantly more likely to support this appointment than others. Not to be outdone, Brett Kavanaugh's confirmation was also controversial because of the ideological shift he would bring to the court and credible accusations of sexual assault against the judge. Kavanaugh was appointed after Justice Anthony Kennedy announced his retirement. Kennedy, who was at the center of the Court's ideological spectrum, would now be replaced by a conservative justice, shifting the entire Supreme Court to the right. Furthermore, Kavanaugh's confirmation hearing garnered heightened publicity due to credible accusations that he had raped a former high school classmate. The hearing also brought to light unflattering details of Kavanaugh's history with alcohol abuse and debauchery. Overall, Americans were split on the confirmation with 46 percent favoring the confirmation and 45 percent opposing it (Jones 2018a). We find that the relationship between adherence to religious exceptionalism and support for Kavanaugh's confirmation is positive, but not significant. As in the earlier analyses, the lack of a significant relationship is due to the strength of partisanship in shaping attitudes toward these appointments. Finally, the confirmation of Justice Amy Comey Barrett was also marked with controversy as she was nominated and confirmed in the middle of the 2020 presidential election. The same Republican leadership in the Senate that refused to offer a hearing for President Obama because of an upcom-ing election quickly processed her nomination and confirmation after the death of Justice Ruth Bader Ginsburg. On top of this, Justice Coney Barrett's nomination was filled with discussions about her religious fundamentalism and how the activities surrounding her confirmation violated various pandemic guidelines. However, even in the face all of these issues, a Gallup poll found 51 percent of Americans supported the confirmation, while a POLITICO/Morning Consult Poll found 55 percent supported it. Our analysis of this situation finds that like the other appointments, the disciples are significantly more supportive of the rushed appointment along with the appointee. When asked if the Senate should confirm a generic replacement for Justice Ginsberg, a dissident has a 25 percent chance of supporting this, while the odds for a disciple are 87 percent. Regarding the specific confirmation of Barrett, a dissident had a 33 percent chance of supporting it, while a disciple had an 85 percent estimated probability of doing so.[11]

The final bit of evidence to demonstrate the close connection between the disciples of American religious exceptionalism and President Trump examines the relationship in the context of the coronavirus pandemic. The toll on President Trump's approval ratings due to his administration's delayed and incoherent response to the COVID-19 pandemic was harsh. Journalists described the pandemic as one of the main reasons why President Trump lost supporters, specifically White suburban women.[12] The results from the analyses shown in Figure 6.7 demonstrate that knowing someone who contracted the virus influenced the relationship between adherence to American religious exceptionalism, presidential approval, and vote choice. In both approval and vote choice, it is clear that the dissidents and laity who knew someone who contracted the virus were significantly less likely to express approval of President Trump's job performance and cast their vote for him. Regarding job approval, a dissident who did not know anyone who contracted the virus has a 27 percent chance of approving of Trump's performance, whereas a dissident who knows someone who contracted the virus has a 4 percent chance. For a laity, the odds of approving are 62 percent if she does not know anyone afflicted, but are just 17 percent if she does know someone. Moving to vote choice, the same pattern emerges. A dissident who does not know anyone stricken with the illness has a 27 percent chance of voting for Trump, but if she does know someone who contracted it, the probability is 3 percent. For laity, the difference is 58 percent and 11 percent, respectively. For a disciple knowing or not knowing someone who had the virus is not associated with any substantive difference in approval or vote choice. These results indicate that for the dissidents and laity the virus had an impact on how they viewed

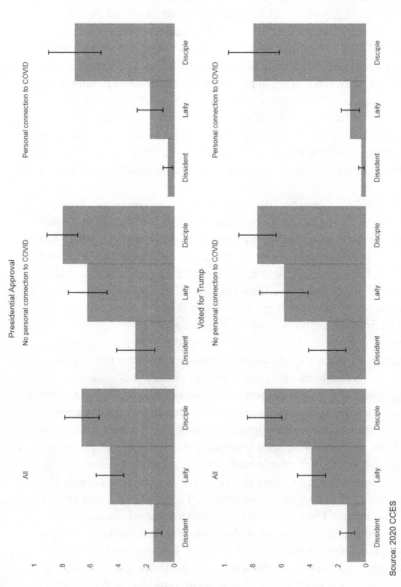

FIGURE 6.7 Predicted probability of approving of President Trump's job performance and voting for him given knowing someone who contracted coronavirus

Note: Predicted probabilities were generated using coefficient estimates from logit regression models that control for biblical literalism, religious tradition, religious importance, worship attendance, personal demographics, political ideology, and partisanship. Capped lines mark the estimated 95 percent confidence intervals.

the president; however, for the disciples this event could not disrupt their support for him.

These results regarding the attraction between the disciples of American religious exceptionalism and President Trump demonstrate that he was their ideal figure no matter what the issue. Several commentators have referenced Christian nationalism as well as support for Trump as being an almost cult-like phenomenon as people have expressed unflinching support for the nation and the president (Phillips 2018; Marti 2019; Posner 2020; Stewart 2019; Whitehead and Perry 2020). Even during various contro- versies, intense opposition, and policy failures this group stuck with *their* president and developed *their* own special reasoning for why he did not have the success they expected. For them any failure was the cause of nefarious forces that worked against an almost godlike figure. These beliefs fomented a variety of conspiracy theories and the acceptance of "alterna- tive" facts. This intense devotion manifested itself on January 6, 2021, as his adherents stormed the US Capitol to prevent the Senate from finalizing the election and confirming the victory of his opponent. Beyond the Capitol insurrection, several states have changed their electoral laws using Trump's false claim as a basis. In line with the arguments of others, our results demonstrate that many of those who participated in this attack on American democracy were the disciples of American religious excep- tionalism and raise questions about what this means about the future of the American democratic process. To help shed light on this, the final section of this chapter will examine the political participation of dissidents, laity, and disciples to see how they operate in the American democracy.

6.6 WORKING IN THE TEMPLE

We conclude this chapter with an examination of patterns of political involvement. Given the disciples' strong attachment to their idea of the nation, we should expect them to have a higher level of engagement compared to the disciples. However, previous scholarship suggests they may in fact be less inclined to be politically engaged. The form of national attachment an individual embraces can influence levels of political engage- ment (Schatz and Lavine 2007). For example, forms of national attach- ment emphasizing an intense emotional identification, unquestioned allegiance, and the rejection of criticism elicit more symbolic behaviors that express a love for the nation and invoke self-esteem. These more symbolic forms of patriotism – "blind patriotism" – lead to equally symbolic gestures, meaning they do not lead to political action and therefore are associated with lower levels of political interest and voter turnout (Schatz, Staub and Lavine 1999; Huddy and Khatib 2007). In contrast, forms of national attachment emphasizing the proper "functioning of the nation's social, political and economic systems" along with its "capability to provide instrumental benefits to citizens" promotes active engagement in the operations of the government (Schatz and Lavine 2007, p. 334).

Given the linkage between religious exceptionalism and forms of national attachment like uncritical patriotism, we might expect the disciples to be less engaged than the dissidents. The results in Figure 6.8 demonstrate that this is not the case as the relationship between adherence to American religious exceptionalism, political engagement, and participation is a U-shaped relationship. The dissidents and disciples are more likely to have a high interest in politics and engage in more political activities than the laity. Similarly, we find that a laity participates in significantly fewer activities than dissidents and disciples in both 2008 and 2018. Furthermore, disciples report engaging in significantly more activities than the dissidents in 2018 and 2020. These results indicate that those on the polar ends of adherence to American religious exceptionalism are most likely to be engaged and participate in American politics, but that the edge for political activism is slanted toward the disciples. All three groupings express significantly higher levels of political interest in 2020 than they did in 2008. This is consistent with the record level of turnout in the 2020 election as almost all Americans wanted to be a part of this momentous election.

6.7 CONCLUSION

Adherence to American religious exceptionalism translates to political views that reflect an ideology that regards America as a temple and the American people as its worshippers. Perhaps, unsurprisingly, due to their penchant for cultural purity and hierarchy, its disciples do not automatically reject the possibility of autocratic governance. Simultaneously, they are also much more likely to express anti-elitism than dissidents, and to support restricting the actions of government, except in promoting religion. This contradiction is explained by the populist nature of disciples' views – the people are sovereign and the only leaders who can be trusted are those who fulfill the people's desires. Finally, exceptionalism's disciples support political parties and officials who act in accordance with the disciples' more authoritarian and culturally threatened views. Despite the

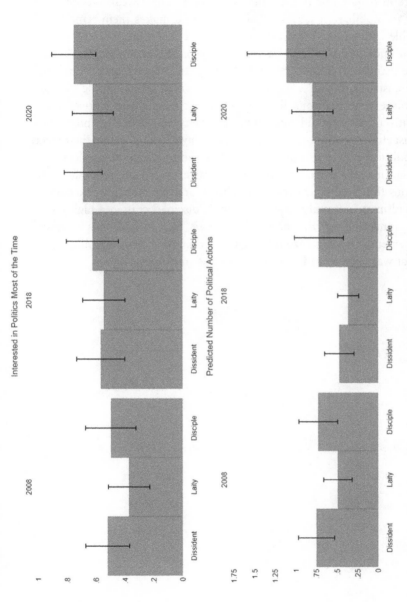

FIGURE 6.8 Predicted probability of being interested in politics most of the time and predicted number of political actions given adherence to American religious exceptionalism

Note: Predicted probabilities were generated using coefficient estimates from logit regression and negative binomial models that control for biblical literalism, religious tradition, religious importance, worship attendance, personal demographics, political ideology, and strength of partisanship. Capped lines mark the estimated 95 percent confidence intervals.

disciples' complacency with autocratic governance, their anti-elitism, and anti-outsider points of view, we do not find disciples are any less likely to engage in democratic politics than dissidents. This reveals disciples are likely to mobilize to support their causes and makes them remarkably valuable voting blocs for savvy candidates seeking office.

Our findings are compatible with an "embattled group identity" many White evangelical Americans hold (Wong 2018; Stewart 2019). Similarly, as defensive actors in an era of unprecedented demographic change, religious exceptionalism's disciples believe the proper role of government and citizens is to uphold cultural homogeneity above all else and so they distrust elites who attempt to change their way of life. They use their voice and political power to support candidates and policies that reflect such beliefs. This pro-active amendment is a far cry from pre-Enlightenment religious thinking, which spurned political activity. Religious exceptionalism ultimately reveals how the nation's disciples crafted a highly religious rendering of the nation's purpose and leaned into political engagement in order to promote this mission, rather than shunning activity that was once considered irreligious and improper.

7

The View from the Back Pews

*A young member of the Black Panther Movement, a confirmed atheist, was
discussing the voter registration drive with his father, a venerable preacher
of the gospel.*

*"I sometimes think that if God himself were to come down to earth in
human form, and He was a black man," said the preacher sadly, "He
wouldn't be allowed to vote in Mississippi."*

*"Pop, with all due respect to you," snorted the atheist son, "if there
really was a God, there wouldn't be a Mississippi!"*

(Spalding 1972, p. 474)

The eighteenth century's Great Awakening yielded many converts to
Christianity in the United States. Many of these converts were Blacks
who joined White congregations. In response, many churches began
creating sections specifically for Blacks to sit. Often referred to as the
"Negro" or "Jim Crow" pew, these sections were located in the back of
sanctuary to keep the Black members out of the White congregants' line
of sight (Asher 1999). This segregated seating arrangement was strictly
enforced. In 1787, several Black members of St. George's Methodist
Episcopal Church in Philadelphia were physically removed from the
altar because they were praying in the "wrong" section. This would
lead to the formation of the first independent Black denomination, the
African Methodist Episcopal Church (Pinn and Pinn 2002; Dickerson
2020). The marginalization of Blacks in predominantly White churches
reflects the wider marginalization of racial and religious minorities in
America. Even though they are members of the congregation, they are
not awarded the same privileges as other members and are shunted to the
periphery. They may have heard the same sermon and sung the same

hymns as the rest of the congregation, but their confinement to the edges of the church community served as a constant reminder that they were not truly equal brothers and sisters in this Holy Family. But, while Black worshippers might have been kept out of the line of sight of White congregants, their view from the back pews was unobstructed and clear, and shaped the understanding of Black citizens of what America is and what it means to be an American (Phillips 2018).[1]

The status of its racial and religious minorities in America's identity has always been tenuous. Neil Visalvanich shows that White voters are more likely to view Latinx and Black Democrats as incompetent and ideologically extreme (2017), though this bias is not evident for Asian candidates. But even this relative acceptance of Asian Americans is fragile. Heightened bigotry and racially motivated attacks against Asian Americans in response to the COVID-19 pandemic demonstrates how a group can one day be accepted, in this case as a "model minority," and the next day be a pariah (Lawrence 2020; Reny and Barreto 2020). Living in constant fear of the ire of "mainstream" American society has made members of these groups cautious to be politically and socially engaged for fear of stoking the dominant group's rage. In some cases, these groups were once banned outright from being a part of American civic and political life. Because they have existed in the periphery of American life, by force or by choice, their exposure and understanding of the American message was distinct. Their experience created their own understanding of what it means to be an American, and what it means for the nation to be favored by God. As this chapter's epigraph demonstrates, some questioned whether there was a God and how could a nation so cruel to them receive God's blessing. For many others, they developed what W. E. B. Du Bois refers to as a "double consciousness" (1990). America's Black, indigenous, and people of color express joy and pride in being part of the American congregation and are willing to defend it in the face of external threats. However, perhaps because they have been forced to watch the services from the back pews, they are not blind to America's shortcomings. Throughout America's history, the myth of American religious exceptionalism has been used by those who have taken the nation to task for the marginalization of some of its members. David Walker's *Appeal*, Frederick Douglass's pleas to the nation, and the fiery preaching of Martin Luther King, all invoked the myth of American religious exceptionalism and called upon the nation to live up to its covenant. In explaining Black political behavior, Hanes Walton notes:

It is a variant form of American political behavior. It is inspired and shaped *by some features and currents that do not form the basis of all American political behavior because it is rooted in the black experience in America.* And this experience is radically different from the experience of other immigrant groups.

(1985, p. 9; emphasis in the original)

Racial and religious minorities might have been exposed to the same message coming from the pulpit, but because they were not allowed to sit with the other congregants, they have always understood the gospel of America from the perspective of an outsider as opposed to accepted congregant. The purpose of this chapter is to explore how racial and religious minorities apply American religious exceptionalism to their beliefs. Specifically, we ask if the influence of the myth on attitudes, candidate evaluations, and policy preferences is conditional upon race and religion.

7.1 PATRIOTISM IN THE PERIPHERY

Racial minorities have supported the United States and urged its success from its inception. African Americans are proud to remind those who are ignorant that Crispus Attucks, a former slave killed in the Boston Massacre in 1770, was one of the first to die for the nation's independence (Quarles 1996; Kachun 2009). Even before this, Blacks served in the military helping the colonists stave off incursions from Native Americans. During the Revolutionary War, a sizable number of Blacks fled to the British with the hope of freedom, while White soldiers and leadership in the Continental Army protested the recruitment of Black soldiers. Even in the face of such racist hostility, at least 5,000 Blacks served in the Continental Army (Quarles 1996; Parker 2009). The hope of many was that by participating in the war effort they would be able to gain the rights promised in the Declaration of Independence. During the independence war effort many Black soldiers distinguished themselves in critical battles on land and sea, but their heroism was not rewarded with full equality. Many of the slaves who fought for the freedom of the nation were given their freedom and many northern states began to repeal slavery and grant Blacks the rights to vote, but in total these rewards went to only a small portion of the Black population and were soon rescinded (Parker 2009).

By grappling with the historic discrimination of Black Americans, including those who fought valiantly for American independence, we begin to understand the duality of patriotism. Blacks show great affection for their nation and will defend it, hoping the nation will remember its debt to them and provide them full citizenship. Todd Shaw refers to this as "invested patriotism" (Shaw 2004, p. 20). In times of struggle, Blacks rebuff classical patriotism and embrace "iconoclastic patriotism." This form of patriotism is displayed by directly confronting racism and demonstrating how it erodes the promise of the nation (Shaw 2004, pp. 20–21). This duality of patriotism is well documented and has demonstrated that, while Blacks are willing to defend their nation, they reject their White brethren's claims of American innocence (Shaw 2004; Johnson 2018; Phillips 2018). As Fredrick Douglass wrote in his denunciation of slavery:

The existence of slavery in this country brands your republicanism as a sham, your humanity as a base pretense, and your Christianity as a lie. It destroys your moral power abroad; it corrupts your politicians at home. It saps the foundation of religion; it makes your name a hissing and a bye-word to a mocking earth.

(1945, pp. 51-52)

Even in the face of slavery's and Jim Crow's hypocrisy, Blacks continued to express a strong devotion to the nation by enlisting in the military and insisting that America was their home. It was this belief that fueled their love of the nation along with their criticisms of it. It is no coincidence nor any surprise that Black military veterans played a key role in organizing during the civil rights movement (Morris 1984; Parker 2009).

For Latinx Americans, their experience with the nation has been as turbulent, but differently so. Unlike their Black counterparts, they were not subjected to slavery, but they too have suffered a long history of second-class citizenship. Similar to the oppressive laws that prevented Blacks from full citizenship in the South, Latinx Americans experienced the same degradation in the American southwest (Weber 2003; Ortiz 2018). A specter that has constantly hung over the heads of Latinx Americans is the perception of their foreignness. Much like Asian Americans (Takaki 1989), Latinx Americans are viewed as foreigners by a large part of the population (Weber 2003). This is especially ironic given Mexicans' settlement in what constitutes today's America pre-dated the latter's takeover of their ancestral homes, an idea captured by an aphorism popular with many Latinx Americans: "we didn't cross the border, the border crossed us." Attempts by majoritarian groups to force assimilation have been short-lived (Fox 2012; Ortiz 2018). Some warn that Latinx Americans will never fully assimilate

(Huntington 2004), even though data demonstrate they are learning English and adopting "American" values as quickly or faster than European immigrants (de la Garza, Falcon and Garcia 1996; Citrin, et al. 2007). This fear of an unassimilable foreign threat at the US border was a critical part of Trump's campaign as well as his presidency as he aggressively championed the detention and deportation of immigrants, and insisted on a border wall. This form of marginalization, which has designated these citizens as irredeemably foreign, while intermittently attempting to bring them into the congregational fold via assimilation, has created a unique relationship between Latinx Americans and their nation.

Much like Black Americans, Latinx Americans have eloquently objected to their second-class citizenship and have demanded to be recognized as true American citizens. However, persistent majoritarian paranoia of foreign invasion has led to policies such as opposing bilingual instruction that actively undermine Latinx advancement in society (Desipio 1996; de la Garza 2004; Ortiz 2018). Furthermore, attempts to assimilate the group reflect the special place Latinxs specifically hold in the American racial hierarchy. Unlike race, which is seen as permanent and inherited, ethnicity is viewed as being fluid and can over time be changed (Smedley 1999). Because Latinx identity is an ethnicity, there have been opportunities for members of the group to move out of this ethnic group and become White. Ngai notes that the distinct Latinx ethnicity was constructed by economic policy entrepreneurs to take advantage of Mexico's cheap labor without breaking racial quotas or norms of racial exclusion that were the crux of twentieth-century immigration laws (2014). The opportunity afforded to some Latinx members to self-categorize as White has effectively undermined group attempts to challenge their subordinate status and work with other marginalized groups (Gómez 2018). This is especially apparent with Cuban Americans, who have historically not found commonality with other Latinxs (Sawyer 2006). Unlike Black Americans, who developed a strong sense of group consciousness because they were constantly viewed as being unassimilable and shared a common American history (Gurin, Hatchett and Jackson 1989; Dawson 1994; Philpot 2017; White and Laird 2020), Latinx Americans have had a much more diverse experience with America, which has hindered the development of a strong sense of group identity and consciousness. However, recent controversies surrounding immigration laws and attempts to minimize the voices of Latinx Americans have fostered a stronger sense of group consciousness that might have longer-term political ramifications (Sanchez 2008; Barreto 2010; Barreto and Segura 2014).

The consequences of pushing these groups to the margins of the American sanctuary have created marked differences in how they apply American rhetoric and ideas to their political lives. For instance, we have seen a clear connection between conservatism and identifying with the GOP among Whites; however, for Blacks and Latinx this connection is less clear. Tasha Philpot demonstrates conservative rhetoric and thought on the part of Blacks means something different than what it does for Whites (2017). For instance, military conservatism on the part of Whites is associated with other forms of conservatism. For Blacks this type of conservatism is associated with some liberal attitudes, such as expanding social welfare. Likewise, Black's religious conservatism does not translate to the same political attitudes that it does for Whites (Wong 2018). The challenges of the Republican Party to recruit both Black and Latinx religious conservatives are largely because they apply their religious views to the world differently than their White counterparts (McDaniel and Ellison 2008; McKenzie and Rouse 2013). These findings suggest Black and Latinx disciples of American religious exceptionalism may behave differently than their White counterparts.

Our results, presented in Figures 7.1 and 7.2, demonstrate there is no need for concern about racial differences among the disciples regarding national attachment and national content.

Regardless of race, disciples express high levels of national identity, pride, hubris, and support for uncritical patriotism. In fact, the relationship between adherence and some of these measures of national attachment is steeper for Blacks and Latinx because Black and Latinx dissidents express significantly lower levels of attachment than White dissidents.[2] And, at the other end of the spectrum, Latinx disciples score significantly higher on uncritical patriotism than do their White counterparts.

We turn then to understandings of the content of American national identity. For both White and Latinx respondents the disciples and the laity are significantly less supportive of freedom of speech than the dissidents. But disciples are significantly more supportive of the civic republicanism and assimilationist traditions of national identity than are the dissidents across all racial groups. We find Latinx disciples are more supportive of assimilationism than Black disciples, while Latinx dissidents are more supportive of multiculturalism than both their White and Black counterparts. Finally, disciples across all racial groups are more likely to support

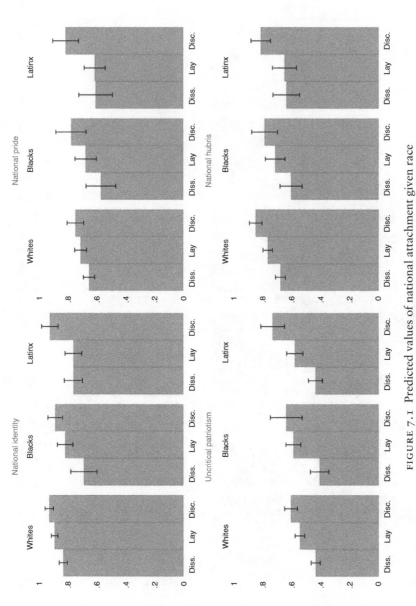

FIGURE 7.1 Predicted values of national attachment given race

Note: Predicted values were generated using coefficient estimates from OLS regression models that control for biblical literalism, religious tradition, religious importance, worship attendance, personal demographics, and political ideology. Capped lines mark the estimated 95 percent confidence intervals.

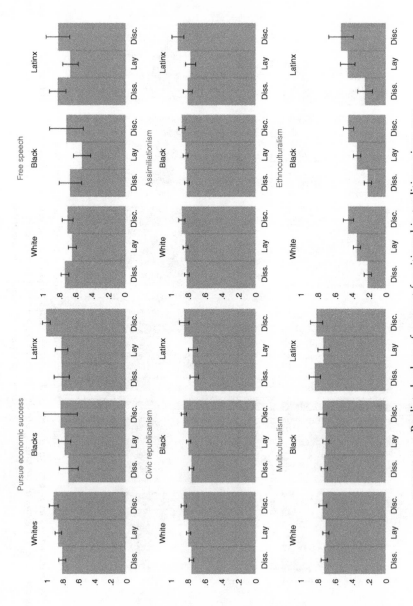

FIGURE 7.2 Predicted values of support for citizenship traditions given race

Note: Predicted values were generated using coefficient estimates from OLS regression models that control for biblical literalism, religious tradition, worship attendance, religious importance, personal demographics, and political ideology. Capped lines mark the estimated 95 percent confidence intervals.

the idea of America as an ethnocultural entity. Black dissidents are least likely to agree with this idea, and significantly less so even than their White and Latino counterparts.

Given the history of both groups as outsiders attempting to gain access to full citizenship rights, we would expect the disciples of these racial groups to be less supportive of a concept such as uncritical patriotism. However, the results show a positive and significant relationship for both Blacks and Latinx. These results indicate that the gospel of American religious exceptionalism emboldens a strong sense of national identity, pride, and hubris even among racial groups that have been historically marginalized. Furthermore, the image of what it means to be an American is shared among the disciples of these various races. The gospel of religious exceptionalism appears to cut across racial lines generating a distinct understanding of what it means to be American.

This racial unity among the disciples appears to be limited to national attachment and content. When we examine the relationship between adherence and political attitudes and behavior, stark racial differences emerge (see Figure 7.3).

First, Black dissidents are significantly more likely to identify as Democrats compared to their White and Latino counterparts. However, Black disciples are significantly less likely to identify as a Democrat than their White and Latino counterparts, and overall increased adherence to American religious exceptionalism moves Blacks to identifying as independents, while moving Latinx respondents to identify more as a Democrat and less as a Republican. For Whites, there is no discernable pattern, indicating that adherence to American religious exceptionalism is not as critical to shaping White partisanship as it is for other racial groups.

Moving to an analysis of vote choice, we see the positive relationship between adherence to American religious exceptionalism and the likelihood of voting for a Republican candidate for White and Latinx respondents. While the figure demonstrates large differences in the probability of voting among Latinx respondents, we find that this relationship is only significant regarding voting for John McCain. What is also notable is the lack of variance among Black respondents. They are excluded from two of the four models shown, because there is no variance among the group. In the two models where they are included, we see a miniscule level of support for the Republican candidate. This suggests that adherence to American religious exceptionalism may attract White and Latinx voters to Republican candidates; however, it has no impact on Black vote choice. Another thing to note is the gap between White dissidents and disciples

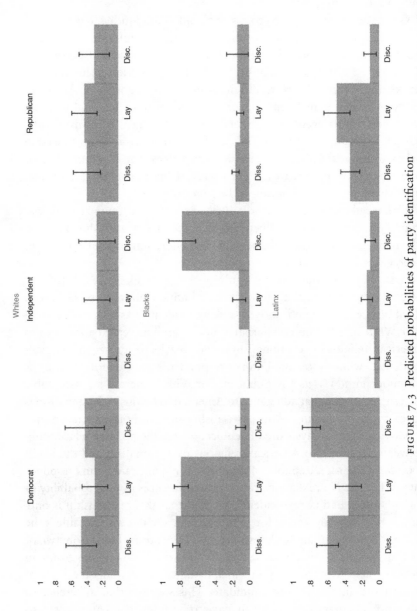

FIGURE 7.3 Predicted probabilities of party identification

Note: Predicted probabilities were generated using coefficient estimates from logit regression models that control for biblical literalism, religious tradition, religious importance, worship attendance, personal demographics, and political ideology. Capped lines mark the estimated 95 percent confidence intervals.

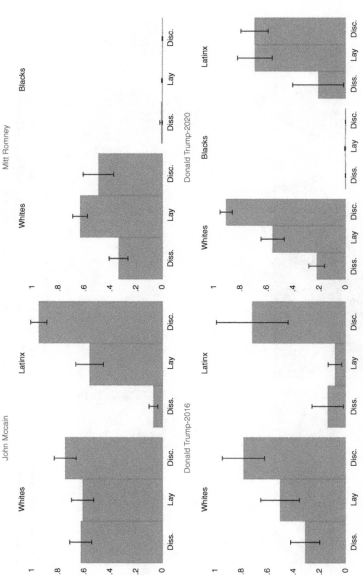

FIGURE 7.4 Predicted probabilities of vote choice

Blacks are excluded in the McCain and the 2016 Trump model because of lack of variance.
Latinos are excluded from the Romney model, because the survey only contained black and white respondents

Note: Predicted probabilities were generated using coefficient estimates from logit regression models that control for biblical literalism, religious tradition, religious importance, worship attendance, personal demographics, and political ideology. Capped lines mark the estimated 95 percent confidence intervals.

Source: Author analysis of the 2008 CCES, 2012 Religious World Views Survey, 2018 CCES, and 2020 CCES.

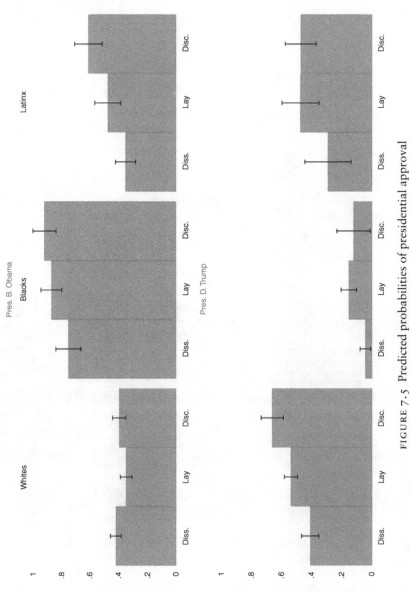

FIGURE 7.5 Predicted probabilities of presidential approval

Note: Predicted probabilities were generated using coefficient estimates from logit regression models that control for biblical literalism, religious tradition, religious importance, worship attendance, personal demographics, and political ideology. Capped lines mark the estimated 95 percent confidence intervals.

Source: Author analysis of 2010 Knowledge Networks Survey and 2020 CCES.

regarding their vote choice. In 2008, the gap was 12 points, but by 2020 it was 68 points. This appears to be attributed to the rise of Donald Trump, who has gained a great deal of favor and admiration among White disciples, while drawing the disdain of White dissidents.

The analysis of presidential approval further demonstrates how the relationship between adherence and evaluation of political figures is dependent upon race. The analysis of President Obama's job approval demonstrates a negative relationship for Whites, but a positive relationship for Black and Latinx respondents. For Whites, the laity and disciples are less likely to approve of Obama's job performance, but the only significant difference is between the laity and the dissidents. For the Latinx respondents, the disciples are more likely to approve of Obama than the laity and dissidents. The positive relationship for Blacks is not significant, but this is primarily an artifact of a ceiling effect as a Black dissident has a 75 percent probability of approving of his job performance. When it comes to Trump, the disciples are more likely to express approval than the dissidents, but this relationship is only significant for Whites. A White disciple's likelihood of approving of Trump's job performance is 25 percentage points higher than for a White dissident.

The last racial comparison we make is regarding political engagement and participation (see Figure 7.6). In Chapter 6, we showed that adherence to religious exceptionalism increases political participation and engagement in a broad national sample, but this effect appears to be driven by White respondents and depends on when the survey was conducted.

White disciples are more engaged than other White respondents, but this effect is strongest in 2008 and more muted in 2018 and 2020. In 2008, Black disciples were much less interested than their dissident counterparts, but this reverses in the later surveys. One interpretation is that national politics – Obama in 2008 versus Trump in 2018 and 2020 – affects the individual-level relationships between American religious exceptionalism and political interest. Interestingly, Latinx respondents express less interest in politics as a group than Whites or Blacks, and Latinx disciples are less interested than other Latinx respondents across the years for which we have data.

7.2 OUTSIDERS LOOKING IN

Whether formally or informally, Americans recognize Christianity, specifically Protestant Christianity, as the dominant religion of the nation. Even though there has been a steady decline in the number of people who

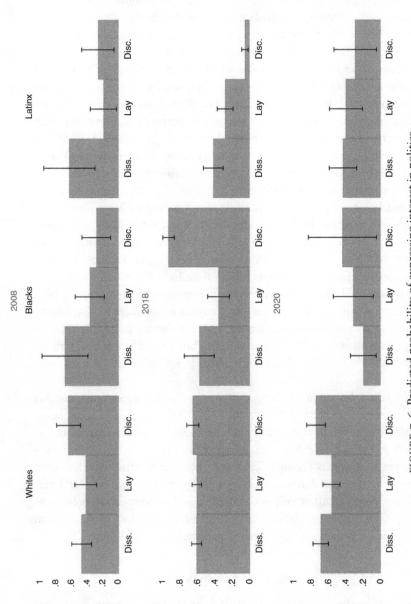

FIGURE 7.6 Predicted probability of expressing interest in politics

Note: Predicted probabilities were generated using coefficient estimates from logit regression models that control for biblical literalism, religious tradition, religious importance, worship attendance, personal demographics, and political ideology. Capped lines mark the estimated 95 percent confidence intervals.

do so, close to two-thirds of Americans still identify as Christian (Pew Research Center 2019).

Of the Christians in the United States, close to a third identify as Catholic (Pew Research Center 2019). As the earlier chapters demonstrated, Catholics once faced the ire of Americans as they were viewed as a threat to the dominance of Protestantism. Catholics were viewed as anti-democratic and were often pushed to the corners of American society (Varacalli 2006; Davis 2017; Hart 2020). Further compounding the problems of American Catholics was that many of them were from racialized groups, such as the Italians and Irish (Guglielmo 2003; Garner 2007; Ignatiev 2009). As these groups came to be accepted as White, the Catholic faith also became more accepted. The culmination of Catholics as truly being a part of the American nation came with the election of John F. Kennedy. However, Kennedy's rise to the presidency came from him distancing himself from his faith. Much like Barack Obama and other Black candidates have distanced themselves from other Blacks to win over White voters (Stephens-Dougan 2020), Kennedy made it clear that his faith would not enter the Oval Office (Hart 2020). Through their demonstrated commitment to the nation during the Cold War, Catholics, specifically conservative Catholics, became prominent members of American society, where their faith was not an issue of concern (Hart 2020; Keeley 2020). Furthermore, their staunch opposition to abortion and homosexuality led conservative Protestants to embrace and promote them. Seven of the nine Supreme Court justices seated today are Catholic; of these seven, six were appointed by Republican Presidents. All of President Trump's Court appointees had some connection to the Catholic Church. Brett Kavanaugh and Amy Comey Barrett identify as Catholic, while Neil Gorsuch was raised Catholic. Even with the growing political presence of conservative Catholics, progressive Catholics have also been able to claim power and attempt to advance a social justice agenda that has been central to the Catholic faith (Varacalli 2006; Davis 2017). The primary example of this is the election of Joe Biden in 2020.

The social and political successes of American Catholics have made them more mainstream, but it is not clear how this affects their internalization of American religious exceptionalism. As noted in Chapter 2, Catholics are less likely to be considered disciples compared to White evangelical Protestants. However, when various social and religion variables are accounted for, Catholics' pattern of adherence mirrors that of White evangelicals. Because of their solid foundation in the mainstream of

American social and political culture, we expect them to behave like their evangelical counterparts.

The most prominently visible non-Christian religious group are Jews, who comprise about 2 percent of the American population (Pew Research Center 2015). Partly because of the history of anti-Semitism that has permeated Europe and America, as well as their ability to find a modicum of economic success in America, Jewish Americans have held a unique status in American culture. Like Black Americans, they have a strong sense of group consciousness which was fostered by centuries of mistreatment, discrimination, and violence, as they were forced to emigrate throughout Europe (Feingold 2002). But unlike Black Americans who viewed coming to America as going to toil in Egypt (Raboteau 1978), Jews who emigrated to the colonies saw it as a potential promised land (Feingold 2002). In many ways the Jewish colonists were the model minority; they achieved financial success through helping set up the colonies' commercial sector and were strongly support-ive of the Revolutionary War – two Jewish officers served on George Washington's staff (*Ibid.*). Anti-Semitism was prevalent, but American Jews benefitted from "pluralistic intolerance," a situation in which the population lacks a consensus on the primary threat (Sullivan, Piereson and Marcus 1982; Gibson 1998; Gibson and Gouws 2003). The constant jostling for position among the various Protestant sects kept them from focusing their ire on Jewish settlers. They also benefitted from the fascination of their religion by groups such as the Puritans, who attempted to emulate Jewish customs. However, this relationship was tenuous as the Puritans became agitated by their unwillingness to convert to Christianity (Feingold 2002).

The innocuous status enjoyed by Jews in early America ended with the mass immigration of southern and eastern Europeans during the nine-teenth century. Once again, the age-old paranoia of being overrun was triggered in White Protestants. Pundits and scientists began categorizing the superiority of groups across and within races. Within the European hierarchy Nordic and northwestern Europeans were at the top and Jews were at the bottom (Brodkin 1998; Smedley 1999; Guglielmo 2003). Much like the Irish and Italians, Jews were pushed out of certain occupa-tions, educational opportunities, and were segregated from larger American society (Brodkin 1998). Rampant anti-Semitism and retrograde views of Jewish Americans would persist in mainstream American society until World War II, in which the battle against the Nazis made scientific racism no longer publicly acceptable. After the war, Jews were more accepted as White and subsequently benefited from the racialized administration of the GI Bill and were able to take advantage of housing, educational, and occupational opportunities that excluded Blacks and other non-Whites. Access to this government-sponsored assistance allowed Jewish Americans to be a part of the rapidly expanding American middle class and elevate their status in the American racial hierarchy (Brodkin 1998). Of course, anti-Semitism persisted after World War II; it just became less socially acceptable to express it publicly (Lerner 1992). Because Jewish Americans held positions of middle management, they became "the recognizable agents of oppression" for racial minorities and poor Whites. As such, these groups often hurled their misplaced blame on Jews, which allowed anti-Semitism to flourish in private even if it could not be shared in public (Lerner 1992; Sifry 1993; Berinsky and Mendelberg 2005).

Complicating further the Jewish experience in America, the opportunity for the group to become White has contributed to some members of the Jewish community's disparaging attitudes toward non-Whites, especially Blacks (Brodkin 1998; Forman 1998). Micah Sifry notes that episodes of Black anti-Semitism are factors of both prejudice and real grievances; however, organizations such as the Anti-Defamation League give harsher scrutiny to Blacks than Whites, who espouse similar rhetoric (1993). Yet American Jews' history of being persecuted has also led them to empathize with marginalized groups and to espouse liberal causes (Feingold 2002). Rabbis and other Jewish leaders who were out front in their support of the civil rights movement continue to be supportive of racial justice causes (Schultz 2001). Furthermore, anxiety over the recent increase in public displays of anti-Semitism, such as the April 13, 2014, shooting at a Jewish community center in Kansas City, along with concerns about the rise of White supremacists in the wake of President Trump's victory (Moshin 2018), demonstrates that American Jews may have been allowed to move closer to the center pews of the American congregation, but that access could be rescinded at any time. Because of this precarious situation, it is unclear if Jewish disciples of American religious exceptionalism will be as distinct from their White counterparts as are their Black counterparts.

A group rapidly growing in the United States is the religiously unaffiliated (Sherkat 2014). In 1990, 8 percent of Americans claimed no religion; today that proportion is between a quarter and a third of all US residents. Another 12–21 percent of respondents claim to be atheist or agnostic, and almost a third say religion is out-of-date (Zuckerman, Galen, and

Pasquale 2016). Americans do not trust the nonreligious who have often been portrayed as being deviant and antisocial (Caplovitz and Sherrow 1977; Bainbridge 2005), though, unsurprisingly of course, data demonstrate they possess the same level of moral commitment to civic life as other Americans. They are more flexible about issues related to sex and sexuality, but express similar disapproval of infidelity. Furthermore, earlier studies suggesting religious individuals are more charitable than the nonreligious were in fact biased, because they did not account for the type of charity in question. While it is true that religious people are more likely to give to religious charities, they are no more likely than the nonreligious to give to secular charities (Zuckerman, Galen and Pasquale 2016).

Clear differences do exist however in the realms of political values and national identity. The nonreligious are less authoritarian and are more supportive of liberal policy positions regarding race, gender, and sexuality. Most important for our concerns, they express lower levels of national pride, hubris, and identification (Zuckerman, Galen and Pasquale 2016). Perhaps the nonreligious are simply less likely to place identities on themselves, but their consistently lower levels of national attachment are noteworthy. They express the lowest levels of support for American religious exceptionalism in our data. Part of this could reflect their rejection of religion, but it could also represent their rejection of intense national devotion. This distinct relationship with the nation may cause their adherence to religious exceptionalism to produce distinctively different results compared to the more mainstream groups.

To what extent do White evangelical Protestants, the prototypical disciples of American religious exceptionalism, drive the connections we found between adherence and attitudes? Answering this question requires understanding how smaller religious groups such as Jews and the religiously unaffiliated apply their beliefs about the nation's divinity to their national attachments, their definitions of what it means to be an American, and the nation's politics. In what follows, we examine if the relationship between adherence to religious exceptionalism and citizen attitudes is contingent upon religious tradition. The analyses will compare White evangelical Protestants to peripheral groups such as Jews, Catholics, and the religiously unaffiliated.[3]

Similar attitudinal trends are evident across the various religious traditions (see Figure 7.7). A disciple, whether she is evangelical or Catholic, expresses significantly higher levels of attachment to the idea of America. The only exception is that an unaffiliated disciple

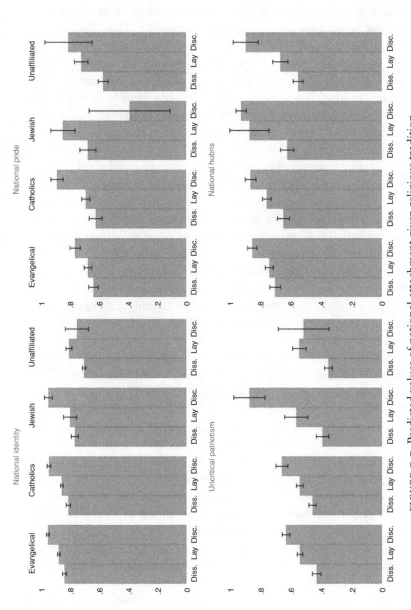

FIGURE 7.7 Predicted values of national attachment given religious tradition

Note: Predicted values were generated using coefficient estimates from OLS regression models that control for biblical literalism, religious tradition, religious importance, worship attendance, personal demographics, and political ideology. Capped lines mark the estimated 95 percent confidence intervals.

does not express significantly higher levels of national identification compared to her dissident counterpart; however, a member of the laity does score significantly higher than a dissident. This pattern is also the case when examining uncritical patriotism. The relationship between adherence and national attachment is similar for Jews. A Jewish disciple of American religious exceptionalism expresses significantly higher levels of national identity, hubris, and uncritical patriotism than her dissident counterpart. The only item where Jewish respondents differentiate from the other traditions examined is national pride on which the laity score significantly higher than the dissidents and disciples.

The correspondence between adherence to American religious exceptionalism and more restrictive definitions of what it means to be an American is highly consistent across the various religious traditions (see Figure 7.8). Two findings are particularly noteworthy. First, there is a negative relationship between adherence to religious exceptionalism and multiculturalism for Jews. It is unclear what is driving this relationship; one possibility is that Jewish Americans who score highly on our American religious exceptionalism scale view multiculturalism as a threat to their well-being as they have worked hard to assimilate and may view opening the nation to more cultures may allow groups antagonistic to their interests to gain more power.

Second, American religious exceptionalism is positively correlated with agreement with an ethnocultural view of America for all the groups. The finding that Jewish and religious unaffiliated disciples are as supportive of ethnoculturalism as their evangelical and Catholic counterparts is striking. Our surveys followed the best practice established by Deborah Schildkraut and instructed respondents to choose how important the criteria *should* be (2011). The notion is that response therefore reflects respondents' personal normative assessment of who is "truly" American as opposed to their observational assessment. While the observational assessment may contribute to this result, this may just as possibly be their true normative assessment of who is American. An examination of the individual items comprising the measure shows the same positive relationship for all groups. It's worth stating this as plainly as possible: The power of the American religious exceptionalism worldview is so strong that Jewish and religiously unaffiliated adherents place a significantly higher level of importance on the notion that being Christian should be a criterion for being a true American compared to their dissident counterparts.

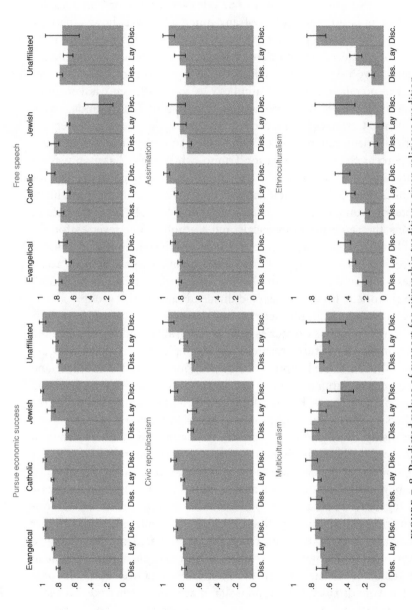

FIGURE 7.8 Predicted values of support for citizenship traditions given religious tradition

Note: Predicted values were generated using coefficient estimates from OLS regression models that control for biblical literalism, religious tradition, religious importance, worship attendance, personal demographics, and political ideology. Capped lines mark the estimated 95 percent confidence intervals.

In domestic politics, we find that adherence moves members of every religious tradition in the same direction, that is, toward a higher probability of identifying as a Republican. The sole exception is for Catholics, for whom there is no relationship of any note.[4] However, how adherence affects presidential vote choice depends on one's religious tradition. In 2008, for instance, we find that evangelical and religiously unaffiliated disciples have a significantly higher probability of voting for McCain, but there was no relationship for Catholics.[5] In 2016, adherence is associated with a significantly higher probability of voting for Trump among evangelicals and Catholics (see Figure 7.9). For Evangelicals, high adherence is practically determinative of a Trump vote. An evangelical dissident has a 36 percent chance of voting for Trump, while a laity has a 79 percent chance, and for a disciple it is 93 percent. A similar pattern exists for Catholics. Interestingly, unaffiliated disciples were significantly less likely to vote for Trump in 2016 than the laity or dissidents. In 2020, the pattern remains the same for evangelicals and Catholics, but reverses for the unaffiliated. Increased adherence on the part of the religiously unaffiliated is associated with a higher probability of voting for Trump in 2020, suggesting that Trump's unabashed use of American religious exceptionalism rhetoric in his campaign paid dividends among this group.[6]

As with the findings for race reported earlier in this chapter, the results for different religious categories offer considerable food for thought and opportunities for future research. For example, the disciples who are religiously unaffiliated express attitudes about national attachment and the content of national identity similar to those of their evangelical and Catholic counterparts, but this does not translate to their politics. For the religiously unaffiliated, adherence is not significantly associated with partisanship, vote choice, or presidential approval. One explanation could be that the authoritarian nature of a belief system like religious exceptionalism may decrease the want or need to be politically engaged (Altemeyer 1996; Schatz, Staub and Lavine 1999). Yet, this is not the case of evangelicals who have long been regarded as one of the most authoritarian groups in American politics and society (Altemeyer 2003). Another explanation may be that the religiously unaffiliated are less likely to engage organized religious institutions, which may make it more difficult from them to translate this belief to politics (Wald, Owen and Hill 1988; Wald and Smidt 1993; Djupe and Calfano 2013b). Furthermore, the lack of access to organized religion may lessen the number of networks for recruitment (Harris 1999; Djupe and Gilbert 2009). Finally, this relationship could be time bound. Our data collection begins with the 2008

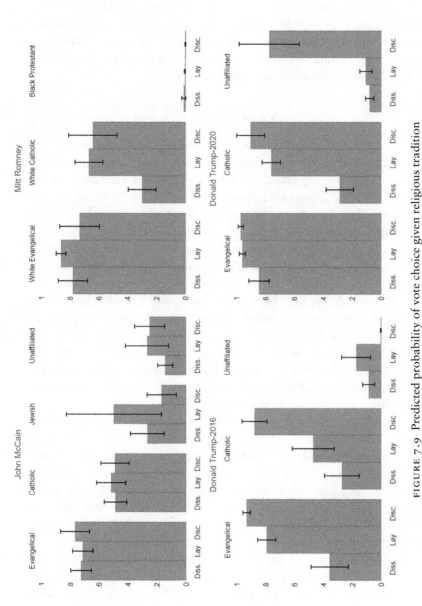

FIGURE 7.9 Predicted probability of vote choice given religious tradition

Note: Predicted probabilities were generated using coefficient estimates from logit regression models that control for biblical literalism, religious tradition, religious importance, worship attendance, personal demographics, and political ideology. Capped lines mark the estimated 95 percent confidence intervals.

presidential election, which has been viewed as the pivotal point in the rise of reactionary conservativism and calls for preserving the nation's heritage (Parker and Barreto 2013). It could be that the mobilizing power of religious exceptionalism for evangelicals is an adverse reaction to the threat presented by the prospect of an African American president in Obama, which found its fullest expression in the racist and xenophobic rhetoric of the Trump campaign and presidency.

CONCLUSION

Many racial and religious minorities subscribe to religious exceptionalism to the same degree if not more than White evangelical Protestants. This is in a sense surprising, as one might expect religious exceptionalism to be unpopular among groups that appear to be alienated by the ideology's notions of cultural purity and hierarchical devotion. In this regard, racial and religious minorities are the nation's most unexpected adherents. However, as this chapter's findings have also shown, minority group members do not relate adherence to their political attitudes and behaviors in the same way as their White counterparts. White disciples vote for and approve of all things Republican, Tea Party, and Trump, and tend to mobilize in support of their causes. In contrast, racial minority disciples are similar to their dissident counterparts in their opposition to all things Republican, Tea Party, and Trump, and appear to be politically demobilized. This is problematic, as it suggests that adherence to American religious exceptionalism undermines racial minorities' political power and democratic representation by demobilizing disciples.

Our findings further suggest that religious minorities often subscribe to religious exceptionalism at the same level as White evangelical Protestants, but as with their racial minority counterparts, they do not link this set of ideas to their political attitudes to the same degree. This is compatible with research showing Latinxs who hold anti-Black sentiments are less likely to apply their racial attitudes to opposition of President Obama (Segura and Valenzuela 2010). Similarly, our research reveals that religious minorities subscribe to the ideology of religious exceptionalism in spite of the ideology's alienation of religious minority groups, but are unlikely to apply their ideology to their understanding and engagement with politics. This speaks to religious exceptionalism's wide acceptance by diverse groups in society, but also to its limited power to shape the attitudes of those positioned at the periphery.

Conclusion

O, yes,
I say it plain,
America never was America to me,
And yet I swear this oath –
America will be!

Langston Hughes, "Let America be America Again"

And so it is marvelous and great that we do have a dream, that we have
a nation with a dream; and to forever challenge us; to forever give us a sense
of urgency; to forever stand in the midst of the "isness" of our terrible
injustices; to remind us of the "oughtness" of our noble capacity for justice
and love and brotherhood.

Martin Luther King, "The American Dream," July 4, 1965

Since the first European settlers arrived in this new and bountiful land, America has occupied a unique place in the imagination. Rich with natural treasure and unsullied by the political machinations and religious intolerance in the European societies that had been left behind, America represented a modern Eden to early arrivals. As the society matured and found its voice to expel the British Crown, the idea that this new nation enjoyed divine favor and an exceptional responsibility to defend freedom and liberty spread widely among the Founders. Since independence, presidents of all stripes have returned to the wellspring of American religious exceptionalism to find inspiration for their articulation of America's purpose in the world. These messages pervade popular culture and are sung out from church pulpits and schoolteachers' desks across America, reinforcing what any blue-blooded citizen takes for granted from birth: that America is exceptional. Defending America against all who might do it harm is then more than a national duty; it is a God-given responsibility.

The key finding of our book is American religious exceptionalism's enduring and powerful relationship to public opinion toward the last two decade's major policy debates and national elections, including George W. Bush's invasion of Iraq, Barack Obama's executive orders on immigration and reform of the national healthcare system, and the election of Donald Trump and his xenophobic America First agenda. The ideology of religious exceptionalism also explains its disciples' willingness to countenance the possibility of autocratic governance, a trend that should make champions of American democracy uneasy to put it mildly. Using the most expansive set of original data ever collected on the topic – nine original surveys spanning over a decade – we demonstrate that religious exceptionalism is an everyday influence that is so commonplace in Americans' lives, most have historically been unable to detect it. This is largely because religious exceptionalism ties religious beliefs closely to one's cherished national identity, making most American patriots unwilling to reject religious exceptionalism's lofty creed, out of the possibility America might not seem as great if its divinity is denied. Indeed, as chapter after chapter of this book describes, disciples of American religious exceptionalism are embarked on an everyday crusade to challenge less-religious visions of American nationhood in every domain where they are called to fight.

FOUNDATIONS OF RELIGIOUS EXCEPTIONALISM

We began our widescale examination of American attitudes and behaviors more than a decade ago with a simple premise: White evangelical identity on its own cannot explain religion's overwhelming influence on American politics. Our book's approach to understanding religion's influence on American attitudes first arose out of sociological and political science research that has repeatedly uncovered the immense role religion plays in the political lives of that nation's most religious group, Black Americans. Our approach seemed even more important to investigate in light of Janelle Wong's research on the divergent ways in which evangelical identity translates to disparate political attitudes for different racial group members (Wong 2018), and Chris Parker and Matt Barreto's study of the Tea Party, which reveals White evangelicals' behavior has changed in response to threats posed by national demographic shifts (2013). These approaches reveal that White evangelical explanations on their own often overlook the expansiveness of religious experiences and their effects, as well as their evolution in light of a diverse and changing America.

Religion's hold over Americans' attitudes and behaviors does not end with White evangelicals. A key takeaway from this book is that religion is far more expansive and reflects a long history of religious ideas enmeshed in America's national identity, which are constantly enforced and reproduced through a set of national myths about the nation's divine purpose, rather than a single racial group's religious tradition. Furthermore, while these myths are born out of national attachments, we are able to theorize with more specificity a Millennialist scriptural origin than current nationalism studies offer. Religion's influence on American attitudes and behaviors is more accurately accounted for by this more expansive ideology of religious exceptionalism with roots in the history of God and nation's fusion.

None of that denies the outsized importance White evangelical identity has in American politics. White evangelicals are today a valuable voting bloc and powerful political coalition, but come to this influence only after a long history of avoiding and railing against political involvement as improper and contrary to the aims of religious sacrifice. For most of American history, they assiduously eschewed the excesses of the material world, of which politics seemed particularly venomous. Our research illuminates a hitherto unidentified link between White evangelicals before the Enlightenment to the point today where they are tried and true supporters of Trump, the least likely of religious leaders (Martí 2018). Religious exceptionalism is pervasive, which means White evangelicals, alongside people of color and other unexpected adherents, internalize dominant and culturally exclusive narratives – in the name of an intense pride and affection for America. This sometimes comes at a great cost to racial minority group members' political mobilization. In other circumstances, these narratives do not translate as well to peripheral group members' attitudes and behaviors, which is in keeping with existing research on minority group behavior (Segura and Valenzuela 2010). Overall, however, our book provides strong evidence that religious exceptionalism underpins the American public's understanding and upholding of religion's link to national identity, ultimately yielding a strong divide between its disciples and dissidents.

Religious exceptionalism is part and parcel of a former inclusive model of civil religion that was justified as an incorporationist tool by elites (see Soper and Fetzer 2018), but, as Chapter 2 documents, it has evolved into a new model that excludes cultural outsiders. Exceptionalism therefore explains how White evangelicals – mainly, but not solely – internalize views of their own position as God's chosen people. To be sure, however, it is not the nation's evangelicals alone who have arrived at exclusionary and religiously bound ideas about who counts as an American, who deserves protections of their rights, and who deserves punishment for breaking norms of social appropriateness. America's history reveals a model of religion's relationship to national identity that began as inclusive, but was captured by well-positioned groups to champion cultural homogeneity, exclusionary policies, and the candidates that advance these aims.

UNDERSTANDING RELIGIOUS EXCEPTIONALISM OUTCOMES

Survey data from nine original polls conducted over a decade-plus period confirm repeatedly that America has become divided into disciples and dissidents. We find a persistent gap in disciples' and dissidents' attitudes and behavior that is incredibly robust across space, time, and political context. Whether or not one adheres to the idea that America is destined by God to spread its values to the rest of the world, is superior to all others, and is by its nature pure predicts strong attachment to American nationalism (Chapter 3), immigration restrictionism (Chapter 4), nationally narcissistic foreign policy attitudes (Chapter 5), a tolerance for the possibility of authoritarian rule (Chapter 6), and increased political engagement on the part of Whites but decreased political mobilization for racial minority group members (Chapter 7). These outcomes ultimately reveal that the American public is fractured as a result of their willingness either to accept or reject a dominant narrative about America as divinely inspired.

The disciple–dissident divide has also revealed to political elites the boundaries by which they can politicize religious issues in order to mobilize this large group of American "patriots". The most obvious case of this is illustrated by the rise of Donald Trump. While we three have long recognized the potential for a candidate like Donald Trump to win over an American electorate primed for a religious crusade at any cost, many scholars were shocked Trump won such a large majority of the White evangelical vote in 2016. Evangelicals voted for Trump over evangelical primary challenger Ted Cruz, and in larger proportions than they had supported fellow evangelical and former Republican President George W. Bush. Trump continues to receive White evangelicals' highest levels of dedication four years later, even after having been impeached (twice) and losing an election. While Trump's 2016 win can be attributed to a successful electoral college strategy, his courting of White evangelical voters still shocked many observers who noted the paradox of God-fearing Americans supporting a man who could not accurately cite the Bible, has been unfaithful to multiple wives, and was caught on tape boasting about his penchant for sexual assault. Trump's popularity is explained by religious exceptionalism, which requires not a leader who embodies religious values, but rather one who is goal-oriented vis-à-vis the nation's religious purpose – to protect its cultural homogeneity and spread its Judeo-Christian values.

In a departure from his Republican predecessors, Trump's use of religious rhetoric relies less on the typical vague language elites use to express in public their commitment to Christianity and more on overt expressions of his willingness to fight for the interests of Judeo-Christian organizations, whom he depicts as marginalized and under constant attack. Trump's success in courting religious exceptionalism's disciples derives from his appeals to a common victimhood narrative that is central to evangelical identity (Parker and Barreto 2013; Wong 2018). He uses a combination of threats, promises, and credit claiming to facilitate this relationship, in keeping with his authoritarian style (Smith and Hanley 2018). In a special meeting with national evangelical leaders, he warned that not mobilizing during the 2018 midterm elections would cause Democrats to enact changes "quickly and violently." He used the occasion to exaggerate the reach of an executive order he had recently issued lifting regulations on religious organizations' ability to receive federal funds after endorsing political candidates. In the same meeting, he warned evangelical leaders they had "really been silenced," but then claimed they were no longer silenced due to his own personal efforts (Martí 2018; Shear 2018). Trump's remarks were hailed by a Black minister who praised Trump for acting as a "warrior at the helm" who would "fight for them." Simply put, religious exceptionalism's disciples are not limited to White evangelicals, and they respond remarkably well to a crusader who promises to keep God's mission at the forefront of the nation's identity.

THE CRUSADE CONTINUES

The imposition of a sentimental, or false, narrative on the disparate and often random experience that constitutes the life of a city or country means, necessarily, that much of what happens in that city or country will be rendered illustrative, a series of set pieces, or performance opportunities.

Joan Didion, "New York: Sentimental Journeys," *New York Review of Books*, January 17, 1991[1]

As Joan Didion so eloquently reminds us, false narratives based on one's pride of place are nothing new. These mythologies are powerful movers of their audience's thoughts and behaviors. In this book, we have shown that the false narratives or myths undergirding the ideology of religious exceptionalism explain Americans' political attitudes and behaviors. This is true for its disciples who fully adhere to and reproduce these religiously laden national myths in order to preserve the cultural homogeneity and dominance of White Christian Protestantism. But these myths also affect its dissidents, who have to combat evolving institutionalized norms and elite rhetoric that reproduce the norms of religious exceptionalism. Whether or not these myths and the internalization of the ideology will lead someday toward a less democratic and more religious national government is uncertain. However, the battle lines have been drawn; enemies abound; the temple must be defended at any cost; and an exceptional nation must be made great again to continue its everyday crusade.

Appendix

This book relies primarily on survey data for its empirical foundations. In this appendix, we first briefly describe the original and other surveys we analyze to generate the insights reported throughout the book. Second, we list the specific items used to measure American religious exceptionalism across our surveys. Third, we report on an internal validity exercise we conducted to strengthen our measure of American religious exceptionalism.

ORIGINAL NATIONAL AND STATE SURVEYS (DESIGNED AND CONDUCTED BY THE AUTHORS SINGLY OR JOINTLY FOR THIS PROJECT)

2010 Knowledge Networks (2010 KN)

This survey was funded by a grant from the Ohio State's Mershon Center for International Security Studies. The survey is a stratified national sample of registered and unregistered adults living in the United States. The survey has 1,273 respondents.

The 2011 Sooner Poll (2011 SP)

To collect Oklahoman attitudes, stratified online and cell phone samples were administered through Survey Sampling International. Every Sooner Poll public opinion poll completed by telephone was conducted within an on-site calling center in Oklahoma City using Computer-aided Telephone Interviewing (CATI) technology during May 2–12, 2011. The survey comprised roughly 500 respondents and had a margin of error of +/– 4.34 percent.

The 2012 Religious Worldviews Survey (2012 RWS)

Funded by the National Science Foundation and administered between October 4 and October 17, 2012. The survey is a stratified national sample of registered and unregistered Black and White adults who identified as Christians. The survey has 1,146 respondents (599 White and 547 Black), and a completion rate of 60 percent. A random sample of panel members was drawn from GfK's KnowledgePanel®. In all, 1,913 (excluding breakoffs) responded to the invitation, yielding a final stage completion rate of 59.9 percent. The recruitment rate for this study, reported by GfK, was 14.9 percent and the profile rate was 64.8 percent, for a cumulative response rate of 5.9 percent. The response summary metrics were calculated using AAPOR RR6, which accounts for the multiple phases of survey recruitment and selection (for a detailed explanation, see Callegaro and DiSogra 2008).

The 2010 Knowledge Networks Survey and the 2012 Religious Worldviews Survey were administered via GfK Knowledge Networks, the only online survey panel based on a representative probability sample of the whole of the United States. While other online panels rely on opt-in recruitment efforts, Knowledge Networks relies on probability-based recruitment. Aware of the biases created by variation in internet access, Knowledge Networks uses "address-based sampling" to select panelists. Furthermore, they provide panelists with internet access if they don't have it.

2014 Kentucky Poll (2014 KYP)

The 2014 Big Red Poll was conducted during October 6–19 through Western Kentucky University's Social Science Research Center. The data collection involved a live-caller, dual frame (landline and cell phone) survey of 601 registered Kentucky voters. The survey has a margin of error of +/– 4 percent. Calls were made from Monday through Friday from 4 PM to 8 PM, and from 1 PM to 5 PM on weekends.

2016 SSI Poll

The 2016 Survey Sampling International Poll was administered during September 14–23, 2016, to roughly 4,800 US residents recruited using its online panel, which was quota-sampled by gender, education, age, and state of residence (based on Current Population Survey estimates). Oversamples of Black, Latinx, and Asian American respondents were collected to facilitate across race comparisons of attitudes and self-assessed behaviors.

The 2019 American Policy Survey (2019 APS)

Administered via Qualtrics between December 20 and December 30, 2019. The survey is an on online convenience sample with quotas, regarding race and gender. The survey has 600 respondents.

Cooperative Congressional Election Study (CCES) Surveys

It is a nationally stratified sample survey administered by YouGov. The survey consists of common content and content designed by specific teams. *The data taken for the 2008, 2018, and 2020 surveys are from the University of Texas team modules.* Each module consists of 1,000 respondents.

PRRI SURVEYS (DESIGNED AND CONDUCTED BY AN EXTERNAL ORGANIZATION)

The Public Religion Research Institute (PRRI) is a nonprofit, nonpartisan organization dedicated to conducting independent research at the intersection of religion, culture, and public policy. Each of the surveys used can be accessed through their website prri.org.

PRRI/Brookings 2012 Race, Class, and Culture Survey

Sample: Nationally representative adults (18+) living in the United States
Total Respondents: 2,501 (1,501 landline; 1,000 cell phone)
Data Collected: August 2–15, 2012

PRRI/Brookings 2013 Economic Values Survey

Sample: Nationally representative adults (18+) living in the United States
Total Respondents: 2,002 (1,202 landline; 800 cell phone)
Data Collected: May 30–June 16, 2013

PRRI/RNS June 2015 Survey

Sample: Nationally representative adults (18+) living in the United States
Total Respondents: 1,007 (501 landline; 506 cell phone)
Data Collected: June 10–14, 2015

PRRI/The Atlantic 2016 Post-Election White Working Class Survey

Sample: Subset of respondents who participated in the PRRI/The Atlantic White Working Class Survey
Total Respondents: 1,162 (540 landline; 622 cell phone)
Data Collected: November 9–20, 2016

ITEMS USED TO CONSTRUCT THE AMERICAN RELIGIOUS EXCEPTIONALISM MEASURE

TABLE A1 *Inclusion of items measuring American religious exceptionalism across surveys*

Items	2008 CCES	2010 KN	2011 OK	2012 RWS	2014 KYP	2016 SSI	2018 CCES	2019 APS	2020 CCES
America holds a special place in God's plan	✓	✓	✓	✓	✓	✓	✓	✓	✓
The success of the United States is not a reflection of divine will	✓	✓		✓	✓	✓	✓	✓	✓
The vast resources of the United States indicate that God has chosen it to lead other nations	✓	✓	✓	✓	✓	✓	✓	✓	✓
The United States is spiritually predestined to lead the world		✓		✓	✓		✓	✓	✓
Mean	.37	.37	.62	.45	.54	.47	.38	.46	.38
Alpha	.73	.82	.68	.80	.84	.60	.80	.79	.84

VALIDATING OUR MEASURE OF AMERICAN RELIGIOUS EXCEPTIONALISM

To establish the internal validity of the measure, we administered several surveys using University of Texas undergraduates in introductory political science courses. Using students from these courses was beneficial because state law requires students to take two government courses, which allowed us to get students from a broader spectrum of majors, not just political science. The Cronbach's alpha scores ranged between .82 and .90. We also conducted a test-retest with a six-week separation between the initial test and the follow-up. The results find the respondent's scores in the test and retest correlated at .72, indicating the measure is stable (Fink 1995).

Additionally, we examined the relationship between our American religious exceptionalism measure and a measure of civil religion taken from Chapp (2013). We find that the measures are moderately correlated with each other with the correlation coefficient ranging from .57 to .66. In addition to the pair-wise correlations, we conducted a series of factor analyses to demonstrate they are distinct dimensions. Table A2 demonstrates the items measuring American religious exceptionalism load on the civil religion factor. However, two of the civil religion items load on the exceptionalism factor. The first item refers to the covenant relationship the United States has with God and highlights a special connection with the divine. The second refers to the sanctity of the US Constitution, which speaks to the role of the divine in its history. These results indicate the measures are positively related, but they are distinct.

TABLE A2 *Principal components factor analysis of the measures of American religious exceptionalism (ARE) and civil religion (CR)*

	Fall 2012		Spring 2013		Fall 2017		Spring 2018	
	ARE	CR	ARE	CR	ARE	CR	ARE	CR
American religious exceptionalism								
America holds a special place in God's plan	.710		.886		.825		.891	
The vast resources of the United States indicate that God has chosen it to lead other nations	.896		.910		.877		.942	

(continued)

TABLE A2 *(continued)*

	Fall 2012		Spring 2013		Fall 2017		Spring 2018	
	ARE	*CR*	*ARE*	*CR*	*ARE*	*CR*	*ARE*	*CR*
The United States is spiritually predestined to lead the world	.851		.834		.802		.914	
The success of the United States is not a reflection of divine will (reverse coded)	.742		.726		.714		.807	
Civil religion								
America as a nation, holds a special higher power		.783		.552		.581		.772
The US Constitution is a holy document	.444	.447		.472		.458	.621	
Being an American citizen is a sacred responsibility		.709		.834		.801		.779
The United States has a special covenant with God	.681		.753		.782		.699	
The office of the president is a sacred position		.745		.954		.808		.835
As Americans, we are blessed with special opportunities		.882		.638		.854		.813
Eigenvalue	5.24	1.35	5.33	1.28	5.05	1.41	5.28	1.76

Note: Varimax rotation and only factor scores above .4 are reported

Notes

1 MYTHS, GODS, AND NATIONS

1. The nation is distinct from the state. Historian Hugh Seton-Watson distinguishes the state from the nation via the Weberian power dynamics implied by the former: "A state is a legal and political organisation, with the power to require obedience and loyalty from its citizens. A nation is a community of people, whose members are bound together by a sense of solidarity, a common culture, a national consciousness" (1977, p. 1).
2. We note with dismay the problematic aspects of scholars continuing to praise America's defense of liberty and equality given the nation's history with the ethnic cleansing of Native Americans; chattel slavery; discrimination against women, non-Whites, and non-Protestants; and disenfranchising non-land-owning Whites. On this dimension, Myrdal's (1944) *The American Dilemma* stands out for its intellectual courage in directly confronting this contradiction in its effort to understand how a nation that claims to prize liberty and justice can so openly oppress – and justify the oppression of – racial minorities.
3. Alpha refers to Cronbach's α, which is a measure of scale reliability. It ranges from 0 to 1 with higher values, indicating that the various items in the measure cohere more tightly on the hypothesized underlying dimension; in other words, higher values indicate that the scale is more reliable. The Appendix provides details for each of the surveys used.
4. Falwell's remarks were made on Pat Robertson's "The 700 Club" radio show on September 13, 2001, two days after the attacks.
5. www.npr.org/2017/09/04/548471362/-he-has-a-reason-how-natural-disasters-test-the-faithful
6. Dobson made these comments on his daily radio show "Dr. James Dobson's Family Talk" on December 17, 2012, three days after the horrific massacre. The radio program is available here: https://drjamesdobson.org/Broadcasts/Broadcast?i=32d0ea7c-eeb2-41fb-9c05-f6e0c733d58a

7. www.huffpost.com/entry/pat-robertson-covid-19_n_5ea0b4abc5b67cf2ad bd78ee
8. The 700 Club, December 30, 1981.
9. Franklin Delano Roosevelt. State of the Union, January 6, 1942: www.c-span .org/video/?152565-1/franklin-d-roosevelt-state-union-address
10. See www.reaganlibrary.gov/research/speeches/30883b. The 1983 speech was the second time Reagan used the "Evil Empire" analogy, but the first time it was intended for the American public. The original occasion was in an address to the British House of Commons in June 1982.
11. The references etched on the rifle sights were to specific biblical passages: 2 Corinthians 4:6 (NIV) "For God, who said, 'Let light shine out of darkness,' made his light shine in our hearts to give us the light of the knowledge of God's glory displayed in the face of Christ" and John 8:12 "When Jesus spoke again to the people, he said, 'I am the light of the world. Whoever follows me will never walk in darkness, but will have the light of life'" (Eckholm 2010). Given the context in which they are used, they further demonstrate the need for religious nationalism to seek a foreign policy agenda of vindicationism.
12. Martin Luther King. "Remaining Awake Through the Great Revolution." Sermon delivered on March 31, 1968, at the National Cathedral in Washington, DC. Accessed May 24, 2020 at https://kinginstitute.stanford.e du/king-papers/publications/knock-midnight-inspiration-great-sermons-rev erend-martin-luther-king-jr-10
13. *Ibid.*

2 WHO ARE THE BELIEVERS?

1. Americans do not necessarily view themselves as being the only ones who receive this protection. Of those who believed the United States receives special protection, three-fourths believe that other nations also receive this special protection, while only 15 percent believed they did not.
2. This item is reverse-worded. Doing so makes the scale measurement more rigorous as it requires the respondent think more carefully about her answer to the question.
3. Whitehead and Perry's (2020) examination of Christian nationalism provide a wider array of measures of private religious behavior. Interestingly, they found that increased engagement in private religious behaviors was associated with lower support for Christian nationalism.
4. It is important to note that the incarnation of the social gospel at the end of the nineteenth and the beginning of the twentieth centuries was closely tied to American religious exceptionalism as supporters argued that through the Progressive movement, the nation perfected itself and should spread its innov-ations to the world. This logic was used to justify American imperialism, such as the colonization of the Philippines (Hunt 2009; McDougall 2019). As time elapsed, critics noted the hypocrisy of linking the social gospel to imperialism. Because of this, the contemporary manifestation of the social gospel is critical

of any belief that the nation has perfected itself and should now go about perfecting the world (Wallis 2005).

5. The social (α = .63) and prosperity (α = .65) gospel measures are taken from McDaniel (2016).

3 WHO DWELLS IN HIS HOUSE?

1. Many works have referred to the former dimension as patriotism and the latter as nationalism (see de Figueiredo and Elkins 2003). Our own published research questions the distinction (McDaniel, Nooruddin, and Shortle 2016), and so we shall not refer to them as such.
2. Huddy and Khatib (2007) also find a negative relationship between this type of national attachment and civic engagement.
3. President Donald Trump's speech in Detroit, Michigan, on May 21, 2020, praised noted anti-Semite Henry Ford's "bloodlines." The speech was condemned as a "dog whistle" to America's ethnoculturalists: www.usatoday.com/story/news/politics/2020/05/22/trump-criticized-praising-bloodlines-henry-ford-anti-semite/5242361002/.
4. www.djournal.com/news/katherine-harris-says-failure-to-elect-christians-will-legislate-sin/article_ffbea32d-7d0b-5e64-b299-f994ddfea766.html (accessed May 30, 2020).
5. www.nytimes.com/2006/12/21/us/21koran.html (accessed May 30, 2020).
6. www.c-span.org/video/?403331-1/donald-trump-remarks-liberty-university (accessed May 30, 2020).

4 WHAT DO WE OWE STRANGERS?

1. On June 7, 2021, Vice President Kamala Harris, in a speech made in Guatemala, plainly told would-be migrants "not to come." See www.npr.org/2021/06/07/1004074139/harris-tells-guatemalans-not-to-migrate-to-the-united-states (accessed June 11, 2021).
2. This myth diverges from earlier national myths of "citizenship by intent," where immigrants were merely expected to formalize their intention to become Americans in order to receive rights. Of course, that earlier myth was in an era when the modal immigrant was a White European, which explains the difference in approach.
3. These results are available in the online appendix.

5 EVANGELIZING AMERICAN RELIGIOUS EXCEPTIONALISM

1. Washington, George. 1796. "Farewell Address." www.loc.gov/resource/mgw2.024/?sp=229&st=text (accessed June 3, 2020).
2. Adams, John Quincy. 1821. "Speech to the U.S. House of Representatives on Foreign Policy" (July 4). Available at https://millercenter.org/the-presidency/

presidential-speeches/july-4-1821-speech-us-house-representatives-foreign-policy (accessed June 3, 2020).

3. McKinley, William. "Inaugural Address" (March 4, 1901). Available at www.inaugural.senate.gov/about/past-inaugural-ceremonies/29th-inaugural-ceremonies/index.html (accessed on June 10, 2020).

4. Wilson, Woodrow. 1914. "Annapolis Commencement Address." Available at www.presidency.ucsb.edu/documents/annapolis-commencement-address (accessed on June 10, 2020).

5. Wilson, Woodrow. 1917. "Address to a Joint Session of Congress Requesting a Declaration of War Against Germany" (April 2). Available at www.presidency.ucsb.edu/documents/address-joint-session-congress-requesting-declaration-war-against-germany (accessed June 10, 2020).

6. The speech is available here: https://shafr.org/sites/default/files/Wallace%2CCommonMan.pdf (accessed December 17, 2021).

7. The full speech can be read here: www.trumanlibrary.gov/library/public-papers/52/address-columbus-conference-federal-council-churches (accessed June 11, 2021).

8. See www.presidency.ucsb.edu/documents/address-the-cornerstone-laying-the-new-york-avenue-presbyterian-church (accessed June 11, 2021).

9. National Security Council Report, NSC 68," United States Objectives and Programs for National Security" (April 14, 1950; declassified February 27, 1975). Available at https://digitalarchive.wilsoncenter.org/document/116191.pdf?v=2699956db534c1821edefa61b8c13ffe (accessed June 13, 2020).

10. "Report to the National Security Council by the Executive Secretary (Lay) on Basic National Security Policy" (October 30, 1953). Available at https://fas.org/irp/offdocs/nsc-hst/nsc-162-2.pdf (accessed June 13, 2020).

11. See www.cfr.org/in-brief/bidens-first-foreign-policy-move-reentering-international-agreements (accessed April 1, 2021).

12. Given the highly partisan nature of these policies, we also estimated the models controlling for partisanship. The results found that the relationships remained even when partisanship is included.

6 GOVERNING THE TEMPLE

1. Rep. Ilhan Omar (D-MN) is a particular object of vitriol and often stands in on talk radio and right-wing television for all Muslim politicians.

2. Our measure is adapted from Schulz, et al. (2017). Later in the chapter, we report the Cronbach α (alpha) score for the measures. This ranges from 0 to 1, with higher values indicating that the items cohere more strongly with each other and therefore bolster confidence that they are capturing a common underlying dimension.

3. Results are available in the online appendix.

4. See www.cnn.com/2018/03/10/politics/trump-campaign-slogan/index.html (accessed June 17, 2020).

5. See www.npr.org/2020/01/16/796864399/exclusive-trump-to-reinforce-protections-for-prayer-in-schools (accessed June 17, 2020).

6. See the online appendix.
7. These results can be found in the online appendix.
8. A dissident has a 20 percent chance sympathizing with the Tea Party, while the odds for a laity and disciple are 37 percent and 50 percent, respectively. These results can be found in the online appendix.
9. We also examined this relationship using the state polls and found the same negative relationship. These results can be found in the online appendix.
10. The Christian flag is a flag with a white banner with a red Latin Cross on a blue canton. The ichthys is the outline of a fish adopted by early Christians.
11. The results from these analyses can be found in the online appendix.
12. See www.washingtonpost.com/elections/interactive/2020/trump-pandemic-c oronavirus-election/ (accessed April 5, 2021).

7 THE VIEW FROM THE BACK PEWS

1. Langston Hughes's magnificent ode to the America that never was captures this idea well: https://poets.org/poem/let-america-be-america-again
2. The predicted value for a White dissident on the national identity measure is .83, but for a Black dissident it is .69 and for a Latinx dissident it is .76. For their disciple counterparts, Whites have a predicted value of .93, while Blacks and Latinx disciples have predicted values of .89 and .92, respectively.
3. Since the modal White and Black respondents in the racial analyses were mainline and Black Protestants, respectively, it would be redundant to include them in this set of analyses. Because of this, we exclude them.
4. These results are available in an online appendix.
5. These results can be found in the online appendix.
6. The online appendix also reports analyses of how adherence to American religious exceptionalism affects presidential approval, voter turnout, and political interest for different religious traditions. The patterns of results are consistent with those for the dependent variables reported earlier.

8 CONCLUSION

1. www.nybooks.com/articles/1991/01/17/new-york-sentimental-journeys/ (accessed June 18, 2020).

References

Abdelal, Rawi, Yoshiko M. Herrera, Alastair Iain Johnston, and Rose McDermott. 2006. "Identity as a Variable." *Perspectives on Politics* 4: 695–711.

Abrajano, Marisa, and Zoltan Hajnal. 2015. *White Backlash: Immigration, Race, and American Politics*. Princeton: Princeton University Press.

Abramowitz, Alan, and Jennifer McCoy. 2019. "United States: Racial Resentment, Negative Partisanship, and Polarization in Trump's America." *The ANNALS of the American Academy of Political and Social Science* 681: 137–56.

Abramowitz, Alan I., and Steven Webster. 2016. "The Rise of Negative Partisanship and the Nationalization of U.S. Elections in the 21st Century." *Electoral Studies* 41: 12–22.

Ackerman, Robert A., Edward A. Witt, M. Brent Donnellan, Kali H. Trzesniewski, Lee N. Robins, and Deborah A. Kashy. 2011. "What Does the Narcissistic Personality Inventory Really Measure?" *Assessment* 18: 67–87.

Adam, Thomas Ritchie. 1937. *The Civic Value of Museums*. Studies in the Social Significance of Adult Education in the United States. New York: American Association for Adult Education.

Alba, Richard D., Rubén G. Rumbaut, and Karen Marotz. 2005. "A Distorted Nation: Perceptions of Racial/Ethnic Group Sizes and Attitudes Toward Immigrants and Other Minorities." *Social Forces* 84: 901–19.

Alba, Richard D., and Victor Nee. 2003. *Remaking the American Mainstream: Assimilation and Contemporary Immigration*. Cambridge, MA: Harvard University Press.

Albrecht, Stan L., and Tim B. Heaton. 1984. "Secularization, Higher Education, and Religiosity." *Review of Religious Research* 26: 43–58.

Aldrich, John H. 1995. *Why Parties? The Origin and Transformation of Political Parties in America*. Chicago: University of Chicago Press.

Aldrich, John H., Christopher Gelpi, Peter Feaver, Jason Reifler, and Kristin Thompson Sharp. 2006. "Foreign Policy and the Electoral Connection." *Annual Review of Political Science* 9: 477–502.

Alexander, Kathryn J. 2017. "Religiosity and Bellicosity: The Impact of Religious Commitment on Patterns of Interstate Conflict." *Journal of Global Security Studies* 2: 271–87.

Allport, Floyd H. 1927. "The Psychology of Nationalism." Harper's Monthly Magazine, August. 291–301. https://harpers.org/archive/1927/08/the-psychology-of-nationalism/

Almond, Gabriel A. 1950. *The American People and Foreign Policy*. 1st ed. New York: Harcourt.

Altemeyer, Bob. 1996. *The Authoritarian Specter*. Cambridge, MA: Harvard University Press.

2003. "Why do Religious Fundamentalists Tend to be Prejudiced?" *International Journal for the Psychology of Religion* 13: 17–28.

Amuedo-Dorantes, Catalina, and Thitima Puttitanun. 2016. "DACA and the Surge in Unaccompanied Minors at the US-Mexico Border." *International Migration* 54: 102–17.

Anderson, Benedict. 1983. *Imagined Communities: Reflections on the Origin and Spread of Nationalism*. London: Verso.

Arkin, William M. 2003. "A General Bind for Rumsfeld." Los Angeles Times, www.latimes.com/archives/la-xpm-2003-oct-26-op-arkin26-story.html (accessed October 19, 2019).

Armstrong, John Alexander. 1982. *Nations before Nationalism*. Chapel Hill: University of North Carolina Press.

Ashcroft, John. 2002. "Prepared Remarks of Attorney General John Ashcroft National Religious Broadcasters Convention Nashville, Tennessee February 19, 2002." United States Department of Justice, www.justice.gov/arch ive/ag/speeches/2002/021902religiousbroadcasters.htm (accessed October 19, 2019).

Asher, Jeremiah. 1999. "Protesting the 'Negro Pew'." In *African American Religious History: A Documentary Witness*, ed. Milton C. Sernett. Durham: Duke University Press. 224–27.

Austin, David. 1794. "The Downfall of Mystical Babylon; or a Key to the Providence of God, in the Political Operations of 1793–1794." In *The Millennium; or, the Thousand Years of Prosperity, Promised to the Church of God, in the Old Testament and in the New, Shortly to Commence, and to be Carried on to Perfection, under the Auspices of Him, Who, in the Vision, was Presented to St. John [Six Lines of Scripture Texts]*, ed. David Austin. Elizabeth Town: Shepard Kollock. 329–432.

Bacevich, Andrew J., and Elizabeth H. Prodromou. 2004. "God Is Not Neutral: Religion and U.S. Foreign Policy after 9/11." *Orbis* 48: 43–54.

Bailey, Thomas Andrew. 1948. *The Man in the Street: The Impact of American Public Opinion on Foreign Policy*. New York: Macmillan.

Bainbridge, William Sims. 2005. "Atheism." *Interdisciplinary Journal of Religion Research* 1: 2–26.

Baker, Joseph O., and Andrew L. Whitehead. 2020. "God's Penology: Belief in a Masculine God Predicts Support for Harsh Criminal Punishment and Militarism." *Punishment & Society* 22: 135–60.

Bald, Vivek. 2013. "Selling the East in the American South: Bengali Muslim Peddlers in New Orleans and Beyond, 1880–1920." In *Asian Americans in Dixie: Race and Migration in the South*, ed. Khyati Y. Joshi and Jigna Desai. Urbana: University of Illinois Press. 33–53.

Banning, Lance. 1986. "Jeffersonian Ideology Revisited: Liberal and Classical Ideas in the New American Republic." *The William and Mary Quarterly* 43: 4–19.

Barbash, Fred. 2019. "Trump's Racist Comments can be Used against Him in Court as Judges Cite Them to Block Policies." The Washington Post, July 16. www.washingtonpost.com/national-security/trumps-racist-comments-can-be-used-against-him-in-court-as-judges-cite-them-to-block-policies/2019/07/16/6ed0ea6a-a7f1-11e9-86dd-d7f0e60391e9_story.html

Barker, David C., Jon Hurwitz, and Traci L. Nelson. 2008. "Of Crusades and Culture Wars: "Messianic" Militarism and Political Conflict in the United States." *The Journal of Politics* 70: 307–22.

Barr, William P. 2019. "Attorney General William P. Barr Delivers Remarks to the Law School and the de Nicola Center for Ethics and Culture at the University of Notre Dame." United States Department of Justice, www.justice.gov/opa/speech/attorney-general-william-p-barr-delivers-remarks-law-school-and-de-nicola-center-ethics (accessed January 3, 2020).

Barreto, Matt A. 2010. *Ethnic Cues: The Role of Shared Ethnicity in Latino Political Participation*. Ann Arbor: University of Michigan Press.

Barreto, Matt A., and Gary M. Segura. 2014. *Latino America: How America's Most Dynamic Population is Poised to Transform the Politics of the Nation*. 1st ed. New York: PublicAffairs.

Bartels, Larry M. 1991. "Constituency Opinion and Congressional Policy Making: The Reagan Defense Build Up." *The American Political Science Review* 85: 457–74.

Barton, David. 1992. *America's Godly Heritage*. Aledo: WallBuilders (sound recording).

2012. *God in the Constitution*. Aledo: WallBuilders (sound recording).

2016. *The Jefferson Lies: Exposing the Myths You've Always Believed about Thomas Jefferson*. Paperback ed. Washington, DC: WND Books.

Bates, Stephen. 2004. "'Godless Communism' and Its Legacies." *Society* 41: 29–33.

Beam, Christopher M. 1976. "Millennialism and American Nationalism, 1740–1800." *Journal of Presbyterian History (1962–1985)* 54: 182–99.

Bellah, Robert N. 1967. "Civil Religion in America." *Daedalus* 96: 1–21.

1975. *The Broken Covenant: American Civil Religion in Time of Trial*. Chicago: University of Chicago Press.

Bercovitch, Sacvan. 1978. *The American Jeremiad*. Madison: University of Wisconsin Press.

Berg, Justin Allen. 2009. "White Public Opinion toward Undocumented Immigrants: Threat and Interpersonal Environment." *Sociological Perspectives* 52: 39–58.

Berger, Stefan. 2009. "On the Role of Myths and History in the Construction of National Identity in Modern Europe." *European History Quarterly* 39: 490–502.

Berinsky, Adam J. 2009. In Time of War: Understanding American Public Opinion from World War II to Iraq, *Chicago Studies in American Politics*. Chicago: The University of Chicago Press.

Berinsky, Adam J., Gregory A. Huber, and Gabriel S. Lenz. 2012. "Evaluating Online Labor Markets for Experimental Research: Amazon.com's Mechanical Turk." *Political Analysis* 20: 351–68.

Berinsky, Adam J. and Tali Mendelberg. 2005. "The Indirect Effects of Discredited Stereotypes in Judgments of Jewish Leaders." *American Journal of Political Science* 49: 845–64.

Beveridge, Albert J. 1898. "The March of the Flag." Modern History Sourcebook, https://sourcebooks.fordham.edu/mod/1898beveridge.asp (accessed September 30, 2019).

1970. "For the Greater Republic." In *Nationalism and Religion in America: Concepts of American Identity and Mission*, ed. Winthrop Still Hudson. New York: Harper AND Row. 117–118.

Billig, Michael. 1995. *Banal Nationalism*. Thousand Oaks, CA: Sage.

Blum, Edward J. 2005. *Reforging the White Republic: Race, Religion, and American Nationalism, 1865–1898, Conflicting Worlds*. Baton Rouge: Louisiana State University Press.

Bonikowski, Bart. 2016. "Three Lessons of Contemporary Populism in Europe and the United States Populism in the Twenty-First Century." *Brown Journal of World Affairs* 23: 9–24.

2019. "Trump's Populism: The Mobilization of Nationalist Cleavages and the Future of US Democracy." In *When Democracy Trumps Populism: European and Latin American Lessons for the United States*, eds. Kurt Weyland and Raul Madrid. Cambridge: Cambridge University Press. 110–31.

Bonikowski, Bart, and Paul DiMaggio. 2016. "Varieties of American Popular Nationalism." *American Sociological Review* 81: 949–80.

Boorstein, Michelle. 2010. "In Flap over Mosque near Ground Zero, Conservative Bloggers Gaining Influence." Washington Post, www.washingtonpost.com/wp-dyn/content/article/2010/08/18/AR2010081802582.html (accessed February 7, 2020).

Borjas, George J. 1999. "The Economic Analysis of Immigration." In *Handbook of Labor Economics*, eds. Orley C. Ashenfelter and David Card. Vol. 3. San Diego: Elsevier. 1697–760.

Bowler, Kate. 2013. *Blessed: A History of the American Prosperity Gospel*. New York: Oxford University Press.

Boyd, Gregory A. 2005. *The Myth of a Christian Nation: How the Quest for Political Power Is Destroying the Church*. Grand Rapids, MI: Zondervan.

Brader, Ted, Nicholas A. Valentino, Ashley E. Jardina, and Timothy J. Ryan. 2010. "The Racial Divide on Immigration Opinion: Why Blacks Are Less Threatened by Immigrants." Paper presented at the American Political Science Association.

Brader, Ted, Nicholas A. Valentino, and Elizabeth Suhay. 2008. "What Triggers Public Opposition to Immigration? Anxiety, Group Cues, and Immigration Threat." *American Journal of Political Science* 52: 959–78.

Braumoeller, Bear F. 2010. "The Myth of American Isolationism." *Foreign Policy Analysis* 6: 349–71.

Breuilly, John. 1985. *Nationalism and the State*. Chicago: University of Chicago Press.

Brodkin, Karen. 1998. *How Jews Became White Folks and What that Says about Race in America*. New Brunswick, NJ: Rutgers University Press.

Brubaker, Rogers. 1996. *Nationalism Reframed: Nationhood and the National Question in the New Europe*. New York: Cambridge University Press.

Bruner, Jerome S. 1959. "Myth and Identity." *Daedalus* 88: 349–58.

Bulman, Raymond F. 1991. "'Myth of Origin', Civil Religion and Presidential Politics." *Journal of Church and State* 33: 525–39.

Bush, George W. 2001. "Remarks at the National Day of Prayer and Remembrance Service." The American Presidency Project, www.presidency.ucsb.edu/docu ments/remarks-the-national-day-prayer-and-remembrance-service-0 (accessed October 19, 2019).

Butler, Anthea D. 2021. *White Evangelical Racism : The Politics of Morality in America*. Chapel Hill: The University of North Carolina Press.

Byrd, James P. 2013. *Sacred Scripture, Sacred War: The Bible and the American Revolution*. New York: Oxford University Press.

Calavita, Kitty. 2014. "The New Politics of Immigration: 'Balanced-Budget Conservatism' and the Symbolism of Proposition 187*." *Social Problems* 43: 284–305.

Callegaro, Mario, and Charles DiSogra. 2008. "Computing Response Metrics for Online Panels." *Public Opinion Quarterly* 72: 1008–32.

Camarota, Steven A. 1997. "The Effect of Immigrants on the Earnings of Low-Skilled Native Workers: Evidence from the June 1991 Current Population Survey." *Social Science Quarterly* 78: 417–31.

Campbell, Angus, Phillip E. Converse, Warren E. Miller, and Donald E. Stokes. 1960. *The American Voter*. New York: John Wiley and Sons.

Campbell, James E. 2006. "Party Systems and Realignments in the United States, 1868–2004." *Social Science History* 30: 359–86.

Caplovitz, David, and Fred Sherrow. 1977. *The Religious Drop-Outs: Apostasy among College Graduates, Sage Library of Social Research v 44*. Beverly Hills: Sage Publications.

Caspary, William R. 1970. "The 'Mood Theory': A Study of Public Opinion and Foreign Policy." *American Political Science Review* 64: 536–47.

Cavari, Amnon. 2012. "Religious Beliefs, Elite Polarization, and Public Opinion on Foreign Policy: The Partisan Gap in American Public Opinion Toward Israel." *International Journal of Public Opinion Research* 25: 1–22.

CBS News and The New York Times. 1984. CBS News/New York Times National and Local Surveys, 1984. Ann Arbor, MI: Inter-university Consortium for Political and Social Research [distributor], 1992-02-16. https://doi.org/10 .3886/ICPSR08399.v1

Center for Political Studies, and University of Michigan. 1992. American National Election Study 1992 (Pre-Election), September, 1992 [survey question] [computer file]. (Study USCPS.92PRE.QG05B) version. University of Michigan Center for Political Studies: Cornell University, Ithaca, NY: Roper Center for Public Opinion Research, iPOLL [distributor]. https://doi .org/10.3886/ICPSR06230.v2

Chambers, William Nisbet. 1972. *The First Party System: Federalists and Republicans, Problems in American History*. New York: Wiley.

Chancey, Mark A. 2014. "Rewriting History for a Christian America: Religion and the Texas Social Studies Controversy of 2009–2010." *The Journal of Religion* 94: 325–53.

2019. "President Trump just Tweeted Support for Bible Courses, but it's already legal to teach about the Bible." *The Washington Post*, January 30. www.washingtonpost.com/religion/2019/01/30/president-trump-just-tweeted-support-bible-courses-its-already-legal-teach-about-bible/

Chang, Iris. 2003. *The Chinese in America: A Narrative History*. New York: Viking.

Chapp, Christopher B. 2013. *Religious Rhetoric and American Politics: The Endurance of Civil Religion in Electoral Campaigns*. Ithaca: Cornell University Press.

Chittick, William O., Keith R. Billingsley, and Rick Travis. 1995. "A Three-Dimensional Model of American Foreign Policy Beliefs." *International Studies Quarterly* 39: 313–31.

Chong, Dennis. 2000. *Rational Lives: Norms and Values in Politics and Society*. Chicago: University of Chicago Press.

Cillizza, Chris. 2013. "Kentucky Senate Race could Top $100 Million." Washington Post, August 11. www.washingtonpost.com/politics/kentucky-senate-race-spending-could-top-100-million/2013/08/11/09280212-0292-11e3-88d6-d5795fab4637_story.html

Cimino, Richard. 2005. "'No God in Common': American Evangelical Discourse on Islam after 9/11." *Review of Religious Research* 47: 162–74.

Citrin, Jack, Donald P. Green, Christopher Muste, and Cara Wong. 1997. "Public Opinion Toward Immigration Reform: The Role of Economic Motivations." *The Journal of Politics* 59: 858–81.

Citrin, Jack, Richard Johnston, and Matthew Wright. 2012. "Do Patriotism and Multiculturalism Collide? Competing Perspectives from Canada and the United States." *Canadian Journal of Political Science / Revue canadienne de science politique* 45: 531–52.

Citrin, Jack, Amy Lerman, Michael Murakami, and Kathryn Pearson. 2007. "Testing Huntington: Is Hispanic Immigration a Threat to American Identity?" *Perspectives on Politics* 5: 31–48.

Citrin, Jack, Beth Reingold, and Donald P. Green. 1990. "American Identity and the Politics of Ethnic Change." *The Journal of Politics* 52: 1124–54.

Citrin, Jack, and David O. Sears. 2009. "Balancing National and Ethnic Identities: The Psychology of E Pluribus Unum." In *Measuring Identity: A Guide for Social Scientists*, eds. Alastair Iain Johnston, Rawi Abdelal, Rose McDermott and Yoshiko M. Herrera. Cambridge: Cambridge University Press. 145–74.

Citrin, Jack, Cara Wong, and Brian Duff. 2001. "The Meaning of American National Identity: Patterns of Ethnic Conflict and Consensus." In *Social Identity, Intergroup Conflict, and Conflict Reduction*, eds. Richard D. Ashmore, Lee Jussim and David Wilder. New York: Oxford University Press. 71–100.

Clarkson, Frederick. 2018. "'Project Blitz' Seeks to do for Christian Nationalism what ALEC does for Big Business." Religion Dispatches, http://religiondispatches.org/project-blitz-seeks-to-do-for-christian-nationalism-what-alec-does-for-big-business/ (accessed November 8, 2019).

Clement, Victoria. 2014. "Articulating National Identity in Turkmenistan: Inventing Tradition through Myth, Cult and Language." *Nations and Nationalism* 20: 546–62.

Clinton, William J. 1998. "Remarks at a Memorial Service for the Victims of the Embassy Bombings in Kenya and Tanzania." The American Presidency Project, www.presidency.ucsb.edu/documents/remarks-memorial-service-for-the-victims-the-embassy-bombings-kenya-and-tanzania (accessed October 19, 2019).

Cohen, Bernard Cecil. 1972. *The Public's Impact on Foreign Policy*. Boston: Little.

Cohen, Cathy J. 1999. *The Boundaries of Blackness: AIDS and the Breakdown of Black Politics*. Chicago: University of Chicago Press.

Coleman, Simon. 1993. "Conservative Protestantism and the World Order: The Faith Movement in the United States and Sweden." *Sociology of Religion* 54: 353–73.

Coles, Roberta L. 2002. "Manifest Destiny Adapted for 1990s' War Discourse: Mission and Destiny Intertwined." *Sociology of Religion* 63: 403–26.

Collingwood, Loren, Nazita Lajevardi, and Kassra A. R. Oskooii. 2018. "A Change of Heart? Why Individual-Level Public Opinion Shifted Against Trump's 'Muslim Ban'." *Political Behavior* 40: 1035–72.

Collins, Todd A., Kenneth A. Wink, James L. Guth, and C. Don Livingston. 2011. "The Religious Affiliation of Representatives and Support for Funding the Iraq War." *Politics and Religion* 4: 550–68.

Compton, John W. 2020. *The End of Empathy: Why White Protestants Stopped Loving their Neighbors*. New York: Oxford University Press.

Converse, Philip. 1964. "The Nature of Belief Systems in Mass Publics." In *Ideology and Discontent*, ed. David Ernest Apter. London: Free Press of Glencoe. 206–61.

Cooper, Richard T. 2003. "THE NATION; general casts war in religious terms; the top soldier assigned to track down Bin Laden and Hussein is an evangelical Christian who speaks publicly of the army of god." *Los Angeles Times*, October 16. A 1.

Cottrell, Leonard S., Jr., and Sylvia Eberhart. 1969. *American Opinion on World Affairs in the Atomic Age*. New York: Greenwood Press.

Cox, Daniel, Rachel Lienesch, and Robert P. Jones. 2017. *Beyond Economics: Fears of Cultural Displacement Pushed the White Working Class to Trump | PRRI/The Atlantic Report*. Washington, DC, May 9, www.prri.org/research/white-working-class-attitudes-economy-trade-immigration-election-donald-trump/#

Creighton, Mathew J., and Amaney Jamal. 2015. "Does Islam Play a Role in Anti-Immigrant Sentiment? An Experimental Approach." *Social Science Research* 53: 89–103.

Crick, Bernard. 2016. "Civic Republicanism and Citizenship: The Challenge for Today." In *Democracy: A Reader*, eds. Ricardo Blaug and John Schwarzmantel, 2nd ed. Edinburgh: Edinburgh University Press. 214–22.

Dahl, Robert A. 1989. *Democracy and Its Critics*. New Haven: Yale University Press.

Dana, Karam, Nazita Lajevardi, Kassra A. R. Oskooii, and Hannah L. Walker. 2019. "Veiled Politics: Experiences with Discrimination among Muslim Americans." *Politics & Religion* 12: 629–77.

Daniels, Joseph P. 2005. "Religious Affiliation and Individual International-Policy Preferences in the United States." *International Interactions* 31: 273–301.

Daniels, Joseph P., and Marc von der Ruhr. 2005. "God and the Global Economy: Religion and Attitudes towards Trade and Immigration in the United States." *Socio-Economic Review* 3: 467–89.

Davis, Darren W. 2017. *Perseverance in the Parish?: Religious Attitudes from a Black Catholic Perspective, Cambridge Studies in Social Theory, Religion, and Politics*. New York: Cambridge University Press.

Davis, Darren W., and Brian D. Silver. 2004. "Civil Liberties vs. Security: Public Opinion in the Context of the Terrorist Attacks on America." *American Journal of Political Science* 48: 28–46.

Dawson, Michael C. 1994. *Behind the Mule: Race and Class in African American Politics*. Princeton: Princeton University Press.

De Cleen, Benjamin. 2017. "Populism and Nationalism." In *The Oxford Handbook of Populism*, eds., Cristóbal Rovira Kaltwasser, Paul Taggart, Paulina Ochoa Espejo and Pierre Ostiguy. New York: Oxford University Press. 342–362.

de Figueiredo, Rui J. P. Jr. , and Zachary Elkins. 2003. "Are Patriots Bigots? An Inquiry into the Vices of In-Group Pride." *American Journal of Political Science* 47: 171–88.

de la Garza, Rodolfo O. 2004. "Latino Politics." *Annual Review of Political Science* 7: 91–123.

de la Garza, Rodolfo O., Angelo Falcon, and F. Chris Garcia. 1996. "Will The Real Americans Please Stand Up: Anglo and Mexican-American Support of Core American Political Values." *American Journal of Political Science* 40: 335–51.

Delli Carpini, Michael X., and Scott Keeter. 1996. *What Americans Know about Politics and Why It Matters*. New Haven: Yale University Press.

Desipio, Louis. 1996. *Counting the Latino Vote: Latinos as a New Electorate*. Charlottesville, VA: University of Virginia Press.

Devos, Thierry, and Mahzarin R. Banaji. 2005. "American=White?." *Journal of Personality and Social Psychology* 88: 447–66.

Dickerson, Caitlin. 2018. "Hundreds of Immigrant Children Have Been Taken From Parents at U.S. Border." *The New York Times*, April 20. www.nytimes.com/2018/04/20/us/immigrant-children-separation-ice.html

Dickerson, Dennis C. 2020. *The African Methodist Episcopal Church: A History*. New York: Cambridge University Press.

Dietz, Mary G. 1987. "Context Is All: Feminism and Theories of Citizenship." *Daedalus* 116: 1–24.

Djupe, Paul A., and Brian Calfano. 2013a. "Divine Intervention? The Influence of Religious Value Communication on U.S. Intervention Policy." *Political Behavior* 35: 643–63.

　　2013b. *God Talk: Experimenting with the Religious Causes of Public Opinion*. Philadelphia: Temple University Press.

Djupe, Paul A., and Christopher P. Gilbert. 2009. *The Political Influence of Churches, Cambridge Studies in Social Theory, Religion, and Politics*. New York: Cambridge University Press.

Dobbs, Lou. 2006. *War on the Middle Class: How the Government, Big Business, and Special Interest Groups are Waging War on the American Dream and How to Fight Back*. New York: Viking.

Domke, David, and Kevin Coe. 2008. *The God Strategy: How Religion Became a Political Weapon in America*. New York: Oxford University Press.

Doty, William G. 1980. "Mythophiles' Dyscrasia: A Comprehensive Definition of Myth." *Journal of the American Academy of Religion* 48: 531–62.

Douglass, Frederick. 1945. "Slavery." In *Frederick Douglass: Selections from His Writings*, ed. Philip Sheldon Foner. New York: International Publishers. 45–62.

Druckman, James N. 2011. "What's It All About?: Framing in Political Science." In *Perspectives on Framing*, ed. Gideon Keren. New York: Psychology Press. 279–301.

Du Bois, W. E. B. 1990. *The Souls of Black Folk*. New York: Vintage Books.

Du Mez, Kristin Kobes. 2020. *Jesus and John Wayne: How White Evangelicals Corrupted a Faith and Fractured a Nation*. 1st ed. New York: Liveright Publishing Corporation, a division of W. W. Norton & Company.

DuBois, W. E. B. 1990. *The Souls of Black Folk*. New York: Vintage Books.

Dunaway, Johanna, Regina P. Branton, and Marisa A. Abrajano. 2010. "Agenda Setting, Public Opinion, and the Issue of Immigration Reform." *Social Science Quarterly* 91: 359–78.

Eckholm, Erik. 2010. "Military Arms Supplier To Drop Bible References." *The New York Times*, January 22.

Edsman, Carl-Martin. 1972. "The Myth of the State, Or the State's Religious Legitimation." *Scripta Instituti Donneriani Aboensis* 6: 170–88.

Eisenhower, Dwight D. 1944. "Document for June 6th: D-day statement to soldiers, sailor, and airmen of the Allied Expeditionary Force, 6/44." National Archives, www.archives.gov/historical-docs/todays-doc/?dod-date =606 (accessed October 12, 2019).

Elkins, Zachary, Tom Ginsburg, and James Melton. 2009. *The Endurance of National Constitutions*. New York: Cambridge University Press.

Emmons, Robert A. 1984. "Factor Analysis and Construct Validity of the Narcissistic Personality Inventory." *Journal of Personality Assessment* 48: 291–300.

1987. "Narcissism: Theory and Measurement." *Journal of Personality and Social Psychology* 52: 11–17.

Farris, Emily M., and Heather Silber Mohamed. 2018. "Picturing Immigration: How the Media Criminalizes Immigrants." *Politics, Groups, and Identities* 6: 814–24.

Feingold, Henry L. 2002. *Zion in America: the Jewish Experience from Colonial Times to the Present*. Mineola, NY: Dover Publications.

Feshbach, Seymour. 1987. "Individual Aggression, National Attachment, and the Search for Peace: Psychological Perspectives." *Aggressive Behavior* 13: 315–25.

Festenstein, Matthew, and Michael Kenny. 2005. *Political Ideologies: A Reader and Guide*. New York: Oxford University Press.

Fink, Arlene. 1995. *The Survey Kit. 9 vols*. Thousand Oaks, CA: Sage Publications.

Fiske, Susan T. 2011. *Envy Up, Scorn Down: How Status Divides Us*. New York: Russell Sage Foundation.

Flaaen, Aaron, and Justin Pierce. 2019. *Disentangling the Effects of the 2018–2019 Tariffs on a Globally Connected U.S. Manufacturing Sector*. Washington: Board of Governors of the Federal Reserve System, www.federalreserve.gov/econres/feds/files/2019086pap.pdf

Forman, Seth. 1998. *Blacks in the Jewish Mind: A Crisis of Liberalism*. New York: New York University Press.

Fox, Cybelle. 2012. *Three Worlds of Relief: Race, Immigration, and the American Welfare State from the Progressive Era to the New Deal, Princeton Studies in American Politics: Historical, International, and Comparative Perspectives*. Princeton: Princeton University Press.

Freeden, Michael. 1998. *Ideologies and Political Theory: A Conceptual Approach*. New York: Oxford University Press.

Frey, William H. 1995. "Immigration Impacts on Internal Migration of the Poor: 1990 Census Evidence for US States." *International Journal of Population Geography* 1: 51–67.

Froese, Paul, and Christopher Bader. 2010. *America's Four Gods: What We Say about God– AND What that Says about Us*. New York: Oxford University Press.

Froese, Paul, and F. Carson Mencken. 2009. "A U.S. Holy War? The Effects of Religion on Iraq War Policy Attitudes." *Social Science Quarterly* 90: 103–16.

Garner, Steve. 2007. *Whiteness: An Introduction*. New York: Routledge.

Gartner, Scott Sigmund, and Gary M. Segura. 1998. "War, Casualties, and Public Opinion." *Journal of Conflict Resolution* 42: 278–300.

2000. "Race, Casualties, and Opinion in the Vietnam War." *Journal of Politics* 62: 115–46.

Gartner, Scott Sigmund, Gary M. Segura, and Bethany A. Barratt. 2004. "War Casualties, Policy Positions, and the Fate of Legislators." *Political Research Quarterly* 57: 467–77.

Gartner, Scott Sigmund, Gary M. Segura, and Michael Wilkening. 1997. "All Politics Are Local: Local Losses and Individual Attitudes toward the Vietnam War." *Journal of Conflict Resolution* 41: 669–94.

Geertz, Clifford. 1973. *The Interpretation of Cultures: Selected Essays.* New York: Basic Books.

Gellner, Ernest. 1983. *Nations and Nationalism, New Perspectives on the Past.* Ithaca: Cornell University Press.

Gelpi, Christopher. 2010. "Performing on Cue? The Formation of Public Opinion Toward War." *Journal of Conflict Resolution* 54: 88–116.

Gerstle, Gary. 1994. "The Protean Character of American Liberalism." *The American Historical Review* 99: 1043–73.

Gest, Justin. 2016. *The New Minority: White Working Class Politics in an Age of Immigration and Inequality.* New York, NY: Oxford University Press.

Gibson, James L. 1998. "Putting Up With Fellow Russians: An Analysis of Political Tolerance in the Fledgling Russian Democracy." *Political Research Quarterly* 51: 37–68.

Gibson, James L., and Amanda Gouws. 2003. *Overcoming Intolerance in South Africa: Experiments in Democratic Persuasion, Cambridge Studies in Political Psychology and Public Opinion.* New York: Cambridge University Press.

Gillion, Daniel Q. 2013. *The Political Power of Protest: Minority Activism and Shifts in Public Policy, Cambridge Studies in Contentious Politics.* New York: Cambridge University Press.

Givens, Terri E. 2005. *Voting Radical Right in Western Europe.* New York: Cambridge University Press.

Givens, Terri E., Rachel Navarre, and Pete Mohanty. 2020. *Immigration in the 21st Century: The Comparative Politics of Immigration Policy.* 1st ed. New York: Routledge.

Glazier, Rebecca A. 2013. "Divine Direction: How Providential Religious Beliefs Shape Foreign Policy Attitudes." *Foreign Policy Analysis* 9: 127–42.

Glock, Charles Y. 1972. "Images of 'God', Images of Man, and the Organization of Social Life." *Journal for the Scientific Study of Religion* 11: 1–15.

Glock, Charles Y., and Rodney Stark. 1965. *Religion and Society in Tension, Rand McNally Sociology Series.* Chicago: Rand McNally.

Gómez, Laura E. 2018. *Manifest Destinies: The Making of the Mexican American Race.* 2nd ed. New York: New York University Press.

Goode, Virgil. 2007. "Save Judeo-Christian Values: Immigration Leaves USA Vulnerable to Muslim Extremists' Infiltration." *USA Today* (January 1). https://web.archive.org/web/20070104055856/http://blogs.usatoday.com/oped/2007/01/opposing_view_s.html

Gorski, Philip S. 2017. *American Covenant: A History of Civil Religion from the Puritans to the Present.* Princeton: Princeton University Press.

Graber, Doris A. 1968. *Public Opinion, the President, and Foreign Policy: Four Case Studies from the Formative Years.* New York: Holt.

Graham, Billy. 1949. "Why A Revival." Billy Graham Center, www2.wheaton.edu/bgc/archives/exhibits/LA49/05sermons01.html (accessed October 18, 2019).

1953. "Spiritual Inventory: Billy Graham's Message of Faith in Tough Times." Billy Graham Evangelistic Association, https://billygraham.org/audio/spiritual-inventory/ (accessed October 17, 2019).

1988. "We Need a Revival." In *The Early Billy Graham Sermon and Revival Accounts*, ed. Joel A. Carpenter. New York: Garland Publishing. 55.

Grant, Susan-Mary. 1997. "Making History: Myth and the Construction of American Nationhood." In *Myths and Nationhood*, eds. Geoffrey A. Hosking and George Schöpflin. London: Hurst & Company in Association with the School of Slavonic and Eastern European Studies, University of London. 88–106.

Granville, Kevin. 2017. "What is TPP? Behind the Trade Deal that Died." *New York Times*, January 23. www.nytimes.com/interactive/2016/business/tpp-explained-what-is-trans-pacific-partnership.html

Gravelle, Timothy B., Jason Reifler, and Thomas J. Scotto. 2017. "The Structure of Foreign Policy Attitudes in Transatlantic Perspective: Comparing the United States, United Kingdom, France and Germany." *European Journal of Political Research* 56: 757–76.

Green, John C. 2007. "Religion and Torture: A View from the Polls." *Review of Faith & International Affairs* 5: 23–27.

Green, John Clifford. 1996. *Religion and the Culture Wars: Dispatches From the Front, Religious Forces in the Modern Political World*. Lanham, Md: Rowman & Littlefield.

Green, Michael J. 2017. *By More than Providence: Grand Strategy and American Power in the Asia Pacific since 1783*. New York: Columbia University Press.

Green, Steven K. 2015. *Inventing a Christian America: The Myth of the Religious Founding*. New York: Oxford University Press.

Guglielmo, Thomas A. 2003. *White on Arrival: Italians, Race, Color, and Power in Chicago, 1890–1945*. New York: Oxford University Press.

Gunn, T. Jeremy. 2009. *Spiritual Weapons: The Cold War and the Forging of an American National Religion, Religion, Politics, and Public Life*. Westport, CT : Praeger Publishers.

Gurin, Patricia, Shirley Hatchett, and James S. Jackson. 1989. *Hope and Independence: Blacks' Response to Electoral and Party Politics*. New York: Russell Sage Foundation.

Gusterson, Hugh. 2017. "From Brexit to Trump: Anthropology and the Rise of Nationalist Populism." *American Ethnologist* 44: 209–14.

Guth, James. 2012. "The Religious Roots of Foreign Policy Exceptionalism." *The Review of Faith & International Affairs* 10: 77–85.

Guth, James L. 2010a. "Economic Globalization: The View from the Pews." *The Review of Faith & International Affairs* 8: 43–48.

2010b. "Religion and American Public Opinion: Foreign Policy Issues." In *The Oxford Handbook of Religion and American Politics*, eds. James L. Guth, Lyman A. Kellstedt and Corwin E. Smidt. New York: Oxford University Press. 243–265.

2013. "Militant and Cooperative Internationalism among American Religious Publics." *Politics and Religion Journal* 7: 315–44.

Guth, James L., Cleveland R. Fraser, John C. Green, Lyman A. Kellstedt, and Corwin E. Smidt. 1996. "Religion and Foreign Policy Attitudes: The Case of Christian Zionism." In *Religion and the Culture Wars: Dispatches from the*

Front, eds. John C. Green, James L. Guth, Corwin E. Smidt and Lyman A. Kellstedt. Lanham, MD: Rowman and Littlefield. 330–60.

Gutmann, Amy. 2003. *Identity in Democracy*. Princeton: Princeton University Press.

Hadden, Jeffery K. 1967. *The Gathering Storm in Churches*. Garden City, NY: Doubleday.

Hainmueller, Jens, and Michael J. Hiscox. 2006. "Learning to Love Globalization: Education and Individual Attitudes Toward International Trade." *International Organization* 60: 469–98.

2010. "Attitudes Toward Highly Skilled and Low-Skilled Immigration: Evidence from a Survey Experiment." *American Political Science Review* 104: 61–84.

Harris-Lacewell, Melissa V. 2004. *Barbershops, Bibles and BET: Everyday Talk and Black Political Thought*. Princeton: Princeton University Press.

Harris, Fredrick C. 1999. *Something Within: Religion in African-American Political Activism*. New York: Oxford University Press.

Hart, D. G. 2020. *American Catholic: The Politics of Faith during the Cold War, Religion and American public life*. Ithaca: Cornell University Press.

Hartz, Louis. 1991. *The Liberal Tradition in America: An Interpretation of American Political Thought since the Revolution*. 2nd Harvest/HBJ ed. San Diego: Harcourt Brace Jovanovich.

Harvard Center for American Political Studies/Harris Poll. 2019. Monthly Harvard-Harris Poll: August 2019 [computer file]. (Study version. Harvard Center for American Political Studies/Harris Poll: [distributor] url: https://harvardharrispoll.com/wp-content/uploads/2019/09/HHP_August2019_Topline_RegisteredVoters.pdf

Haselby, Sam. 2015. *The Origins of American Religious Nationalism*. New York: Oxford University Press.

Hauslohner, Abigail. 2019. "Trump wants a different kind of immigrant: Highly skilled workers who speak English and have job offers." *Washington Post*, May 15. www.washingtonpost.com/immigration/trump-wants-a-different-kind-of-immigrant-highly-skilled-workers-who-speak-english-and-have-job-offers/2019/05/15/9c1d8eca-772b-11e9-bd25-c989555e7766_story.html

Held, David. 2006. *Models of Democracy*. 3rd ed. Malden, MA: Polity Press.

Henderson, Errol Anthony. 2019. *The Revolution Will Not Be Theorized: Cultural Revolution in the Black Power Era, SUNY Series in African American Studies*. Albany: State University of New York Press.

Hero, Alfred O. 1973. *American Religious Groups View Foreign Policy: Trends in Rank-and-File Opinion, 1937–1969*. Durham, NC: Duke University Press.

Herzog, Jonathan P. 2011. *The Spiritual-Industrial Complex: America's Religious Battle against Communism in the early Cold War*. New York: Oxford University Press.

Hjerm, Mikael. 2001. "Education, Xenophobia and Nationalism: A Comparative Analysis." *Journal of Ethnic and Migration Studies* 27: 37–60.

Hobsbawm, E. J. 1992. *Nations and Nationalism since 1780: Programme, Myth, Reality*. Vol. 2nd. New York: Cambridge University Press.

Holsti, Ole R. 2004. *Public Opinion and American Foreign Policy. Rev. ed, Analytical Perspectives on Politics*. Ann Arbor: University of Michigan Press.

Holsti, Ole R., and James N. Rosenau. 1990. "The Structure of Foreign Policy Attitudes among American Leaders." *The Journal of Politics* 52: 94–125.

1993. "The Structure of Foreign Policy Beliefs Among American Opinion Leaders-After the Cold War." *Millennium* 22: 235–78.

Honko, Lauri. 1984. "The Problem of Defining Myth." In *Sacred Narrative: Readings in the Theory of Myth*, ed. Alan Dundes. Berkeley: University of California Press. 41–52.

Howe, Daniel Walker. 2007. *What hath God Wrought: The Transformation of America, 1815–1848, The Oxford History of the United States*. New York: Oxford University Press.

Huber, Gregory A., and Thomas J. Espenshade. 1997. "Neo-Isolationism, Balanced-Budget Conservatism, and the Fiscal Impacts of Immigrants." *International Migration Review* 31: 1031–54.

Huddy, Leonie, and Nadia Khatib. 2007. "American Patriotism, National Identity, and Political Involvement." *American Journal of Political Science* 51: 63–77.

Hudson, Winthrop Still. 1970. *Nationalism and Religion in America: Concepts of American Identity and Mission*. 1st ed. New York: Harper and Row.

Hughes, Richard T. 2004. *Myths America Lives By*. Urbana: University of Illinois Press.

Hunt, Michael H. 2009. *Ideology and U.S. Foreign Policy*. New Haven: Yale University Press.

Huntington, Samuel P. 1996. *The Clash of Civilizations and the Remaking of World Order*. New York: Simon & Schuster.

2004. *Who Are We? The Challenges to America's National Identity*. New York: Simon & Schuster.

Hurwitz, Jon, and Mark Peffley. 1987. "How are Foreign Policy Attitudes Structured? A Hierarchical Model." *American Political Science Review* 81: 1099–120.

Ignatiev, Noel. 2009. *How the Irish became White, Routledge Classics*. New York: Routledge.

Inboden, William. 2008. *Religion and American Foreign Policy, 1945–1960: The Soul of Containment*. New York: Cambridge University Press.

ISSP Research Group. 2020. International Social Survey Programme: Religion IV – ISSP 2018 [computer file]. (Study ZA7570) 2.1.0 version. Cologne: GESIS Data Archive [distributor]. https://doi.org/10.4232/1.13629

Jacobs, Lawrence R., and Robert Y. Shapiro. 1995. "The Rise in Presidential Polling: The Nixon White House in Historical Perspective." *Public Opinion Quarterly* 59: 163–95.

Jefferson, Thomas. 1999. *Notes on the State of Virginia, Penguin Classics*. New York: Penguin Books.

Jelen, Ted G. 1994. "Religion and Foreign Policy Attitudes." *American Politics Research* 22: 382–400.

Jenkins, Jack. 2019. "From cruise ships to Trump's hotel, Calvinist Christian nationalism is making moves." Religious News Service, https://religion

news.com/2019/07/08/from-cruise-ships-to-trumps-hotel-calvinist-christian-nationalism-is-making-moves/ (accessed November 10, 2019).

Johns, Robert, and Graeme A. M. Davies. 2012. "Democratic Peace or Clash of Civilizations? Target States and Support for War in Britain and the United States." *The Journal of Politics* 74: 1038–52.

Johnson, Micah E. 2018. "The Paradox of Black Patriotism: Double Consciousness." *Ethnic and Racial Studies* 41: 1971–89.

Johnson, Paul E. 2004. *A Shopkeeper's Millennium: Society and Revivals in Rochester, New York, 1815–1837*. 1st rev. ed. New York: Hill and Wang.

Johnson, Stephen D., Joseph B. Tamney, and Ronald Burton. 1989. "Pat Robertson: Who Supported His Candidacy for President?" *Journal for the Scientific Study of Religion* 28: 387–99.

Jonason, Peter K., and Gregory D. Webster. 2010. "The Dirty Dozen: A Concise Measure of the Dark Triad." *Psychological Assessment* 22: 420–32.

Jones, Jeffery M. 2017. "Support for Gorsuch Lower Than for Other Recent Court Picks." Gallup, https://news.gallup.com/poll/203339/support-gorsuch-lower-recent-court-picks.aspx (accessed February 24, 2020).

2018a. "Americans Still Closely Divided on Kavanaugh Confirmation." Gallup, https://news.gallup.com/poll/243377/americans-closely-divided-kavanaugh-confirmation.aspx (accessed February 24, 2020).

2018b. "In U.S., Positive Attitudes Toward Foreign Trade Stay High." Gallup, https://news.gallup.com/poll/228317/positive-attitudes-toward-foreign-trade-stay-high.aspx (accessed February 11, 2020).

Jones, Robert P. 2016. *The end of White Christian America*. New York: Simon & Schuster.

2020. *White Too Long: The Legacy of White Supremacy in American Christianity*. New York: Simon & Schuster.

Joyner, Daniel. 2016. *Iran's Nuclear Program and International Law: From Confrontation to Accord*. New York: Oxford University Press.

Judd, Dennis R., and Todd Swanstrom. 2012. *City Politics: The Political Economy of Urban America*. 8th ed. Boston: Longman.

Juergensmeyer, Mark. 1996. "The Worldwide Rise of Religious Nationalism." *Journal of International Affairs* 50: 1.

Kachun, Mitch. 2009. "From Forgotten Founder to Indispensable Icon: Crispus Attacks, Black Citizenship, and Collective Memory, 1770–1865." *Journal of the Early Republic* 29: 249–86.

Kalkan, Kerem Ozan, Geoffrey C. Layman, and Eric M. Uslaner. 2009. ""Bands of Others"? Attitudes toward Muslims in Contemporary American Society." *The Journal of Politics* 71: 847–62.

Kaltenthaler, Karl, and William J. Miller. 2014. "Social Psychology and Public Support for Trade Liberalization." *International Studies Quarterly* 57: 784–90.

Kanno-Youngs, Zolan. 2020. "Trump Administration Adds Six Countries to Travel Ban." *The New York Times*, January 31. www.nytimes.com/2020/01/31/us/politics/trump-travel-ban.html

Kaysen, Ronda. 2017. "Condo Tower to Rise Where Muslim Community Center Was Proposed." *New York Times*, May 12, 2017. www.nytimes.com/2017/05/12/realestate/muslim-museum-world-trade-center.html

Keddie, G. Anthony. 2020. *Republican Jesus: How the Right has Rewritten the Gospels*. Oakland, California: University of California Press.

Keeley, Theresa. 2020. *Reagan's Gun-Toting Nuns: The Catholic Conflict over Cold War Human Rights Policy in Central America*. Ithaca: Cornell University Press.

Kellas, James G. 1998. *The Politics of Nationalism and Ethnicity*. 2nd ed. New York: St. Martin's Press.

Kellstedt, Lyman A., and Corwin E. Smidt. 1991. "Measuring Fundamentalism: An Analysis of Different Operational Strategies." *Journal for the Scientific Study of Religion* 30: 259–78.

   1993. "Doctrinal Beliefs and Political Behavior: Views of the Bible." In *Rediscovering the Religious Factor in American Politics*, eds. David C. Leege and Lyman A. Kellstedt. New York: M. E. Sharpe. 177–198.

Kelman, Herbert C. 1965. *International Behavior: A Social-Psychological Analysis*. New York: Holt.

Kent, Stephen A., and James V. Spickard. 1994. "The 'Other' Civil Religion and the Tradition of Radical Quaker Politics." *Journal of Church and State* 36: 373–87.

Kertzer, Joshua D., Kathleen E. Powers, Brian C. Rathbun, and Ravi Iyer. 2014. "Moral Support: How Moral Values Shape Foreign Policy Attitudes." *The Journal of Politics* 76: 825–40.

Kertzer, Joshua D., and Thomas Zeitzoff. 2017. "A Bottom-Up Theory of Public Opinion about Foreign Policy." *American Journal of Political Science* 61: 543–58.

Kibria, Nazli, Cara Bowman, and Megan O'Leary. 2014. *Race and immigration*. Malden, MA: Polity Press.

Kil, Sang Hea. 2012. "Fearing Yellow, Imagining White: Media Analysis of the Chinese Exclusion Act of 1882." *Social Identities* 18: 663–77.

Kilburn, H. Whitt., and Brian J. Fogarty. 2015. "American Religious Traditions, Orthodoxy, and Commitment in Public Opinion toward Torture." *Politics and Religion* 8: 36–59.

Kinder, Donald R. 1998. "Communication and Opinion." *Annual Review of Political Science* 1: 167–97.

Kinder, Donald R., and Cindy D. Kam. 2009. *Us Against Them: Ethnocentric Foundations of American Opinion, Chicago Studies in American Politics*. Chicago: University of Chicago Press.

Kinder, Donald R., and Lynn M. Sanders. 1996. *Divided by Color*. Chicago: University of Chicago Press.

Kinnvall, Catarina. 2004. "Globalization and Religious Nationalism: Self, Identity, and the Search for Ontological Security." *Political Psychology* 25: 741–67.

Kleinberg, Katja B., and Benjamin O. Fordham. 2010. "Trade and Foreign Policy Attitudes." *Journal of Conflict Resolution* 54: 687–714.

Kohn, Hans. 1944. *The Idea of Nationalism: A Study in Its Origins and Background*. New York: Macmillan Company.

Kosterman, Rick., and Seymour Feshbach. 1989. "Toward a Measure of Patriotic and Nationalistic Attitudes." *Political Psychology* 10: 257–74.

Kramnick, Isaac, and R. Laurence Moore. 2005. *The Godless Constitution: A Moral Defense of the Secular State*. Rev. ed. New York: W.W. Norton.

Kreps, Sarah, and Sarah Maxey. 2018. "Mechanisms of Morality: Sources of Support for Humanitarian Intervention." *Journal of Conflict Resolution* 62: 1814–42.

Kriesberg, Martin. 1949. "Public Opinion: Dark Areas of Ignorance." In *Public Opinion and Foreign Policy*, ed. Lester Markel. New York: Harper. 49–64.

Krutchik, Laurence M. 2007. "Down but Not out: A Comparison of Previous Attempts at Immigration Reform and the Resulting Agency Implemented Changes Symposium Notes and Comment." *Nova Law Review* 32: 455–94.

Kymlicka, Will. 1995. *The Rights of Minority Cultures*. New York: Oxford University Press.

La Feber, Walter. 1977. "American Policy-Makers, Public Opinion and the Outbreak of the Cold War, 1945–1950." In *The Origins of the Cold War in Asia*, eds. Yonosuke Nagia and Akira Iriye. New York: Columbia University Press. 43–65.

Lacorne, Denis. 2011. *Religion in America: A Political History, Religion, Culture and Public Life*. New York: Columbia University Press.

Lajevardi, Nazita. 2020. "Access Denied: Exploring Muslim American Representation and Exclusion by State Legislators." *Politics, Groups, and Identities* 8: 957–85.

Landler, Mark. 2017. "Trump Recognizes Jerusalem as Israel's Capital and Orders U.S. Embassy to Move." *New York Times*, December 6. www.nytimes.com/2017/12/06/world/middleeast/trump-jerusalem-israel-capital.html

2018. "Trump Abandons Iran Nuclear Deal He Long Scorned." *New York Times*, May 8. www.nytimes.com/2018/05/08/world/middleeast/trump-iran-nuclear-deal.html

Lawrence, Jordun. 2020. "Coronavirus Fallout Highlights Asian American Discrimination in the U.S." Public Religion Research Institute, www.prri.org/spotlight/coronavirus-fallout-highlights-asian-american-discrimination-in-the-u-s/ (accessed March 28, 2020).

Layman, Geoffrey C. 1997. "Religion and Political Behavior in the United States: The Impact of Beliefs, Affiliations, and Commitment From 1980 to 1994." *The Public Opinion Quarterly* 61: 288–316.

2001. *The Great Divide: Religious and Cultural Conflict in American Party Politics*. New York: Columbia University Press.

Lei, Richard. 2003. "Christian Soldier." *The Washington Post*, November 6. www.washingtonpost.com/archive/lifestyle/2003/11/06/christian-soldier/95b8f359-3aa6-428e-981e-2310d94aaa14/

Lee, Michael J. 2006. "The Populist Chameleon: The People's Party, Huey Long, George Wallace, and the Populist Argumentative Frame." *Quarterly Journal of Speech* 92: 355–78.

Lee, Yueh-Ting, and Victor Ottati. 2002. "Attitudes Toward U.S. Immigration Policy: The Roles of In-Group-Out-Group Bias, Economic Concern, and Obedience to Law." *The Journal of Social Psychology* 142: 617–34.

Lee, Yueh-Ting, Victor Ottati, and Imtiaz Hussain. 2001. "Attitudes toward "Illegal" Immigration into the United States: California Proposition 187." *Hispanic Journal of Behavioral Sciences* 23: 430–43.

Leege, David C. 1993. "Religion and Politics in Theoretical Perspective." In *Rediscovering the Religious Factor in American Politics*, eds. David C. Leege and Lyman A. Kellstedt. New York: M. E. Sharpe. 3–25.

Leonard, Scott A., and Michael McClure. 2004. *Myth and Knowing: An Introduction to World Mythology*. Boston: McGraw-Hill.

Lerner, Michael. 1992. *The Socialism of Fools: Anti-Semitism on the Left*. Oakland, CA: Tikkun.

Levendusky, Matthew S., and Michael C. Horowitz. 2012. "When Backing Down Is the Right Decision: Partisanship, New Information, and Audience Costs." *The Journal of Politics* 74: 323–38.

Lévi-Strauss, Claude. 1981. *The Naked Man*. 1st U.S. ed, Introduction to a Science of Mythology. New York: Harper & Row.

Lewis, Amy C., and Steven J. Sherman. 2010. "Perceived Entitativity and the Black-Sheep Effect: When Will We Denigrate Negative Ingroup Members?". *The Journal of Social Psychology* 150: 211–25.

Lewis, Donald M. 2010. *The Origins of Christian Zionism: Lord Shaftesbury and Evangelical Support for a Jewish Homeland*. New York: Cambridge University Press.

Lieven, Anatol. 2004. *America Right or Wrong: An anatomy of American Nationalism*. New York: Oxford University Press.

Lincoln, Abraham. 1865. "Inaugural Address." The Presidency Project, www.presidency.ucsb.edu/documents/inaugural-address-35 (accessed January 5, 2020).

Lincoln, Bruce. 1999. *Theorizing Myth: Narrative, Ideology, and Scholarship*. Chicago: University of Chicago Press.

Lippmann, Walter. 1955. *Essays in the Public Philosophy*. 1st ed. Boston: Little.

Lipset, Seymour Martin. 1979. *The First New Nation: The United States in Historical and Comparative Perspective*. New York: Norton.

Long, Heather. 2019. "Trump's steel tariffs cost U.S. consumers $900,000 for every job created, experts say." *Washington Post*, May 7. www.washingtonpost.com/business/2019/05/07/trumps-steel-tariffs-cost-us-consumers-every-job-created-experts-say/

Lorenz, Chris. 2008. "Drawing the Line: 'Scientific' History between Myth-making and Myth-breaking." In *Narrating the Nation: Representations in History, Media, and the Arts*, eds. Stefan Berger, Linas Eriksonas and Andrew Mycock, New York: Berghahn Books.

Lynch, David J. 2021. "Even as supply lines strain, Biden is in no rush to scrap Trump's steel tariffs." *Washington Post*, April 17. www.washingtonpost.com/us-policy/2021/04/17/biden-steel-tariffs-trade/

Lynch, David J., Josh Dawsey, and Damian Paletta. 2018. "Trump imposes steel and aluminum tariffs on the E.U., Canada and Mexico." *Washington Post*,

May 31. www.washingtonpost.com/business/economy/trump-imposes-steel-and-aluminum-tariffs-on-the-european-union-canada-and-mexico/2018/05/31/891bb452-64d3-11e8-a69c-b944de66d9e7_story.html

Malhotra, Neil, Yotam Margalit, and Cecilia Hyunjung Mo. 2013. "Economic Explanations for Opposition to Immigration: Distinguishing between Prevalence and Conditional Impact." *American Journal of Political Science* 57: 391–410.

Malinowski, Bronislaw. 1954. *Magic, Science and Religion, and Other Essays, Doubleday Anchor Books.* Garden City, NY: Doubleday.

Malka, Ariel, and Christopher J. Soto. 2011. "The Conflicting Influences of Religiosity on Attitude Toward Torture." *Personality and Social Psychology Bulletin* 37: 1091–103.

Mansfield, Edward D., and Brian M. Pollins. 2001. "The Study of Interdependence and Conflict: Recent Advances, Open Questions, and Directions for Future Research." *The Journal of Conflict Resolution* 45: 834–59.

Maoz, Zeev, and Errol Anthony Henderson. 2020. *Scriptures, Shrines, Scapegoats, and World Politics: Religious Sources of Conflict and Cooperation in the Modern Era.* Ann Arbor: University of Michigan Press.

Marques, José M., and Dario Paez. 1994. "The 'Black Sheep Effect': Social Categorization, Rejection of Ingroup Deviates, and Perception of Group Variability." *European Review of Social Psychology* 5: 37–68.

Marrow, Helen B. 2011. *New Destination Dreaming: Immigration, Race, and Legal Status in the Rural American South.* Palo Alto, CA: Stanford University Press.

Marston, Sallie Ann. 1990. "Who are 'The People'?: Gender, Citizenship, and the Making of the American Nation." *Environment and Planning D: Society and Space* 8: 449–58.

Marti, Gerardo. 2019. *American Blindspot: Race, Class, Religion, and the Trump Presidency.* Lanham, MD: Rowman & Littlefield.

Martí, Gerardo. 2018. "The Unexpected Orthodoxy of Donald J. Trump: White Evangelical Support for the 45th President of the United States." *Sociology of Religion* 80: 1–8.

Marty, Martin. 1974. "The Two Kinds of Civil Religion." In *American Civil Religion*, eds. Russell E. Richey and Donald G. Jones. New York: Harper and Row. 139–159.

Massey, Douglas S. 1999. "International Migration at the Dawn of the Twenty-First Century: The Role of the State." *Population and Development Review* 25: 303–22.

Massey, Douglas S., Jorge Durand, and Nolan J. Malone. 2002. *Beyond Smoke and Mirrors: Mexican Immigration in an Era of Economic Integration.* New York: Russell Sage Foundation.

Massey, Douglas S., and Karen A. Pren. 2012. "Unintended Consequences of US Immigration Policy: Explaining the Post-1965 Surge from Latin America." *Population and Development Review* 38: 1–29.

Mayer, Jeremy D. 2004. "Christian Fundamentalists and Public Opinion Toward the Middle East: Israel's New Best Friends?." *Social Science Quarterly* 85: 695–712.

Mayer, William G. 1992. *The Changing American Mind: How and Why American Public Opinion Changed Between 1960 and 1988*. Ann Arbor: University of Michigan Press.

McCartney, Paul T. 2004. "American Nationalism and U.S. Foreign Policy from September 11 to the Iraq War." *Political Science Quarterly* 119: 399–423.

2011. "Religion, the Spanish-American War, and the Idea of American Mission." *Journal of Church and State* 54: 257–78.

McCleary, Daniel F., and Robert L. Williams. 2009. "Sociopolitical and Personality Correlates of Militarism in Democratic Societies." *Peace and Conflict: Journal of Peace Psychology* 15: 161–87.

McDaniel, Eric L. 2008. *Politics in the Pews: The Political Mobilization of Black Churches*. Ann Arbor: University of Michigan Press.

2016. "What Kind of Christian Are You? Religious Ideologies and Political Attitudes." *Journal for the Scientific Study of Religion* 55: 288–307.

McDaniel, Eric L., and Christopher G. Ellison. 2008. "God's Party?: Race, Religion, and Partisanship Over Time." *Political Research Quarterly* 61: 180–91.

McDaniel, Eric L., Irfan Nooruddin, and Allyson F. Shortle. 2011. "Divine Boundaries: How Religion Shapes Citizens' Attitudes Toward Immigrants." *American Politics Research* 39: 205–33.

2016. "Proud to be an American?: The Changing Relationship of National Pride and Identity." *The Journal of Race, Ethnicity, and Politics & Policy* 1: 145–76.

McDougall, Walter A. 1997. *Promised Land, Crusader State: The American Encounter with the World since 1776*. Boston: Houghton Mifflin.

2019. *The Tragedy of U.S. Foreign Policy: How America's Civil Religion Betrayed the National Interest*. Paperback edition. ed. New Haven: Yale University Press.

McKenzie, Brian D. 2011. "Barack Obama, Jeremiah Wright, and Public Opinion in the 2008 Presidential Primaries." *Political Psychology* 32: 943–61.

McKenzie, Brian D., and Stella M. Rouse. 2013. "Shades of Faith: Religious Foundations of Political Attitudes among African Americans, Latinos, and Whites." *American Journal of Political Science* 57: 218–35.

McNeill, William Hardy. 1986. *Mythistory and Other Essays*. Chicago: University of Chicago Press.

Mead, Walter Russell. 2001. *Special Providence: American Foreign Policy and How it Changed the World*. 1st ed. New York: Knopf.

Melville, Herman. 1988. *White-jacket, or, The World in a Man-of-war, Classics of Naval Literature*. Annapolis: Naval Institute Press.

Merolla, Jennifer, S. Karthick Ramakrishnan, and Chris Haynes. 2013. "'Illegal', 'Undocumented', or 'Unauthorized': Equivalency Frames, Issue Frames, and Public Opinion on Immigration." *Perspectives on Politics* 11: 789–807.

Meyer, Carter Jones, and Diana Royer. 2001. *Selling the Indian: Commercializing & Appropriating American Indian Cultures*. Tucson: University of Arizona Press.

Miles, Jack. 2004. "Religion and American Foreign Policy." *Survival* 46: 23–37.

Miller, Hunter. 1931. "Document 20 Tripoli: November 4, 1796 and January 3 1797." In *Treaties and Other International Acts of the United States of America*, ed. Hunter Miller. Vol. 2. Washington, DC: Government Printing Office. 349–85.

Miller, Joshua D., Jessica L. Maples, Laura Buffardi, Huajian Cai, Brittany Gentile, Yasemin Kisbu-Sakarya, Virginia S. Y. Kwan, Alex LoPilato, Louise F. Pendry, Constantine Sedikides, Lane Siedor, and W. Keith Campbell. 2015. "Narcissism and United States' Culture: The View from Home and Around the World." *Journal of Personality and Social Psychology* 109: 1068–89.

Miller, Warren E., and Donald E. Stokes. 1963. "Constituency Influence in Congress." *American Political Science Review* 57: 45–56.

Millon, Theodore. 1996. *Disorders of Personality: DSM-IV and Beyond*. 2nd ed. New York: Wiley.

Milner, Helen V., and Dustin Tingley. 2015. *Sailing the Water's Edge: The Domestic Politics of American Foreign Policy*. Princeton, New Jersey: Princeton University Press.

Monten, Jonathan. 2005. "The Roots of the Bush Doctrine: Power, Nationalism, and Democracy Promotion in U.S. Strategy." *International Security* 29: 112–56.

Moore, Colin D. 2017. *American Imperialism and the State, 1893–1921*. New York: Cambridge University Press.

Morgenthau, Hans J. 1948. *Politics among Nations: The Struggle for Power and Peace*. 1st ed. New York: A. A. Knopf.

Morone, James A. 2003. *Hellfire Nation: The Politics of Sin in American History*. New Haven: Yale University Press.

Morris, Aldon D. 1984. *The Origins of the Civil Rights Movement: Black Communities Organizing for Change*. New York: Free Press.

Moses, Wilson Jeremiah. 1982. *Black Messiahs and Uncle Toms: Social and Literary Manipulations of a Religious Myth*. University Park: Pennsylvania State University Press.

Moshin, Jamie. 2018. "Hello Darkness: Antisemitism and the Rhetorical Silence in the 'Trump Era'." *Journal of Contemporary Rhetoric* 8: 26–43.

Motomura, Hiroshi. 2006. *Americans in Waiting: The Lost Story of Immigration and Citizenship in the United States*. New York: Oxford University Press.

2014. *Immigration Outside the Law*. New York: Oxford University Press.

Mueller, John E. 1973. *War, Presidents, and Public Opinion*. New York: Wiley.

Mutz, Diana C. 2018. "Status Threat, Not Economic Hardship, Explains the 2016 Presidential Vote." *Proceedings of the National Academy of Sciences* 115: E4330–E4339.

Myrdal, Gunnar. 1944. *An American Dilemma: The Negro Problem and Modern Democracy*. New Brunswick: Transaction Publishers.

Nagel, Joane. 1998. "Masculinity and Nationalism: Gender and Sexuality in the Making of Nations." *Ethnic and Racial Studies* 21: 242–69.

National Opinion Research Center, and University of Chicago. 2014. General Social Survey 2014, March, 2014 [survey question] [computer file]. (Study USNORC.GSS14A.Q0412D) version. University of Chicago National Opinion Research Center: Cornell University, Ithaca, NY: Roper Center for Public Opinion Research, iPOLL [distributor]. https://doi.org/10.3886/ICPS R36319.v2

New York Times. 1953. "PRESIDENT SEES EDITORS; Tells Them Communism Can Be Beaten Through Religion." *New York Times*, April 10. www.nytimes .com/1953/04/10/archives/president-sees-editors-tells-them-communism-can-be-beaten-through.html

Newport, Frank. 2016. "Most Americans Still Believe in God." Gallup https://news .gallup.com/poll/193271/americans-believe-god.aspx (accessed January 12, 2020).

———. 2020. "Impeachment From the American Public's Perspective." Gallup, https:// news.gallup.com/opinion/polling-matters/284030/impeachment-american-public-perspective.aspx (accessed February 24, 2020).

Ngai, Mae M. 2014. *Impossible Subjects: Illegal Aliens and the Making of Modern America*. Princeton: Princeton University Press.

Niebuhr, Reinhold. 2008. *The Irony of American History*. Chicago: University of Chicago Press.

Nincic, Miroslav. 1992. *Democracy and Foreign Policy: The Fallacy of Political Realism*. New York: Columbia University Press.

Norris, Pippa, and Ronald Inglehart. 2011. *Sacred and Secular: Religion and Politics Worldwide*. 2nd ed. Cambridge: Cambridge University Press.

Obama, Barack H. 2007. "Renewing American Leadership Campaign 2008." *Foreign Affairs* 86: 2–16.

———. 2009a. "Interview With Laurence Haim of Canal Plus Television." University of California Santa Barbara, www.presidency.ucsb.edu/documents/inter view-with-laurence-haim-canal-plus-television (accessed May 9, 2020).

———. 2009b. "Nobel Lecture." The Nobel Prize, www.nobelprize.org/prizes/peace/ 2009/obama/26183-nobel-lecture-2009/ (accessed October 19, 2019).

Ockenga, Harold John. 1961. "The Communist Issue Today." *Christianity Today* 5: 9–12.

Oliver, J. Eric., and Thomas John Wood. 2018. *Enchanted America: How Intuition and Reason Divide our Politics*. Chicago: The University of Chicago Press.

Olson, Laura R., and Adam L. Warber. 2008. "Belonging, Behaving, and Believing: Assessing the Role of Religion on Presidential Approval." *Political Research Quarterly* 61: 192–204.

Olzak, Susan. 1992. *The Dynamics of Ethnic Competition and Conflict*. Stanford, CA: Stanford University Press.

Ortiz, Paul. 2018. *An African American and Latinx history of the United States, ReVisioning American History Series*. Boston: Beacon Press.

Overing, Joanna. 1997. "The Role of Myth: An Anthropological Perspective, or: 'The Reality of the Really Made-up'." In *Myths and Nationhood*, eds. Geoffrey A. Hosking and George Schöpflin. London: Hurst & Company in

Association with the School of Slavonic and Eastern European Studies, University of London. 1–18.

Page, Benjamin I., and Robert Y. Shapiro. 1982. "Changes in Americans' Policy Preferences, 1935–1979." *Public Opinion Quarterly* 46: 24–42.

1983. "Effects of Public Opinion on Policy." *American Political Science Review* 77: 175–90.

1992. *The Rational Public: Fifty Years of Trends in Americans' Policy Preferences.* Chicago: University of Chicago Press.

Paine, Thomas. 1776. *Common Sense: With the Whole Appendix: The Address to the Quakers: Also, the Large Additions, and A Dialogue between the Ghost of General Montgomery, Just Arrived from the Elysian Fields and an American Delegate in a Wood, Near Philadelphia, on the Grand Subject of American Independency.* Philadelphia: Printed and sold by R. Bell, in Third-street.

Palmer, J. Jioni, and Molly Igoe. 2019. "How Americans Feel About DREAM, the Wall, and Family Separation." PRRI, www.prri.org/spot light/how-americans-feel-about-dream-the-wall-and-family-separation/ (accessed May 10, 2020).

Parker, Christopher S. 2009. *Fighting for Democracy: Black Veterans and the Struggle against White Supremacy in the Postwar South, Princeton Studies in American Politics.* Princeton: Princeton University Press.

2010. "Symbolic versus Blind Patriotism: Distinction without Difference?". *Political Research Quarterly* 63: 97–114.

2018. "The Radical Right in the United States of America." In *The Oxford Handbook of the Radical Right,* ed. Jens Rydgren. New York: Oxford University Press. 630–649.

Parker, Christopher S., and Matt A. Barreto. 2013. *Change They can't Believe in: The Tea Party and Reactionary Politics in America.* Princeton: Princeton University Press.

Pateman, Carole. 1980. "'The Disorder of Women': Women, Love, and the Sense of Justice." *Ethics* 91: 20–34.

Pérez, Efrén Osvaldo. 2008. "*No Way José: The Nature and Sequence of US Anti-Immigrant Opinion.*" Durham, NC: Duke University Press.

Petrikova, Ivica. 2018. "Religion and Foreign-policy Views: Are Religious People More Altruistic and/or More Militant?" *International Political Science Review* 40: 535–57.

Pew Research Center. 2015. *America's Changing Religious Landscape.* May 12, www.pewforum.org/2015/05/12/americas-changing-religious-landscape/

2019. In *U.S., Decline of Christianity Continues at Rapid Pace: An update on America's changing religious landscape.* October 17, www.pewforum.org/2 019/10/17/in-u-s-decline-of-christianity-continues-at-rapid-pace/

Phillips, Nichole Renée. 2018. *Patriotism Black and White: The Color of American Exceptionalism.* Waco, TX: Baylor University Press.

Philpot, Tasha S. 2017. *Conservative but Not Republican: The Paradox of Party Identification and Ideology among African Americans.* New York: Cambridge University Press.

Pierard, Richard V., and Robert Dean Linder. 1988. *Civil Religion & the Presidency*. Grand Rapids, MI: Academie Books.

Pinn, Anne H., and Anthony B. Pinn. 2002. *Fortress Introduction to Black Church History*. Minneapolis, MN: Fortress Press.

Posner, Sarah. 2020. *Unholy: Why White Evangelicals Worship at the Altar of Donald Trump*. New York: Random House.

Pratto, Felicia, Jim Sidanius, Lisa M. Stallworth, and Bertram F. Malle. 1994. "Social Dominance Orientation: A Personality Variable Predicting Social and Political Attitudes." *Journal of Personality and Social Psychology* 67: 741–63.

Preston, Andrew. 2012. "Why is American Foreign Policy so Religious?" John C. Danforth Center on Religion and Politics, https://religionandpolitics .org/2012/05/07/why-is-american-foreign-policy-so-religious/2/ (accessed September 11, 2019).

Prior, Markus. 2010. "You've Either Got It or You Don't? The Stability of Political Interest over the Life Cycle." *Journal of Politics* 72: 747–66.

Prothero, Stephen R. 2012. *The American Bible: How Our Words Unite, Divide, and Define a Nation*. 1st ed. New York: HarperOne.

Public Agenda Foundation. 1984. Nuclear Arms and National Security, May, 1984 [survey question] [computer file]. (Study USPAF.84B790.R083) version. Public Agenda Foundation: Cornell University, Ithaca, NY: Roper Center for Public Opinion Research, iPOLL [distributor]. https://doi .roper.center/?doi=10.25940/ROPER-31094224

Public Religion Research Institute. 2010. Public Religion Research Institute Post-election American Values Survey 2010, Nov, 2010 [survey question] [computer file]. (Study USPRRI.10POSTELVAL.R24B) version. Public Religion Research Institute: Cornell University, Ithaca, NY: Roper Center for Public Opinion Research, iPOLL [distributor]. https://doi.roper.center/? doi=10.25940/ROPER-31096412

2012. Public Religion Research Institute American Values Survey, Sep, 2012 [survey question] [computer file]. (Study USPRRI.12VALUES.R27D) version. Public Religion Research Institute: Cornell University, Ithaca, NY: Roper Center for Public Opinion Research, iPOLL [distributor]. https://doi .roper.center/?doi=10.25940/ROPER-31096438

2013. Public Religion Research Institute Religion & Politics Tracking Survey, Jan, 2013 [survey question] [computer file]. (Study USPRRI.13RELPOL01. R03) version. Public Religion Research Institute: Cornell University, Ithaca, NY: Roper Center for Public Opinion Research, iPOLL [distributor]. https:// doi.roper.center/?doi=10.25940/ROPER-31096451

Public Religion Research Institute, Brookings Institution, and Ford Foundation. 2013. Public Religion Research Institute Economic Values Survey, May, 2013 [survey question] [computer file]. (Study USPRRI.071813.R23D) version. Public Religion Research Institute: Cornell University, Ithaca, NY: Roper Center for Public Opinion Research, iPOLL [distributor]. https://doi .roper.center/?doi=10.25940/ROPER-31113248

Public Religion Research Institute, and Religion News Service. 2012. PRRI/RNS Religion News Survey, Dec, 2012 [computer file]. (Study

USPRRI.12RELNEWSDC.R04B) version. Public Religion Research Institute: Cornell University, Ithaca, NY: Roper Center for Public Opinion Research, iPOLL [distributor]. https://doi.roper.center/?doi=10.25940/RO PER-31096437

Putnam, Robert D. 1995. *Bowling Alone: The Collapse and Revival of American Community*. New York: Simon & Schuster.

Putnam, Robert D., and David E. Campbell. 2010. *American Grace: How Religion Divides and Unites Us*. New York: Simon & Schuster.

Quarles, Benjamin. 1996. *The Negro in the American Revolution*. Chapel Hill: University of North Carolina Press.

Quinley, Harold E. 1974. *The Prophetic Clergy: Social Activism among Protestant Ministers*. New York: Wiley.

Raboteau, Albert J. 1978. *Slave Religion: The "Invisible Institution" in the Antebellum South*. Oxford: Oxford University Press.

Rainsford, William Stephen. 1902. *The Reasonableness of Faith, and other addresses*. New York: Doubleday, Page.

Rathbun, Brian C. 2007. "Hierarchy and Community at Home and Abroad: Evidence of a Common Structure of Domestic and Foreign Policy Beliefs in American Elites." *Journal of Conflict Resolution* 51: 379–407.

Rathbun, Brian C., Joshua Kertzer, Jason Reifler, Paul Goren, and Thomas Scotto. 2016. "Taking Foreign Policy Personally: Personal Values and Foreign Policy Attitudes." *International Studies Quarterly* 60: 124–37.

Rauschenbusch, Walter. 1918. *A Theology for the Social Gospel*. New York: The Macmillan Company.

Reagan, Ronald. 1983. "Remarks at the Annual Convention of the National Association of Evangelicals in Orlando, Florida." The American Presidency Project, www.presidency.ucsb.edu/documents/remarks-the-annual-convention-the-national-association-evangelicals-orlando-florida (accessed September 23, 2019).

Religion News Service. 2011. Public Religion Research Institute PRRI/RNS Poll: May 2011 Religion News, May, 2011 [dataset] [computer file]. (Study USPRRI2011-05, Version 4) version. Public Religion Research Institute: Cornell University, Ithaca, NY: Roper Center for Public Opinion Research, RoperExpress [distributor]. https://doi.roper.center/?doi=10.25940/ROPER-31096418

Renan, Ernest. 1990. "What is a Nation?" *Nation and Narration* 11: 8–22.

Reny, Tyler T., and Matt A. Barreto. 2020. "Xenophobia in the Time of Pandemic: Othering, Anti-Asian Attitudes, and COVID-19." *Politics, Groups, and Identities*: 1–24.

Rhodes, Edward. 2018. "The Search for Monsters to Destroy: Theodore Roosevelt, Republican Virtu, and the Challenges of Liberal Democracy in an Industrial Society." In *US Grand Strategy in the 21st Century: The Case For Restraint*, eds. A. Trevor Thrall and Benjamin H. Friedman. London: Routledge. 157–178.

Riker, William H. 1996. *The Strategy of Rhetoric: Campaigning for the American Constitution*. New Haven: Yale University Press.

Ritter, Gretchen. 2006. *The Constitution as Social Design: Gender and Civic Membership in the American Constitutional Order.* Stanford, CA.: Stanford University Press.

Rokeach, Milton. 1973. *The Nature of Human Values.* New York: Free Press.

Roof, Wade Clark. 1976. "Traditional Religion in Contemporary Society: A Theory of Local-Cosmopolitan Plausibility." *American Sociological Review* 41: 195–208.

Roosevelt, Franklin D. 1940. "Annual Message to the Congress." The Presidency Project, www.presidency.ucsb.edu/documents/annual-message-the-congress (accessed October 12, 2019).

Rosenson, Beth A., Elizabeth A. Oldmixon, and Kenneth D. Wald. 2009. "U.S. Senators' Support for Israel Examined Through Sponsorship/Cosponsorship Decisions, 1993–2002: The Influence of Elite and Constituent Factors." *Foreign Policy Analysis* 5: 73–91.

Rozell, Mark J., and Gleaves Whitney, eds. 2018. *Religion and the American Presidency.* 3rd ed. Switzerland: Palgrave Macmillan.

Russett, Bruce M., and John R. Oneal. 2001. *Triangulating Peace: Democracy, Interdependence, and International Organizations.* New York: Norton.

Ryo, Emily. 2019. "How ICE enforcement has changed under the Trump administration." The Conversation, https://theconversation.com/how-ice-enforcement-has-changed-under-the-trump-administration-120322 (accessed May 10, 2020).

Sanchez, Gabriel R. 2008. "Latino Group Consciousness and Perceptions of Commonality with African Americans." *Social Science Quarterly* 89: 428–44.

Sanger, David. 2009. "Biblical Quotes Adorned Pentagon Reports." *New York Times,* May 18. www.nytimes.com/2009/05/18/us/18rumsfeld.html

Savelle, Max. 1962. "Nationalism and Other Loyalties in the American Revolution." *American Historical Review* 67: 901–23.

Sawyer, Mark Q. 2006. *Racial Politics in Post-revolutionary Cuba.* New York: Cambridge University Press.

Schattschneider, E. E. 1975. *The Semisovereign People: A Realists View of Democracy in America.* New York: Harcourt Brace Jovanovich College Publishers.

Schatz, Robert T., and Howard Lavine. 2007. "Waving the Flag: National Symbolism, Social Identity, and Political Engagement." *Political Psychology* 28: 329–55.

Schatz, Robert T., Ervin Staub, and Howard Lavine. 1999. "On the Varieties of National Attachment: Blind Versus Constructive Patriotism." *Political Psychology* 20: 151–74.

Schildkraut, Deborah J. 2002. "The More Things Change ... American Identity and Mass and Elite Response to 9/11." *Political Psychology* 23: 511–35.

2005. *Press One for English: Language Policy, Public Opinion, and American Identity.* Princeton: Princeton University Press.

2011. *Americanism in the Twenty-first Century: Public Opinion in the Age of Immigration.* New York: Cambridge University Press.

Schneider, Anne L., and Helen M. Ingram. 1997. *Policy Design for Democracy, Studies in Government and Public Policy*. Lawrence, KS: University Press of Kansas.

Schöpflin, George. 1997. "The Functions of Myths and the taxonomy of Myths." In *Myths and Nationhood*, eds. Geoffrey A. Hosking and George Schöpflin. London: Hurst & Company in Association with the School of Slavonic and Eastern European Studies, University of London. 19–35.

Schrag, Peter. 2010. *Not Fit for Our Society: Nativism and Immigration*. Berkeley: University of California Press.

Schultz, Debra L. 2001. *Going South: Jewish Women in the Civil Rights Movement*. New York: New York University Press.

Schulz, Anne, Philipp Müller, Christian Schemer, Dominique Stefanie Wirz, Martin Wettstein, and Werner Wirth. 2017. "Measuring Populist Attitudes on Three Dimensions." *International Journal of Public Opinion Research* 30: 316–26.

Schwadel, Philip. 2015. "Explaining Cross-National Variation in the Effect of Higher Education on Religiosity." *Journal for the Scientific Study of Religion* 54: 402–18.

Schwartz, Shalom H. 1992. "Universals in the Content and Structure of Values: Theoretical Advances and Empirical Tests in 20 Countries." *Advances in Experimental Social Psychology* 25: 1–65.

1994. "Are There Universal Aspects in the Structure and Contents of Human Values?" *Journal of Social Issues* 50: 19–45.

Sears, David O., Jim Sidanius, and Lawrence Bobo, eds. 2000. *Racialized Politics*. Chicago: University of Chicago Press.

Segal, Robert A. 2001. "Myth in Religion." In *International Encyclopedia of the Social & Behavioral Sciences*, eds. Neil J. Smelser and Paul B. Baltes. Oxford: Pergamon. 10273–78.

Segura, Gary M., and Ali A. Valenzuela. 2010. "Hope, Tropes, and Dopes: Hispanic and White Racial Animus in the 2008 Election." *Presidential Studies Quarterly* 40: 497–514.

Seton-Watson, Hugh. 1977. *Nations and States: An Enquiry into the Origins of Nations and the Politics of Nationalism*. Boulder, CO: Westview Press.

Shapiro, Robert Y., and Benjamin I. Page. 1988. "Foreign Policy and the Rational Public." *Journal of Conflict Resolution* 32: 211–47.

Shaw, Todd. 2004. "'Two Warring Ideals': Double Consciousness, Dialogue, and African American Patriotism post-9/11." *Journal of African American Studies* 8: 20–37.

Shear, Michael D. 2017. "Trump Will Withdraw U.S. From Paris Climate Agreement." *New York Times*, June 1. www.nytimes.com/2017/06/01/climate/trump-paris-climate-agreement.html

2018. "If G.O.P. Loses Hold on Congress, Trump Warns, Democrats Will Enact Change 'Quickly and Violently'." *New York Times*, August 28. www.nytimes.com/2018/08/28/us/politics/trump-evangelical-pastors-election.html

Sherkat, Darren E. 2014. *Changing Faith: The Dynamics and Consequences of Americans' Shifting Religious Identities*. New York: NYU Press.

Shklar, Judith N. 1993. "Obligation, Loyalty, Exile." *Political Theory* 21: 181–97.

Shortle, Allyson F., and Ronald Keith Gaddie. 2015. "Religious Nationalism and Perceptions of Muslims and Islam." *Politics and Religion* 8: 435–57.

Sidanius, Jim, Seymour Feshbach, Shana Levin, and Felicia Pratto. 1997. "The Interface Between Ethnic and National Attachment: Ethnic Pluralism or Ethnic Dominance?" *Public Opinion Quarterly* 61: 102–133.

Sidanius, Jim, and Felicia Pratto. 1999. *Social Dominance: An Intergroup Theory of Social Hierarchy and Oppression.* New York: Cambridge University Press.

Sifry, Micah L. 1993. "Anti-Semitism in America." *The Nation* (January 25). 92–99.

Smedley, Audrey. 1999. *Race in North America: Origin and Evolution of a Worldview.* 2nd ed. Boulder, CO: Westview.

Smidt, Corwin E. 2005. "Religion and American Attitudes Toward Islam and an Invasion of Iraq." *Sociology of Religion* 66: 243–61.

Smith, Anthony D. 1991. *National Identity, Ethnonationalism in Comparative Perspective.* Reno: University of Nevada Press.

2000. "The 'Sacred' Dimension of Nationalism." *Millennium – Journal of International Studies* 29: 791–814.

2001. *Nationalism: Theory, Ideology, History, Key Concepts.* Malden, MA: Polity Press.

Smith, David Norman, and Eric Hanley. 2018. "The Anger Games: Who Voted for Donald Trump in the 2016 Election, and Why?" *Critical Sociology* 44: 195–212.

Smith, Joseph, and Church of Jesus Christ of Latter-Day Saints. 1971. *Doctrine and Covenants of the Church of the Latter Day Saints: Carefully Selected from the Revelations of God.* Independence, Mo: Herald House.

Smith, Rogers M. 1997. *Civic Ideals: Conflicting Visions of Citizenship in U.S. History.* New Haven: Yale University Press.

Sniderman, Paul M., Louk Hagendoorn, and Markus Prior. 2004. "Predisposing Factors and Situational Triggers: Exclusionary Reactions to Immigrant Minorities." *American Political Science Review* 98: 35–49.

Snyder, Jack L. 2000. *From Voting to Violence: Democratization and Nationalist Conflict.* 1st ed. New York: Norton.

Somerville, John. 1981. "Patriotism and War." *Ethics* 91: 568–78.

Soper, J. Christopher., and Joel S. Fetzer. 2018. *Religion and Nationalism in Global Perspective, Cambridge Studies in Social Theory, Religion and Politics.* Cambridge: Cambridge University Press.

Spalding, Henry D. 1972. *Encyclopedia of Black Folklore and Humor.* Middle Village, NY: Jonathan David Publishers.

Spry, Carmen. , and Matthew Hornsey. 2007. "The Influence of Blind and Constructive Patriotism on Attitudes toward Multiculturalism and Immigration." *Australian Journal of Psychology* 59: 151–58.

St. John de Crèvecoeur, J. Hector. 1782. *Letters from an American Farmer: Describing Certain Provincial Situations, Manners, and Customs … and Conveying Some Idea of the Late and Present Interior Circumstances of the British Colonies in North America.* London: Printed for T. Davies etc.

Stanley, Ben. 2008. "The Thin Ideology of Populism." *Journal of Political Ideologies* 13: 95–110.

Steiner, George. 1998. *Language and Silence: Essays on Language, Literature, and the Inhuman*. New Haven: Yale University Press.

Stephens-Dougan, LaFleur. 2020. *Race to the Bottom: How Racial Appeals Work in American Politics*. Chicago: University of Chicago Press.

Stewart, Katherine. 2018. "A Christian Nationalist Blitz." *New York Times*, May 26. www.nytimes.com/2018/05/26/opinion/project-blitz-christian-nationalists.html

2019. *The Power Worshippers: Inside the Dangerous Rise of Religious Nationalism*. New York: Bloomsbury Publishing.

Stewart, Maria W. 2001. "Productions." In *Pamphlets of Protest: An Anthology of Early African American Protest Literature, 1790–1860*, eds. Richard Newman, Patrick Rael and Phillip Lapansky. New York: Routledge. 122–131.

Stone, Deborah. 2012. *Policy Paradox: The Art of Political Decision Making*. 3rd ed. New York: W.W. Norton.

Stone, Geoffrey R. 2010. "The Second Great Awakening: A Christian Nation?" *Georgia State Law Review* 26: 1305–33.

Stout, Harry S. 1977. "Religion, Communications, and the Ideological Origins of the American Revolution." *The William and Mary Quarterly* 34: 519–41.

Strong, Josiah. 1893. *The New Era*. New York: Baker & Taylor.

Sullivan, John L., James Piereson, and George E. Marcus. 1982. *Political Tolerance and American Democracy*. Chicago: University of Chicago Press.

Tajfel, Henri. 1981. *Human Groups and Social Categories: Studies in Social Psychology*. New York: Cambridge University Press.

Takaki, Ronald. 1989. *Strangers from a Different Shore: A History of Asian Americans*. New York: Penguin Books.

Taydas, Zeynep, Cigdem Kentmen, and Laura R. Olson. 2012. "Faith Matters: Religious Affiliation and Public Opinion About Barack Obama's Foreign Policy in the 'Greater' Middle East." *Social Science Quarterly* 93: 1218–42.

Terracciano, Antonio, and Robert R. McCrae. 2007. "Perceptions of Americans and the Iraq Invasion: Implications for Understanding National Character Stereotypes." *Journal of Cross-Cultural Psychology* 38: 695–710.

Theiss-Morse, Elizabeth. 2009. *Who Counts as an American?: The Boundaries of National Identity*. Cambridge: Cambridge University Press.

Thomas, George M. 1989. *Revivalism and Cultural Change: Christianity, Nation Building, and the Market in the Nineteenth-Century United States*. Chicago: University of Chicago Press.

Thomson Jr, Robert A., and Paul Froese. 2016. "God versus Party: Competing Effects on Attitudes Concerning Criminal Punishment, National Security, and Military Service." *Journal for the Scientific Study of Religion* 55: 839–58.

Thucydides, Rex Warner, and M. I. Finley. 1972. *History of the Peloponnesian War*. Rev. ed. Baltimore: Penguin Books.

Tichenor, Daniel J. 2002. *Dividing Lines: The Politics of Immigration Control in America*. Princeton, NJ: Princeton University Press.

Tipton, Steven M. 2007. *Public Pulpits: Methodists and Mainline Churches in the Moral Argument of Public Life*. Chicago: University of Chicago Press.

Tiryakian, Edward A. 1982. "Puritan America in the Modern World: Mission Impossible?" *Sociological Analysis* 43: 351–67.

Tocqueville, Alexis de. 1945. *Democracy in America*. Toronto: Vintage Books.

Toosi, Nahal. 2018. "Some see Christian First Bias in Trump Foreign Policy." Politico, www.politico.com/story/2018/10/04/christian-bias-trump-foreign-policy-870853 (accessed October 20, 2019).

Towler, Christopher C., and Christopher S. Parker. 2018. "Between Anger and Engagement: Donald Trump and Black America." *Journal of Race, Ethnicity, and Politics* 3: 219–53.

Truman, Harry S. 1945a. "Address on Foreign Policy at the Navy Day Celebration in New York City." www.presidency.ucsb.edu/documents/address-foreign-policy-the-navy-day-celebration-new-york-city (accessed October 12, 2019).

1945b. "Proclamation 2651—Victory in Europe: Day of Prayer." The Presidency Project, www.presidency.ucsb.edu/documents/proclamation-265 1-victory-europe-day-prayer (accessed October 12, 2019).

1946. "Address in Columbus at a Conference of the Federal Council of Churches." Harry S. Truman Presidential Library & Museum, www.trumanlibrary.gov/library/public-papers/52/address-columbus-conference-federal-council-churches (accessed October 16, 2019).

1951. "Address at the Cornerstone Laying of the New York Avenue Presbyterian Church." The American Presidency Project, www.presidency.ucsb.edu/documents/address-the-cornerstone-laying-the-new-york-avenue-presbyterian-church (accessed October 16, 2019).

Tuveson, Ernest Lee. 1968. *Redeemer Nation: The Idea of America's Millennial Role*. Chicago: University of Chicago Press.

U.S. Congress. 1955. "Congressional Record." ed. 1st Session 84th Cong. Vol. 101. 7764.

Uddin, Asma T. 2019. *When Islam is not a Religion: Inside America's Fight for Religious Freedom*. New York: Pegasus Books.

Varacalli, Joseph A. 2006. *The Catholic Experience in America, The American Religious Experience*. Westport, CT: Greenwood Press.

Verba, Sidney, Kay Lehman Schlozman, and Henry E. Brady. 1995. *Voice and Equality: Civic Voluntarism in American Politics*. Cambridge: Harvard University Press.

Vernant, Jean Pierre. 1988. *Myth and Society in Ancient Greece*. New York: Zone Books.

Visalvanich, Neil. 2017. "When does Race Matter? Exploring White Responses to Minority Congressional Candidates." *Politics, Groups, and Identities* 5: 618–41.

von der Ruhr, Marc, and Joseph P. Daniels. 2003. "The Relationship Between Religious Affiliation, Region, Race, and Attitudes Toward Globalization." *Faith and Economics* 42: 26–39.

Wald, Kenneth D. 1994. "The Religious Dimension of American Anti-Communism." *Journal of Church and State* 36: 483–506.

Wald, Kenneth D., Dennis E. Owen, and Samuel S. Hill, Jr. 1988. "Churches as Political Communities." *American Political Science Review* 82: 531–48.

Wald, Kenneth D., and Corwin E. Smidt. 1993. "Measurement Strategies in the Study of Religion and Politics." In *Rediscovering the Religious Factor in American Politics*, eds. David C. Leege and Lyman A. Kellstedt. Armonk, NY: M.E. Sharpe. 26–49.

Walker, David. 1995. *David Walker's Appeal*. New York: Macmillan.

Wallace, Henry. 1942. "The Century of the Common Man delivered 8 May 1942, Grand Ballroom, Commodore Hotel, New York, NY." American Rhetoric, www.americanrhetoric.com/speeches/henrywallacefreeworldassoc.htm (accessed October 12, 2019).

Wallace, Sophia J. 2014. "Papers Please: State-Level Anti-Immigrant Legislation in the Wake of Arizona's SB 1070." *Political Science Quarterly* 129: 261–91.

Wallis, Jim. 2005. *God's Politics: Why The Right Gets It Wrong and the Left Doesn't Get It*. San Francisco: Harper.

2019. *Christ in Crisis: Why We Need to Reclaim Jesus*. 1st ed. San Francisco: HarperOne.

Walton, Hanes, Jr. 1985. *Invisible Politics: Black Political Behavior*. Albany: State University of New York Press.

Warner, Carolyn M., and Stephen G. Walker. 2010. "Thinking about the Role of Religion in Foreign Policy: A Framework for Analysis." *Foreign Policy Analysis* 7: 113–35.

Weaver, Vesla M. 2007. "Frontlash: Race and the Development of Punitive Crime Policy." *Studies in American Political Development* 21: 230–65.

Weber, David J. 2003. *Foreigners in their Native Land: Historical Roots of the Mexican Americans*. 30th anniversary pbk. ed. Albuquerque: University of New Mexico Press.

Weber, Max. 1946. *From Max Weber: Essays in Sociology*. Translated by Hans Heinrich Gerth and C. Wright Mills. New York: Oxford University Press.

Weisman, Jonathan. 2014. "Tea Party Candidate in Kentucky Hits Snags." *New York Times*, May 2. www.nytimes.com/2014/05/03/us/politics/tea-party-challenge-to-mcconnell-hits-a-skid.html

Wettstein, Martin, Frank Esser, Sven Engesser, Werner Wirth, Dominique Wirz, Anne Schulz, Florin Büchel, Nicole Ernst, Daniele Caramani, Luca Manucci, Laurent Bernhard, Marco Steenbergen, Regula Haenggli, Caroline Dalmus, and Edward Weber. 2016. "The appeal of populist ideas, strategies and styles: A theoretical model and research design for analyzing populist political communication." www.nccr-democracy.uzh.ch/publications/work ingpaper/pdf/wp_88.pdf (February 21, 2020).

White, Ismail K., and Chryl Nicole Laird. 2020. *Steadfast Democrats: How Social Forces Shape Black Political Behavior*. Princeton: Princeton University Press.

Whitehead, Andrew L., and Samuel L. Perry. 2020. *Taking America Back for God: Christian Nationalism in the United States*. New York: Oxford University Press.

Whitehead, Andrew L., Samuel L. Perry, and Joseph O. Baker. 2018. "Make America Christian Again: Christian Nationalism and Voting for Donald Trump in the 2016 Presidential Election." *Sociology of Religion* 79: 147–71.

Wilcox, Clyde. 1989. "The Fundamentalist Voter: Politicized Religious Identity and Political Attitudes and Behavior." *Review of Religious Research* 31: 54–67.

Williams, Robert L., Stacy L. Bliss, and R. Steve McCallum. 2006. "Christian Conservatism and Militarism among Teacher Education Students." *Review of Religious Research* 48: 17–32.

Wilson, Peter. 1998. "The Myth of the 'First Great Debate'." *Review of International Studies* 24: 1–15.

Winters, Jeffrey A. 2011. *Oligarchy*. New York: Cambridge University Press.

Winthrop, John. 1630. Sermon: "A Model of Christian Charity." Delivered 1630. This version published in 1838 in Collections of the Massachusetts Historical Society, 3rd series 7:31–48; accessed as a digital edition via the Hanover Historical Texts Collection, Hanover College. https://history.hanover.edu/texts/winthmod.html

Wittkopf, Eugene R. 1986. "On the Foreign Policy Beliefs of the American People: A Critique and Some Evidence." *International Studies Quarterly* 30: 425–45.
  1990. *Faces of Internationalism: Public Opinion and American Foreign Policy*. Durham: Duke University Press.

Wlezien, Christopher. 1996. "Dynamics of Representation: The Case of US Spending on Defence." *British Journal of Political Science* 26: 81–103.

Wong, Janelle. 2018. *Immigrants, Evangelicals, and Politics in an era of Demographic Change*. New York: Russell Sage Foundation.

Wood, Gordon S. 1998. "Religion and the American Revolution." In *New Directions in American Religious History*, eds. Harry S. Stout and Darryl G. Hart. Oxford: Oxford University Press, 173–205.

Woodward, Bob. 2004. *Plan of Attack*. New York: Simon & Schuster.

Woodward, Kenneth. 1997. "Is God Listening?" *Newsweek* (March 30). www.newsweek.com/god-listening-170460 (accessed on December 17, 2021).

Wu, Joshua Su-Ya, and Austin J. Knuppe. 2016. "My Brother's Keeper? Religious Cues and Support for Foreign Military Intervention." *Politics and Religion* 9: 537–65.

Wuthnow, Robert. 1988. *The Restructuring of American Religion*. Princeton: Princeton University Press.

Wuthnow, Robert, and Valerie Lewis. 2008. "Religion and Altruistic U.S. Foreign Policy Goals: Evidence from a National Survey of Church Members." *Journal for the Scientific Study of Religion* 47: 191–210.

Yee, Vivian. 2017. "Judge Blocks Trump Effort to Withhold Money from Sanctuary Cities." *New York Times*, April 25. www.nytimes.com/2017/04/25/us/judge-blocks-trump-sanctuary-cities.html

Zaller, John R. 1992. *The Nature and Origins of Mass Opinion*. Cambridge: Cambridge University Press.

Zelinsky, Wilbur. 1988. *Nation into State: The Shifting Symbolic Foundations of American Nationalism*. Chapel Hill: University of North Carolina Press.

Zolberg, Aristide R. 2006. *A Nation by Design: Immigration Policy in the Fashioning of America*. New York: Russell Sage Foundation; Harvard University Press.

Zolberg, Aristide R., and Long Litt Woon. 1999. "Why Islam is like Spanish: Cultural Incorporation in Europe and the United States." *Politics & Society* 27: 5–38.

Zuckerman, Phil, Luke W. Galen, and Frank L. Pasquale. 2016. *The Nonreligious: Understanding Secular People and Societies*. New York: Oxford University Press.

Index